Severe Emotional Disturbance in Children and Adolescents

Severe Emotional Disturbance in Children and Adolescents conveys the experiences of severely emotionally disturbed children in detailed accounts of psychoanalytic psychotherapy, and explores the life and death struggles against severe self-harm to body and mind by the most distressed sections of adolescents.

Different applied contexts for psychotherapy are discussed together with the work of the multi-professional teams who understand, provide care and reduce the level of risk. Theoretical and practical accounts are given of psychotherapy with borderline children and adolescents, in methods of treatment that address deficit and internal conflict, issues of splitting and staff conflict. Illustrated by clinical material, topics addressed include:

- The inpatient therapeutic setting.
- Family rehabilitation after physical, sexual and emotional abuse.
- The adoptive father.
- Work with adolescent inpatients with spina bifida.
- Assessment, treatment and clinical management of adolescent disturbance.

Severe Emotional Disturbance in Children and Adolescents underlines the value of intensive psychoanalytic psychotherapy as a coherent method of treatment in even the most severe cases of emotional disturbance. Psychotherapists, mental health workers, and social workers will find it a valuable resource for difficult work in a variety of contexts.

Denis Flynn is a Child Psychotherapist and is now Head of the Inpatient Adolescent Unit at The Cassel Hospital, London. He is a Member and Child Analyst of the British Psychoanalytical Society and also works as a Psychoanalyst in private practice.

Severe Emotional Disturbance in Children and Adolescents

Psychotherapy in applied contexts

Denis Flynn

Brunner-Routledge
Taylor & Francis Group

HOVE AND NEW YORK

First published 2004 by Brunner-Routledge
27 Church Road, Hove, East Sussex BN3 2FA

Simultaneously published in the USA and Canada
by Brunner-Routledge
29 West 35th Street, New York NY 10001

Brunner-Routledge is an imprint of the Taylor & Francis Group

Copyright © 2004 Denis Flynn

Typeset in Times by Mayhew Typesetting, Rhayader, Powys
Printed and bound in Great Britain by TJ International Ltd, Padstow,
Cornwall

This publication has been produced with paper manufactured to strict
environmental standards and with pulp derived from sustainable
forests.

British Library Cataloguing in Publication Data
A catalogue record for this book is available from the British Library

Library of Congress Cataloging-in-Publication Data
Flynn, Denis Christopher.
  Severe emotional disturbance in children and adolescents :
psychotherapy in applied contexts / Denis Christopher Flynn. – 1st ed.
      p. cm.
Includes bibliographical references and index.
  ISBN 1-58391-211-8 (hardback : alk. paper) – ISBN 1-58391-212-6
(paperback : alk. paper)
  1. Child psychotherapy–Case studies. 2. Adolescent
psychotherapy–Case studies. 3. Mentally ill children–Treatment–
Case studies. I. Title.
RJ504.F59 2004
618.92'8914–dc22

                                                    2003024562

ISBN 1-58391-211-8 (hbk)
ISBN 1-58391-212-6 (pbk)

For my parents, Francis Joseph and Cecilia,
and for Caroline

Contents

List of plates

These illustrations are the drawings of the child described in Chapter 2.

You can also view these in colour at www.brunner-routledge.co.uk/Flynn

Preface and acknowledgements

I have wanted to write this book about my work with children and adolescents for some time. The efforts and struggles to actually do it have not however dimmed my initial enthusiasm. I was aware that papers I had written at different times were linked, yet they had been dispersed in different places. In many of them there had been a continuity of theme and in my interest in the use of psychoanalytic psychotherapy in public service settings. I decided then to bring together some of these papers, with other new material and ideas, to present in a book.

I have been continuously struck, and often moved, by the power and meaningfulness of psychotherapy, especially with these very emotionally disturbed children and adolescents, and I want here to convey something of what psychotherapy can do. There are complexities and constraints, of course, in this work, which I shall discuss. The settings of treatment also provide particular challenges in terms of understanding and agreement in treatment teams, but the work can be done. It has value, and its effects can be seen, often vividly and graphically, in the experiences of the individual children and adolescents, in their changes of outlook and in their capacity to change and progress, despite adversity.

I would now like to express my thanks and appreciation to my many teachers during my years of training in psychotherapy and psychoanalysis and in my subsequent work. I cannot mention everyone personally by name, but I thank them nevertheless. In my child and adolescent training at the Tavistock Clinic, I remain indebted to the late Matti Harris, whose approach was inspiring and who gave help with such selfless kindness, and then to Margaret Rustin, Edna O'Shaughnessy and Donald Meltzer, for their creative thinking. I felt a whole new world was opened up for me. In nearly two decades of non-stop intensive and fulfilling work at the Cassel Hospital, I wish to acknowledge the work and unflagging support of many colleagues, nurses, psychotherapists and psychoanalysts, consultants and other staff, in our shared work on the Families Unit, especially Roger Kennedy, and on the Adolescent Unit. In my training at the Institute of Psychoanalysis and since, I am grateful for the rigorous thinking and support of many teachers and colleagues, especially Eric Rayner, Elizabeth Spillius, Betty Joseph, Michael Parsons, and John Steiner. My most special thanks are to the late Doreen Waddell, Isabel Menzies Lyth, Yolanda Glaser and Brendan MacCarthy.

I am indebted to the children and adolescents themselves and their parents, whose experiences are described in the book, and whose courage in psychotherapy is often remarkable and humbling. Some colleagues have contributed some material I have included in the case studies: I acknowledge nurses Isobel McGrory, Karyn Chiesa, Maria Huk and Joanne Turner; teachers Margaret Childs, Catherine Evans and Claudette Miles; psychotherapists of adolescents, Helga Skogstad, Fiona Fullerton and Lisa Morice. Also I am grateful to the many different people who have helped me with comments and criticisms about earlier forms of the papers behind the chapters: to Margaret Rustin for supervision of my work with the child in Chapter 2; to Trevor Lubbe for helpful comments about a draft of Chapter 3; and to Donald Meltzer for earlier supervision. I would like to thank Deirdre Dowling for reading a draft of Part 2, and particularly to thank Lesley Day for reading a whole draft of the book and giving me valuable guidance at different times. Lastly my thanks go to Cheryl Pavitt for secretarial support and to Helen Goodman, librarian at the Cassel.

I am also grateful for the many invitations to speak at conferences, hospitals and universities both in the UK and abroad, which have given me the incentive to put down my ideas and to develop them.

Finally, in all my discursions about 'family' in this book, I recognise the powerful and positive benefits I have received from my own family, before and now. That personal experience can make this most difficult work possible. I lastly owe a special gratitude, for their encouragement and forbearance during the preparation of the book, to Caroline, Dan and Izzy.

Permissions acknowledgements

Acknowledgement is due to the following publishers for permission to reprint papers, in whole or part:

To Free Association Books for 'The Child's View of the Hospital: An Examination of the Child's Experience of an In-Patient Setting', Chapter 13 in *The Family as In-Patient* (1987), edited by Roger Kennedy, Ann Heymans and Lydia Tischler. First published by Free Association Books Ltd, England 1986 copyright © The editors of this collection and the individual contributors 1986.

To Brunner-Routledge and *The Journal of Child Psychotherapy* (website http:/www.tandf.co.uk) for 'Internal Conflict and Growth in a Child Preparing to Start School' (1987) 13:1; for 'The Assessment and Psychotherapy of a Physically Abused Girl during In-Patient Family Treatment' (1988) 14:2; for 'Adolescent Group Work in a Hospital In-Patient Setting with Spina Bifida Patients and Others' (1992) 18:2; for 'Psycho-Analytic Aspects of In-Patient Treatment' (1998) 24:2.

To Brunner-Routledge for 'The Challenges of In-patient Psychotherapy' (1999), Chapter 13 in *Handbook of Child and Adolescent Psychotherapy*, eds. Ann Horne and Monica Lanyado; for 'The Adoptive Father' (2002), Chapter 13 in Book of Papers on *The Importance of Fathers*, eds. Alicia Etchagoyen and Judith Trowell, New Library of Psychoanalysis, General Editor, Susan Budd.

To the Institute of Psychoanalyis, London, for 'Adolescence' (2000) Chapter 4 in *Adolescence*, ed. Inge Wise, Psychoanalytic Ideas Series, Series Editor, Inge Wise.

To Karnac Books for 'The Containment of Borderline Adolescents' (2003), Chapter 8 in *The Internal and External Worlds of Children and Adolescents: Collaborative Therapeutic Care*, eds. Lesley Day and Denis Flynn, Cassel Monograph No. 3.

Chapter 1

General introduction

Psychotherapy in applied contexts

This book gives clinical and theoretical accounts of psychoanalytic psychotherapy in applied contexts in work with severely emotionally disturbed
children and adolescents. These applied contexts include inpatient settings
for both children and families and adolescents, work in other hospital or
day service applied contexts including a surgical ward and a children's day
centre, and settings where psychotherapy is focused in some particular
subject or application, such as psychotherapy in the complex fields of family
rehabilitation, adoption and dangerously at risk adolescents. In applied
contexts the clinical descriptions given go beyond the psychotherapist–
child/adolescent dyad usual in conventional psychoanalytic psychotherapy.
I shall discuss the work involved in coordinating team work with different
groups of professionals, who together with the parents are jointly concerned
with the therapeutic treatment of the child or adolescent and their overall
care. Psychotherapy in applied contexts brings with it a number of important and complex considerations, which I shall discuss in each chapter.
Despite these complexities I aim not to lose and indeed to convey throughout *a sense of the child or adolescent's experience of their severe emotional
disturbance* and *the particular use of psychoanalytical understanding and
techniques for treatment of the disturbance in the applied setting*. To do this
the book has a combination of theoretical discussions, vignettes and longer
case studies. In all cases I have changed the names of the child and
adolescent, and either limited or disguised details of the background history,
to protect confidentiality.

My overall aim too is to *show the impact of disturbance upon the everyday
reality of the child and adolescent, and the interplay between internal and
external reality*. The book looks at how unconscious internal disturbance
affects capacities and social adjustment, for example, going to school, or
dealing with long-term illness or adolescent transitions. It looks too at how
external traumatic events disturb inner awareness and capacities where, for
example, there is physical, emotional or sexual abuse, disturbed parenting

with a mentally ill parent, or where there has been a family breakdown. It also looks at how such outside events can cause a breakdown of mental functioning and emotional life in the child and adolescent. It considers severe consequences of such emotional disturbance, including borderline functioning in the child and adolescent, the impact of psychosis and experiences of self-harm, aggression against others and attempts at suicide.

In reality these studies of psychotherapy in applied contexts add something for all psychotherapists to think about, for there can be no artificial distinction between our 'inner self' and the 'external world', since both are continuously related, and as 'subjects' we constantly stand in meaningful relations to the external world, which needs to be understood and interpreted, in its social, conscious and unconscious dimensions (Merleau-Ponty 1945; Matthews 2002: 34, 38). By studying the relation of inner experience and outer reality, and what Winnicott calls 'the continuity of being' in a 'holding environment', we can understand better the full continuous interplay between internal and external reality (Winnicott 1960; Abram 1996: 57–68).

Emotional disturbance becomes manifest in children and adolescents in a number of ways and may lead to ongoing difficulties in personal development even when the emotional disturbance appears relatively minor. When the disturbance is very severe there may be a breakdown of functioning in the child or adolescent, compounding family difficulties and affecting the child or adolescent's environment. *Psychotherapy* by psychoanalytic methods *looks centrally at the present experience of the emotional disturbance*, and *examines the roots of the disturbance as the treatment progresses and deepens.* Different settings for treatment may be appropriate, both outpatient and inpatient, depending on the severity of disturbance and the degree of need. I aim to stress that within these new applied contexts too the influence and power of the present experience of the child and adolescent can be made meaningful and new possibilities for change opened up. Then the child or adolescent's sense of their own personal value and identity may be increased, obstacles to development recognised and processes of psychic growth enhanced.

Psychoanalytic psychotherapy is of value and can be adapted for more serious cases in applied settings, especially when the problems are too severe for a conventional setting – one-to-one in a consulting room or clinic – and there are attendant overriding issues of management of risk and disturbance. My belief is that *effective and meaningful psychotherapy can occur in such applied settings when the main elements of psychoanalytic technique are adhered to and employed, especially a focus on the use of transference and countertransference*, including the child's use of the relationship to the psychotherapist and the treatment setting to gain awareness of their internal world, their personal situation and social context. Psychoanalytic *psychotherapy can be used for cases of the most severe disturbance in applied settings*, including the inpatient setting, when due attention is given to creating a setting that is consistent with psychoanalytic methods and technique, and where there is a shared clear rationale with co-workers as to how the work fits together.

Related types of emotional disturbance – of varying severity – are discussed in turn, with reference to very young children, latency age children, younger adolescents and older adolescents or young persons aged up to about 21 years. The book divides into three parts: Parts 1 and 2 on children, Part 1 in outpatient treatment and Part 2 in inpatient treatment, and Part 3 with adolescents and young persons in group and individual treatments, both inpatient and outpatient. Each part, or chapter, can be read separately and independently in whatever order, but there is an intended progression throughout the book. I start in Part 1 with two detailed studies of intensive outpatient psychoanalytic treatments of young children. Then in Part 2 I explore the treatment of young and latency aged children in relation to their family, and the treatment of mothers and infants, particularly after child abuse or severe parental psychiatric disturbance. Finally, in Part 3, I look at severe disturbance in adolescence in contrast to normal developmental processes, the particular plight of the disabled adolescent, assessment of severe disturbance in the most disturbed adolescents and containment during treatment, especially management of risk of severe self-harm and suicide.

Skogstad (2003) surveys how inpatient settings run according to psychoanalytic principles developed in Germany (Simmel 1929) and the USA (Menninger 1936) in attempts to treat more disturbed patients. The dangers of regression and confusion in the inpatient treatment process are very real, and ways of working together meaningfully and therapeutically will be discussed here. Tom Main (1946, 1989), as a psychoanalyst and as Medical Director, pioneered a method in the UK at the Cassel Hospital of *using the whole inpatient experience to therapeutic effect*, combining psychosocial nursing, developed by Doreen Waddell (a matron who became a psychoanalyst) and psychoanalytic psychotherapy within the inpatient context. While such a procedure has had its critics, because of the confusion of the splitting processes (Enke 1965) or because the whole 'bi-polar model' is seen as faulty (Janssen 1987), the approach continues to develop with success, spawning an increasing literature and reflected in positive research outcomes (Chiesa 1997; Chiesa and Fonagy 2000). As noted throughout, my particular perspective is on psychotherapy with children and adolescents in this applied context, and my aim is to illustrate a number of successful cases as well as some of the pitfalls and difficulties in such applied work.

Some of the chapters have full treatment studies around particular issues, such as the development in a young child of a capacity for symbolic expression that helped her deal with intense internal conflict (Chapter 2); the issue of the loss of psychic containment in a borderline child (Chapter

3); and the internal struggles in a child to make sense of experiences of severe abuse (Chapter 5). Most chapters give treatment examples that are intensive in terms of frequency (seen up to three times per week) and duration (for up to two years), and occur in the context of interdisciplinary work, with the parents and the family, and with the professional network. The work with children in Parts 1 and 2 about trauma, abuse and family breakdown also underlies the subsequent work in Part 3 with adolescents, many of whom have had a similar childhood history. It is important with adolescents that elements of previous childhood experience and disturbance be understood as part of making sense of specific adolescent aspects of emotional disturbance.

This book fits alongside two of Roger Kennedy's books, *The Family as In-Patient* (Kennedy, Heymans, and Tischler 1987), and *Child Abuse, Psychotherapy and the Law* (Kennedy 1997), but it aims to give more detailed clinical discussions of the assessment and treatment of children and adolescents, linking one area to another, as well as explaining more fully the rationale of the inpatient treatment as it affects them. It complements and adds to my recent book with Lesley Day (edited), *The Internal and External Worlds of Children and Adolescents: Collaborative Therapeutic Care* (Day and Flynn 2003), but with a more sustained look in a number of clinical studies at linked areas of the work with children and fuller theoretical discussions of the work with adolescents. The aim is to complement a number of other studies of psychotherapy of children and adolescents in mainly conventional settings (Waddell 1988; Alvarez 1992; Lubbe 2000a), and diverse applied contexts (Anastasopoulos, Laylou-Lignos and Waddell 1999; Lanyado and Horne 1999). My intention is to outline a rationale for inpatient psychotherapy with children and adolescents as practised at the Cassel Hospital, UK (and in similar ways in some other parts of Europe), at a time when medium and long-term inpatient psychotherapeutic treatment is strongly under threat in the USA.

By bringing together these case studies on a sustained common theme of psychotherapy in applied contexts, I hope to appeal to those interested and involved in the psychotherapy of children and adolescents, and to those professionals who are our essential co-workers in such difficult work in applied contexts – psychologists, doctors, psychiatrists, nurses, social workers and probation officers, counsellors, lawyers and the judiciary. Besides wanting to bring together some of my papers and work in this important area, the aim is to 'give something back' to this group of professional co-workers, by showing the value of psychotherapy in their complex work.

Part 1 on The Young Child discusses two cases of psychotherapy of young children of pre-school age, both of whom were treated in outpatient settings, the first in a child guidance clinic and the second in a hospital day children's centre. The roots of emotional disturbance in each child developed from early infancy onwards. Chapter 2 describes the emotional turmoil of a young child about to start school. Her level of disturbance, in the normal or 'neurotic' range, is less than for many of the other children discussed in the rest of the book. This child's emotional contact with her mother had been ruptured and affected in her earliest years in ways that substantially affected her internal psychic development. In the run-up to starting school we see the various levels of internal conflict that became manifest in behavioural and emotional disturbance; and in psychotherapy the growth of her ability to manage her intense feelings of anger and jealousy of her younger brother and envy of the parental couple. In particular we see how facing and working through internal conflicts was shown in an increase in her capacity for symbolic expression, which elucidated in detail the relation of her inner world and her external life. This is illustrated in the sequence of drawings she produced throughout the psychotherapy.

In Chapter 3 the child's level of disturbance was greater and had developed from chronically inconsistent emotional care, in particular traumatic separations and loss of parents. This had resulted in severe behavioural difficulties and constant unsettled emotional turmoil that meant continued problems of containment. This child was in the 'borderline' range and she required a type of treatment that allowed for psychotherapy of her inner disturbance and conflicts, along with nurturing care in the children's centre by her nurse and teacher, and from her social worker outside. This helped her deal with the reality of her lack of personal nurturing experience and was an attempt partly to remedy the deficit. I shall discuss the diagnosis 'borderline child' and the modifications in the treatment modality in a day treatment setting.

In Part 1, I illustrate how the conflict and emotional turmoil of such children gets expressed in the process of psychotherapy. This emphasis sets the scene for the process of intensive psychotherapy as used in more complex applied contexts discussed in the rest of the book. We see how the intensity of the whole therapeutic process is relived in the psychotherapy setting itself, allowing the formation and repetition of internal conflicts in the transference relationship to the psychotherapist. This is a live process involving shifts in feeling and belief in the child and shifts in their view of the psychotherapist. At successive stages we see the emergence at different levels of primary figures, of mother and father, and of archaic figures and primitive early identifications. I look at how talking to the child at an in-depth level, and recognition of meaning in their play, involves the use of interpretative techniques to identify, name and understand such figures, bringing them alive in the here and now of the interactive dialogue and play in the psychotherapy session.

In these studies I make full use of Melanie Klein's techniques of child analysis in particular to develop an in-depth understanding of the child and to harness the power of the transference relationship. I incorporate into this, influenced by the work of Bowlby and Winnicott, a sense of the realities of the life of the child – the restraining facts of their family, the trauma, the separations (and in this part and in Part 2 in particular) any abuse they may have suffered. Most especially I make use of Bion's concepts of 'containment' and 'thinking', and his emphasis on the work of developing feeling and awareness of internal processes – the work of 'α-function'. This work of differentiating thinking and feelings can lead to psychic growth, free from disturbed and bizarre elements, which can cloud understanding with types of delusive awareness that lead to ongoing emotional disturbance. I shall return to this (Bion's) emphasis on distortions that effect the development and psychic growth of adolescents in Part 3.

In Part 1 I look at the impact of the psychological on the social both in terms of the formation of the type of emotional disturbance – the manifestation of internal disturbance in the symptoms – and in terms of the aim of therapeutic work and the indistinguishable link between psychological readjustment or inner growth and reorientation to social task (Jaques 1953, 1955). In Chapter 2 this is the inner growth required for the young child to adjust to the social reality of going to school; in Chapter 3 it is the inner growth which the child needs to achieve in order to develop a personal relationship so that she could be contained within a family.

The relation between the internal and external world is continuously explored using concepts I outline later – transference, countertransference, phantasy, containment and psychic growth. The child who is severely emotionally disturbed is caught in his or her own view, which means an awareness of reality and the external world that is largely influenced, indeed dictated, by their internal states and inner emotional turmoil, without the possibility of an emotionally shared view of the world. The task of psychotherapy is to help the child make contact with these internal states and make shifts in their internal awareness and their view of the external world. I shall outline movements from more primitive psychic functioning to a type of relating that implies an acceptance of loss and a capacity for self-awareness, in movements from the paranoid–schizoid position to the depressive position, and reversals of these processes (PS ↔ D). With more positive change in the direction of Klein's depressive position comes the development of a capacity for concern, including a concern not just for the survival of the object (the parent, the 'lost good object') but a concern for the survival of the self that allows a more sustained individual growth and the development of personal identity.

Part 2 on The Child in the Family comprises Chapters 4 to 8, and describes the child in the context of the family. Chapters 4 to 7 outline specialist work with children and their families in the inpatient context of the Cassel Hospital Families Unit in work towards rehabilitation of children with families. In turn I look at assessment of children in this context and their experience of a residential setting; problems of childhood disturbance and adult mental health; physical, sexual and emotional abuse of children and the complex work of rehabilitating such children with their families. I shall also look at the experience of children when rehabilitation fails and there is a need for a new family. Finally in this part, in Chapter 8, I discuss some aspects of the new family for the child by focusing on the role of the adoptive father and by giving case examples of adopted children.

In Part 2 I fully discuss the structure and importance of this inpatient applied context not just as planned by staff but as experienced by the child. The overall themes of this part are: *What do children have to do to make sense of their experience? How are children able to think about their family experience?* Whether they have been through separation, abuse or a breakdown in parenting, these are recurrent questions. Equally I shall look at how difficult it is for children to work through early real-life experiences that have caused a level of emotional disturbance and fragmentation, and how precarious the path to recovery can be. Another theme running through is the importance of the containing environment provided by the child psychotherapist in the institution, working cooperatively with the staff team, for the parent to rebuild the family and for the child to regain a capacity to think.

The children's images in their play in the case studies provide a fascinating and revealing thread throughout this part, showing the child's experience of the hospital and the changing patterns of relationships in the family, indicating different levels of transference to the child psychotherapist and others working with the family, especially adult psychotherapists and nurses. Like the images and drawings of the children discussed in Part 1, the images that occur in the children's phantasy, play and dreams show the impact of their internal world and view of themselves and their family, in their perception of the external world. Equally some images show how the external world is experienced and incorporated into their unconscious inner view of reality. Some examples of the children's images from the child's psychotherapy that occur in Part 2 are:

- *the fishtank* as the stuck family
- *the house with windows facing in* as the family with secrets without outside influences
- *the oxygen cylinders* as the unsafe hospital/family
- *the ladder leading nowhere* as the collapsed family and the child's despair
- *the lacerated neck of the horse* and the remembered abuse injury
- *the dandelion which rises and dies again* as the collapse of progress
- *the monster man Stewart* and the dangerous stepfather/psychotherapist
- *Tarzan and the bad monster* as the exciting powerful man and the threat to safety
- *the knee-knaw police car* and the cruel mocking superego
- *the dangerous crocodile* and the immediacy of the danger of abuse

- *the falling tree person* and the effect on the child of the neglectful parent
- *the plasticine covered holes* and the terror of anal abuse
- *the alien child* and the loss of maternal contact and rejection of the child
- *the man watching TV* and the psychotherapist's protective attention
- *the fat man on the ceiling* and the dream screen memory of the death of a sibling
- *the dummy mummy* as the mother who blocks out awareness
- *the child belonging in a bin* as the rejection of the adoptive child.

Many of the case examples in this part bring out the impact of trauma on the child's thinking and relating. The child asks questions and also explores in his or her mind in an invaluable even indispensable way, in play and interactions in psychotherapy and in their progress towards recovery. They question *what has gone wrong? . . . Do my parents love me or hate me? . . . How do I deal with my feelings of love and hate towards them?* Trauma can cause a closedown or disintegration of functioning. But sometimes the impact of trauma creates a spur or impetus in the child to make sense of what has happened and who they are. This can cause a sudden spurt of emotional work that can be enriching if it is not overwhelming. We can sometimes see the same thing in very disturbed adolescents, as I discuss in Part 3. We see how important this is in adoption, where children have lost their original or birth parents and they have extra work to do to integrate this experience in their minds – work that can be enriching if it is not too painful to manage. To help the adopted child with this work the adoptive parents face the dual task of care and nurture, and understanding and integration of their experience and the child's experience.

In the rehabilitation of families after abuse this work by the child of integrating their experience can only occur if the family can establish during treatment some degree of normality of family life and some stability in their lives. Work in an applied context aims to provide and understand the conditions necessary for this. Current risks are carefully managed, parents receive intensive parallel work in psychotherapy, family meetings and psychosocial nursing, and the whole thing is held together in a coherent way, both in regard to the management of care and the therapeutic work and with regard to relations between the inside and the outside, other agencies or parties involved, including social services, health authorities and the courts (Kennedy 1997).

During family rehabilitation children take part in a difficult and painful process, seeing their parents' weaknesses and flaws, and facing conflicts over accepting their parents' guilt. Their view of their parents may suffer considerable damage, but effective work aimed in particular to improve the quality of relating and the love and care the child gets in the present can help repair the damage. In this process the child may get to know the real parents with their flaws and can develop further, knowing more of the reality, both internally and externally. We underestimate the capacity of children to face reality, which they can often do better than adults. At times, however, children may need to use their psychotherapy to communicate their stark despair at their parents' failure to repair their parenting and their own feeling that their world is falling apart. Experience of a whole spectrum of difficult cases allows for a better assessment of when rehabilitation has a more hopeful diagnosis. We then see that specific parenting capacities need to be acquired to help children reintegrate their experience during family rehabilitation.

Part 3 on The Adolescent discusses severe emotional disturbance in adolescence and some special requirements in applied treatment contexts for adolescents. These four chapters highlight the powerful physical forces of sexuality and aggression that become active in the body of the adolescent and the increasingly strong mental processes of introjection and projection that are active as adolescents detach from parental figures and make real steps towards becoming independent adults. Old ideals are modified or rejected and new ideals and an individual approach to life taken on, influenced at this stage for most adolescents by the peer group. Individual approaches (Chapters 10, 11, 12) and group approaches (Chapters 9, 10, 11) to adolescents are examined in the light of the most severe forms of adolescent disturbance. There is a continuity of intrapsychic conflicts from childhood, including those that occur in central relationship issues – new Oedipal configurations – and those influenced by adverse upbringing or environment, including neglect, physical, sexual and emotional abuse. Issues about health, disability, physical and sexual maturation; issues about body image and identity, and disturbed thinking and bizarre thoughts; about self-harm and suicidal risk are discussed. My final two chapters look at the containment of severely disturbed borderline adolescents in an inpatient therapeutic unit (Day and Flynn 2003), and crucial issues in the assessment of severely disturbed adolescents.

At the start of Part 3 in Chapter 9 is a discussion of a group of adolescents who are frequently overlooked – those with severe disabilities, and therapeutic work in a ward group for patients who mainly have spina bifida. We see the impact of illness on their lives, their sense of self and their overall development. We see the impact of early deaths in adolescence, how the deprivations of disability affect personal progress and development, and the impact of the institution on the individual in the absence of normal family life. Next, in Chapter 10, there is a short survey of psychoanalytic theories of adolescence, starting with Freud's crucially important but somewhat sparse views on the subject and the centrality of the Oedipal conflict in adolescence as in childhood, with examples of younger adolescents and their transition into adolescence. Some developments in psychoanalytic theory about adolescents particularly post-1945 are traced, and a theoretical understanding for differentiating normal adolescent processes from those where there is the eruption of more severe pathology is considered, with examples differentiating more normal and more pathological aspects.

This continues as a main theme in the last two chapters. In Chapter 11, I describe how a therapeutic process for severely disturbed adolescents aims to achieve change and progress, to deal with, understand and importantly contain and manage risk. Some practical ways of doing this and its theoretical underpinning are then examined. We see how important it is for both staff and adolescents to attempt to understand disturbed institutional processes, and how the work with the unleashed powerful life forces and destructive forces within the adolescent and the adolescent group needs to be addressed. In Chapter 12 the focus is again on the interplay of these forces and the consequent splitting processes in relation to different workers, and on the possible eclipse of normal adolescent functioning in the individual adolescent and in the adolescent group processes. There are difficulties inherent in the therapeutic task for those facing such splits, including strong countertransference reactions that can affect the capacities of different members of staff. There are particular issues to consider for making emotional contact with adolescents during assessment, including importantly the need to gather in and respond to split perceptions (both negative and positive) in the adolescent.

Throughout adolescence, and indeed in any adolescent's day, there are constant shifts backwards and forwards, and there occur frequent changes of emotional state and mood. In effect the adolescent moves in and out of different mental states and in some respects these changes reflect the movements between more conflictual internal states in what Klein called the 'paranoid-schizoid position' to more emotionally responsive and self-reflective states, accepting of depressive pain and loss and not so rent by intense turbulent conflicts, which are moves characteristic of Klein's 'depressive position'. I shall return repeatedly to movements between 'healthy adolescent development' and 'healthy adolescent disturbance', both part of what I shall call 'the adolescent function', and movements to disturbed often highly volatile and dramatic states and actually bizarre and distorted types of thinking of a psychotic nature, both of which are part of what I call 'the borderline function', where self-harm and suicidal thoughts and behaviour squeeze out both the more healthy and the more 'healthily disturbed' sides of normal adolescent functioning.

As in other parts of the book, I shall discuss applications of central psychoanalytic concepts in work in applied contexts with adolescents; the transference of the adolescent to an individual, a group, an institution such as the ward or inpatient unit; and issues of countertransference experienced in the workers especially faced with the group processes. Important in this is the concept of 'tolerance' of disturbance (see also Chapters 3 and 6), including the need for human limits in respect of negative behaviour and especially with regard to the degree of tolerable risk over self-harming and suicidal behaviour. In all of this I stress the importance of 'containment' in adolescence, in the adolescent of their own mind and body, on the ward or in the inpatient unit, in and between the staff, and with the adolescents' peers and family.

Central concepts in psychoanalytic understanding

Before going on to the detailed exploration of the case studies, I shall now outline certain central psychoanalytic terms, which help us unlock and understand the child and adolescent's emotional state, and which need to be applied in later chapters to understand some of the complexities of this work with children and adolescents in applied contexts. These central psychoanalytic concepts that underlie all the case discussions throughout the book are 'transference', 'countertransference', the Kleinian concept of 'phantasy', Bion's concept of 'containment' and finally some issues about 'psychic growth'. In Parts 2 and 3 I discuss some additional technical modifications of 'transference', 'countertransference' and 'containment' within the inpatient setting.

Transference

Freud first described transference as 'new editions or facsimiles of the impulses and phantasies which are aroused and made conscious during the process of analysis . . . they replace some earlier person by the person of the physician . . . a whole series of psychological experiences are revived, not as belonging to the past, but as applying to the physician at the present moment' (Freud 1905a: 7–124; see also 1912: 97–108).

Klein thought that 'in some form or other transference operates throughout life and influences all human relations'. She extended Freud's theory to include not just direct references to persons but aspects or parts of persons or experiences that date from the earliest stages of the child's life (Klein 1952: 48–52; see also Brenman-Pick 1985). Klein recognised that the nature and quality of the transference develops from the nature of the earliest mental experiences and stages of development in its positive and negative aspects (Klein 1952: 48). This makes it possible within the psycho-analytic procedure to extend knowledge to the deepest layers of the personality and the earliest unconscious phantasies that constitute the earliest forms of transference (Segal 1964).

In the earliest stages of life the infant is vulnerable, dependent on the mother and the emotional 'environment' (Winnicott), and mental processes of splitting, denial, omnipotence and idealisation are at their height, in the 'paranoid-schizoid' position' (Klein 1946). Many of the child's anxieties are of a persecutory nature out of fear of annihilation and disintegration (Winnicott 1945; Klein 1946: 4, footnote 2), or out of fears of retaliation, because the infant's frustration or discomfort may have aroused aggressive or destructive impulses against his/her mother. Klein, following Ferenczi and Abraham, thought that the infant was exposed to his/her own raw emotional states that enhanced the quality of emotions and the nature of defences (Likierman 2001: 21). These raw emotions then become the content of phantasies whereby the infant directs his love to the 'good breast' and his persecutory feelings to the 'bad breast': this develops the ego and is the beginning of superego formation (Klein 1952: 49).

In time with the onset of the 'depressive position', which Klein dates from the time that the infant is six months old, anxieties of a depressive nature come into focus, as anxieties about sheer survival lessen and as good and bad aspects of experience are synthesised. The infant's aggressive impulses and desires are now felt instead as a danger to the preservation of the loved internal and external objects (primarily the mother), which then brings a new and intensive anxiety and guilt, and forms early Oedipal relations (Klein 1935, 1937, 1940). In the turbulent to-and-fro of early projective and introjective forces, phantasies are formed with increasing reality modifications, which become the basis of what abstractly we would call early identifications (Segal 1964: 43) and which influence the growing personality, and ego and superego structures. Klein stresses the need to appreciate the interconnection of positive and negative transferences, the interplay of love and hate and conflicting emotions and anxieties, which manifest life and death instincts.

Joseph (1985) develops Klein's view that the transference extends to 'the total situation' of the psychoanalytic encounter and is 'a framework in which something is always going on, where there is more or less constant movement and activity'. This extends Bion's idea of constant movements between more integrated and less integrated mental states, PS ↔ D (see Chapter 10 for application of this to adolescent mental states). The assumption of this approach is that the patient's immediate anxieties and the nature of his/her relationship with internal figures emerges in the whole situation lived out in the transference. This can lead to a complex subtlety of interpretation particularly as the part of the patient that is really needing to be understood is often (unconsciously) communicated through the pressures brought to bear on the psychoanalyst psychotherapist (to be unduly active, pleasant, seduced, parental etc.). Joseph believes that if one sees transference as basically living, experiencing and shifting – as movement – then interpretations have to express this, and they are then less constructions linking present and past. When the underlying unconscious assumptions in the transference–countertransference encounter are out 'in the open', however uncomfortable and painful this sometimes can be, then the transference can be experienced as a real live psychic reality. Later links can be made between this present live psychic reality and the patient's past that is again becoming more alive to the patient in the analytic process. This can help them build a sense of their own continuity and individuality and assist them to achieve some detachment from previous distortions (Joseph 1985: 164).

With young children especially, these links with the past may also be very psychically real and very recent in time, and access to internal figures that influence current mental states very immediate, so staying in the present and being aware of the unconscious influence of the child not only on the psychotherapist but in the whole situation is essential so as not to lose track of the child's communications. Adolescents too generally expect a direct and genuine interpersonal contact, even if they themselves are very cut off or depressed, so staying with them at an affective level tuned to underlying unconscious themes is especially important (see Chapter 12 on adolescent assessment). Such emphases in the use of the concept of transference give special importance to understanding the child and adolescent's experience of the setting of psychotherapy, especially complex applied settings, such as inpatient treatment (see especially Chapters 4, 6, 7, 9 and 11).

Countertransference

Countertransference has been increasingly important in psychoanalytic thinking for the last 50 years (Winnicott 1949; Heimann 1950; Racker 1957; Grinberg 1962; Money-Kyrle 1978). Heimann (1950) initially used the term 'to cover all the feelings which the analyst experiences towards his patient'. Since it is the psychoanalyst/psychotherapist's emotional response to his patient within the analytic situation, the countertransference is an instrument of research into the patient's unconscious (Heimann 1950: 74). In part the concept had been developed to lessen the sense of emotional detachment of the psychotherapist to the patient, who could be seen as somewhat coldly 'analysing' all sorts of levels of transference and emotions from the patient to him/her without himself/herself being emotionally involved.

Freud warned against over-involvement, writing that the psychoanalyst must 'recognise and master' his/her countertransference (Freud 1912; Heimann 1950: 77), so as not to enact unworked through aspects of his/her own unconscious thoughts and emotions, since this would distort the analytic process and then they may confuse their own countertransference with the transference. Most psychoanalysts/psychotherapists would now agree that neglect of countertransference limits the efficacy of analytic work. Also if the psychoanalyst/psychotherapist avoids routine self-screening processes of their own conscious and unconscious reactions to the patient, there will be a greater possibility of the very danger being avoided happening – unduly influencing the patient from one's own unconscious processes (Casement 1985).

Our changing view of countertransference is in part related to changing views of transference. If the transference is rooted in primitive preverbal infantile experience and is consistent with the Kleinian view of projective identification (Segal 1977: 82), it becomes more three dimensional – 'into' not 'onto' the psychoanalyst/psychotherapist. The child or adolescent may not only communicate a distorted view, but do things to the analyst's mind, projecting *into* the analyst in a way which affects the analyst (Joseph 1989).

Segal maintains that the major part of the countertransference like the transference is always unconscious and what we become aware of are 'conscious derivatives'. When at depth our countertransference is in a good state we have a double relation to the patient: one is receptive, containing and understanding of the patient's communications; the other is active, producing or giving understanding, knowledge or structure to the patient in the interpretation. It is 'analogous to the breast as containing and the nipple as feeding, or to maternal/paternal functions' (Segal 1964). (See Chapter 2, and modifications of this in an inpatient setting, with children in Chapter 6, with adolescents Chapter 11.)

Some issues about countertransference slide over into questions about analytic style, when in fact they are different issues. Personal disclosures from the analyst to the patient can be seen as reasonable and 'natural' extensions of countertransference – the patient perceives not just the analyst's unconscious process and can be allowed to see all sorts of levels of thought and feeling in the psychotherapist – allowing for 'more mutual' interchanges between psychotherapist and patient. Winnicott wrote of trying 'to avoid breaking up the natural process by making interpretations' (Winnicott 1969a: 711). Balint believed that each analyst is unique and contributes his own atmosphere to the particular analysis (Balint 1950: 123). Bollas (1989) recognised that the analyst's style and the atmosphere engendered offer the patient an equal partnership in a process that 'restores a normal mutuality in "affective response" of one to the other'. Winnicott thought that inter-pretations let the patient know the limits of his understanding and wrote 'the principle is that it is the patient and only the patient who has the answers'. I think this view goes too far in dispensing with the central purpose of the interpretation and the function of the analyst to use the special tool of the transference to attempt to describe psychic truth, including its deepest layers. In applied settings, such as a hospital inpatient unit, the psychotherapist may be known in many ways by his patients. However, my view is that psychotherapy even in such contexts requires a structured setting and an analytic technique that is not too personally involved with the patient and which can allow an understanding of primitive levels of experience to emerge.

Phantasy

Freud (1911b) drew no distinction between instincts and mental expressions or psychical representatives of instinct, regarding the instinct itself as the psychical representative of somatic forces. Strachey (1957) pointed out that an instinct could never become an object of consciousness. It was Isaacs

(1948) who pointed out that it was 'phantasy' which was the mental expression of instinct. Phantasies are in part conscious and in part unconscious, initially the product of hallucinatory wish fulfilment, but gradually becoming more attuned to reality and combining conscious elements and perceptions, in line with the development of the reality principle.

Phantasies relating to life-giving or destructive drives retain elements of infantile omnipotent phantasies and something of the live, almost tangible somatic quality of the impact of the instinctual experience upon the infant. The omnipotence of phantasy however is never complete, since from the beginning there is an interaction between phantasy and reality. The phantasy of the ideal breast breaks down if the frustration is too prolonged or intense. Equally persecutory phantasies can be alleviated or overcome by the reality of a good experience. At the same time the infant perceives reality in terms of his omnipotent phantasy, with good experiences merging with ideal phantasies, and frustration and deprivation being experienced as persecution by bad objects.

Isaacs (1948) links phantasy with higher mental function ('thinking', 'imagination', 'anticipation', 'counting'), because of the use of *symbolism* in phantasy and other mental functions. Segal (1964) more explicitly explains that higher mental functioning arises out of phantasy because of *reality testing* and hence allows a move away from hallucinatory ways of construing experience. But phantasy has a defensive function too insofar as it aims at fulfilling instinctual striving in the absence of reality satisfaction. There can be a regression to manic omnipotent phantasies in situations of stress or to depressive masochistic phantasies when a more courageous reality orientation is lacking, and so on.

Freud (1911b) wrote in 'Two Principles of Mental Functioning': 'With the introduction of the reality principle, one mode of thought activity was split off; it was kept free from reality testing and remained subordinated to the pleasure principle alone. This activity is phantasying.' Thought on the other hand was developed in the service of reality testing, primarily as a means of sustaining tension and delaying satisfaction. But he understood it is both phantasy and thoughts that enables the ego to sustain tension without immediate motor discharge. The infant can sustain his desire for some time with the help of phantasy until satisfaction in reality is available. As Segal points out, phantasy underlies thinking in that 'the richness, depth and accuracy of a person's thinking will depend on the quality and malleability of the unconscious phantasy life and the capacity to subject it to reality testing' (Segal 1964: 46).

Containment and psychic growth

Bion (1959, 1962a, 1962b, 1963, 1965, 1970) developed a new theory of the psychoanalytic procedure as a process of containment, a system of meaning of 'container' and 'contained', both interpersonally and intra-psychically. To understand is essentially to 'contain', which involves not just gathering in systematically or extensively different types of emotional perception and expression, but also means dealing with highly disturbed, bizarre and concrete elements of emotional experience, appreciating and thinking and then being able to 'digest' or 'metabolise'. Psychoanalysis/psychotherapy becomes something different with this model of container and contained, for rather than the process being mainly about giving the patient under-standing about their past and present psychic states, it means helping the patient in the process of thinking through their most difficult emotions and thoughts and helping them face what is preventing their being able to think and their development. What Bion called α-function is this process of making sense of various levels of experience, from the most primitive and concrete to more symbolical or higher levels of thinking, so that at each stage new 'realisations' of what is psychically true can be appreciated and experienced.

As the capacity for α-function is taken on and used within the individual, in their mind, it becomes a process whereby the mind develops giving emotional meaning to experiences and thoughts. This process is beautifully described by Wordsworth in a passage from the *1799 Prelude* (see Britton 1998: 128–45), which describes a kind of *vital response* of the mother to the infant, and the psychoanalyst/psychotherapist to the patient, which helps create the capacity to make sense of experience:

> Blest the infant babe
>   . . . who when his soul
> Claims manifest kindred with an earthly soul
> Does gather passion from his mother's eye.
> Such feelings pass into his torpid life
> Like the awakening breeze, and hence his mind,
> Even in the first trials of its powers,
> Is prompt and watchful, eager to combine
> In one appearance all the elements
> And parts of the same object, else detached
> And loth to coalesce. Thus day by day
> Subjected to the discipline of love,
> His organs and recipient faculties
> Are quickened, are more vigorous; his mind spreads,
> Tenacious of the forms which it receives.
>   (Wordsworth *1799 Prelude*: 267, 271–284)

Bion emphasised, as Wordsworth has in the *1799 Prelude*, how the quality of early maternal nurture helps the infant develop a capacity to link experiences in a meaningful way. This linking capacity provided by 'α-function' and 'thinking' acts by waiting and drawing together the meaning of experiences, not rushing at premature and thoughtless constructions. It draws on the 'life instincts', its *vital* quality, and aims to appreciate and deal with threatening and destructive elements and processes, summed up in the concept of the 'death instinct' (Bion 1963: 35). It is not an isolated process, but is in *response* to needs and anxieties, as is the mother's response to the infant. Progressively, as the process is internalised, it becomes the basis wherein the individual can give adequate response to their own bodily and mental experiences and thoughts, and as such leads to an internal *vital response* in return, from the infant to the mother and within the infant's own mind, so the infant uses his faculties to bring together experiences in a vital and alive way. It also underlies the response from the patient to the psychoanalyst/ psychotherapist as they make use of the analyst.

Bion's concept of 'containment' is similar to Winnicott's ideas (and Milner's; see Chapter 2) about allowing a transitional space where the infant can fully explore their omnipotence and come to feel they create new experiences, in line with progressive attunements to the reality principle. Steiner points out that before being able to take in and internalise a capacity for containment, there is a need to accept fully the loss of the desired good object: *only if* the loss of the good object is accepted internally, can it be recreated internally or a substitute created instead in a reparative way. 'What is internalised in the first stage is an object containing parts of the self, so that true separateness is not achieved, and the lessening of anxiety which results during this first stage depends on a narcissistic type of object relationship' (Steiner 1993: 60). This is an important point, which I think is implicit in what both Freud and Klein write in respect of the reparative element in the healthy process of mourning (Freud 1917; Klein 1940).

Bion simplifies types of emotional experience into three elements: K, learning from experience and L (love) and H (hate). In psychoanalytic work if the psychoanalyst/psychotherapist engages in L and H links to experience, it will be related to issues of emotional gratification or grievance. In Bion's view, 'whatever kind of link the patient uses L, H, or K with whatever part of the analyst's mind, the analyst seeks to use K' (Hinshelwood 1999). Bion writes (1962b: 47, #1) 'L and H may be relevant to K, but . . . neither is by itself conducive to K'.

In order to provide a point of reference to the emotional contact with the patient, the psychoanalyst/psychotherapist selects a focus from what the patient is saying and doing – the *selected fact* – to guide his attention and possible future line of intervention or interpretation. Where learning from experience breaks down by turning away from it, there is non-K (or relatively non-L or non-H). Where there is more severe disturbance and more severe splitting there is –K (or –L, or –K), the psychotherapist is felt enviously to remove the good or valuable element (in the communication) and force the worthless residue back into the infant (Bion 1963: 95, ch. 28, #5). This may feel to a child or adolescent like trying to project into a psychotherapist who does not want to know. It can puzzle, enrage and disturb thinking and produce a puzzled or enraged response from the infant or child in return.

Conversely the child or adolescent may use –K (minus K), so that anything valuable in the analyst, including their analytic function cannot survive (Bion 1962b; O'Shaughnessy 1992b). What Bion calls 'β-elements', indigestible elements of experience whose psychical quality cannot be perceived and that sometimes are experienced as events happening to the person, somewhat concretely rather than part of their psychological processes, may literally clutter up thinking capacity and contribute to defences against learning. Additionally 'bizarre objects', like β-elements but split off and projected objects, imbued with negative superego qualities ('critical', 'depriving', 'enviously destroying') contribute to the destruction of learning and literally can invade more healthy thinking processes.

Learning from experience depends on the capacity for containment to remain integrated, not losing it and keeping out rigidity (Bion 1962b: 93, ch. 27, #19). Essential for psychic growth is receptivity to the new idea: K and α-function is 'about something that is unknown' (Bion 1962b: ch. 27, p. 89, #1) and allowing or creating the new experience or idea (Bion 1962b, 1963, 1965, 1970; cf. Britton on PS $\leftrightarrow$ D $\leftrightarrow$ PS, 1998, ch. 6: pp. 69–81).

The theme of 'psychic growth' is the continuing theme of Bion's works after *Learning from Experience* (1962b). Our own subjective experience at the time may leave us in considerable uncertainty or doubt about whether what we are doing and thinking constitutes growth (Bion 1963: 63). While confidence and ego-strength are gained in the process of learning, and the process of learning itself is reinforced by a deepening of the transference relationship, the patient will remain unsure of the influence of the balance of negative forces and what Bion calls 'the spontaneous bleakness of the genuine PS $\leftrightarrow$ D' (i.e. movements to a more perceptive, understanding, 'depressive' and responsive state of mind). The patient may instead seek a false certainty or false sense of well-being and cut off from the painfulness of the process of learning (Bion 1963: 52; 1970: 102–3; Riesenberg-Malcolm 1999).

Bion's concept of "O" represents an emotional reality that is always changing however much of the emotional facts or truth we know (Bion 1965: 17, 1970: 103). Bion recognised that each new step in learning from experience involves painful work, but if it is sustained, progress can be made to overcome or move beyond emotional disturbance: 'the impact of the evolving "O" domain on the domain of the thinker is signalled by persecutory feelings in the paranoid-schizoid position . . . if the thoughts are entertained, they are conducive to mental health; if not, they initiate disturbance' (Bion 1970: 103). In this sense the patient is inevitably in an isolated position as they go through this struggle. Bion recognises the importance of accepting and allowing this inevitable sense of isolation as an essential part of their own struggle to use α-function and try to make sense of their own experience: 'at no time must either analyst or analysand lose the sense of isolation within the intimate relationship of analysis'. I emphasise this theme in the case accounts of children and adolescents and explain further the underlying theoretical issues with adolescents (Chapter 10).

To be able to move on, for true psychic growth, the patient needs to deal with the emotional understanding within him/herself. There is a stark and frank reality to Bion's perception that 'once he has expressed a truth the thinker is redundant' (Bion 1970: 104). Analyst and patient however closely involved in the process remain separate, and at times potentially may feel and be isolated. But as I discussed earlier, to internalise a capacity for containment implies the capacity to accept loss, even loss of the analyst who has helped to bring along the process of emotional understanding. Psychotherapy involves the crucial work to try to recreate the lost good object internally anew, which Melanie Klein recognised as a core element of coming to the 'depressive position' (1935, 1940).

Part 1

The Young Child

Chapter 2

Internal conflict and growth in a pre-school child

Introduction

The transition from home to school is one of the most important changes in the life of a developing child. Separation problems, which have their roots in the child's earliest experiences, generally become more evident at this time. The child's own progress through early stages of development and individuation receives a jolt when they are faced with the demands of a more social situation with its increased need for restraint and uniformity, and its new challenge to make relationships with different children and adults outside the family especially teachers.

I shall outline a case study of a girl of three and a half years called Georgina who came for three times weekly psychotherapy for one and a half years before starting school, when she reduced to once weekly. I shall describe her internal conflicts as her anxieties about going to school increased, and the parallel between the separation from home and parents and her experience of separation in the transference relationship with me, her psychotherapist. I aim to show that her achievement in working through intense infantile conflicts was of central importance to her making a successful social change, the transition from home to life at school.

Georgina was referred to a child guidance clinic at the age of three and a half. Georgina was reportedly progressing well in some areas, but her mother felt something was holding up her development and was intensely upset about her behaviour, especially her repeated aggression towards her 9-month-old brother, Jason. Also although she had been toilet trained before the age of two she was now repeatedly wetting and soiling again. Her mother found Georgina alternately clingy then distant and unmanageable and she was dismayed that children in the vicinity and at playgroup hated her because of her attacks on them. She dated the beginning of these difficulties from the time Georgina went to nursery, aged two and a half. The difficulties had increased after Jason's birth and ever since then there had been a strained relationship with her.

Further relevant details of her history emerged in the family assessment, from which the father absented himself. Her parents had longed for a child but they had had fertility problems for many years, and were then disappointed by the birth of a girl rather than a boy. Georgina had then been born by Caesarean section. Some deterioration in the relationship between Georgina and her mother may have begun almost straightaway (Trowell 1982). She did however enjoy a seven-month-long breastfeeding but was weaned abruptly in a week. Her mother was thinking about her next child and went into hospital to have an operation to widen her cervix to prevent another Caesarean. After these early difficulties Georgina was again separated from her mother when she went into hospital to have her second baby and was then also displaced by the longed for boy child. It seems there was an early good start when mother and child were deeply immersed with each other. They had now literally become 'cut off' from and unresponsive towards each other.

After her first few months there was a significant history of early illness in Georgina. At ten months she had measles and at eleven months, just before Christmas, she was hospitalised for croup. She was again hospitalised with croup the next Christmas, just before her second birthday. These early illnesses, which meant repeated experiences of separation from mother, seemed to set a pattern for further frequent and irregular minor illnesses in her pre-school years. In many instances the onset of the illness seemed to relate to some particular stressful event for her or in her family and therefore indicated the likelihood that there was a psychosomatic element.

In my first contact with Georgina, when I first saw her with her mother and her brother Jason, she presented as a small, slim, fair-haired child, with an intent, glazed, impassive look, some facial twitches, a stilted and almost incomprehensible speech, and an active daring manner. She was very inquisitive, keen that I should like her and vindictive towards Jason, pushing him, stuffing crayons in his mouth, and trying to pull him out of mother's lap. She showed no anxiety and spoke in a light monotonous growl. At one point Jason was holding a toy giraffe just near his genitals. Georgina laughed, took it away forcibly and pressed her own genitals with it whilst giggling and looking sideways at her mother. I found the giraffe in the waste bin at the end. Later, as mother and I spoke about breastfeeding, Georgina spontaneously said that she had tasted mummy's milk, liked it and wanted more of it. I found that the most striking aspect of Georgina's behaviour was her lack of any obvious anxiety, particularly with regard to her determined wish actively to push her brother away from mother. Georgina was attempting then to place herself in a central position not only in the family, but also in this first contact with her psychotherapist in the consulting room.

Early stages of psychotherapy: first three months

During the first part of her treatment, Georgina made a strong positive contact with me. As she became aware that our relationship would not exclude troubling feelings and ideas about other people in her life or mine, and she came to experience some losses and separations, she exhibited increasingly disturbed behaviour. This allowed us to examine in some depth phantasies and conflicts which underlay her disturbance.

In her first psychotherapy session she was initially timid and withdrawn. She showed intense frustration over her difficulty in sorting out from her box of toys the ones she wanted. There was a twist to her pretty facial features. She wanted my help and looked up at me without speaking – a look partly of supplication and partly of reproof. I thought she had a way of asking for something she wished for, while holding on to the thing in her mind, as if it could not be denied her: if she did not experience gratification, she would also not allow herself to experience deprivation.

She became calmer as she began making 'kites' consisting of painted pictures with elastic bands or string either glued or sellotaped on (Plates 2.1 and 2.2). She told me that she 'flew a kite with three boys' and that when she flew the kite she 'nearly wanted to do wee-wees'. She then said that she was 'wearing trousers and not a dress'. In this first session and later she told me stories of exciting occasions at the weekend when she had gone with her daddy and boys to fly kites. She repeatedly made these kites in her early sessions. Simultaneously her excited movements and gestures indicated that she wanted to maintain an excited relationship with the psychotherapist. The kite began to signify that her relationship to the psychotherapist was like that to an exciting daddy. Yet one could see too as some anxiety seeped through that the kite on a string also signified the tenuous contact she had with her mother.

In part she seemed to have picked up the message that to be a boy was more important. As a consequence she felt the need to seek out a special relationship to her daddy, particularly when her relationship with her mummy was strained. During the first week of psychotherapy she frequently became quite manic, rushing around and tipping over furniture and chairs. She talked of liking her daddy, but also recounted stories where there was a clear aggressive element against him. She resented him if he were not hers. She regarded herself as like the lady in the Superman film, who would hang onto the helicopter and be saved, i.e. a sort of rescue fantasy where daddy would 'save' her. But then she talked with glee of her daddy falling over and hitting his head and of her fighting with the boys and 'teaching them a lesson'.

In some water play, in the session before the first weekend break, she put a cloth in a jug and floated them in a water-tray saying 'they are like mummy and daddy'. She then tipped the cloth out of the jug and pressed a bowl on top of them so that they were smothered underneath in the water. I said that something seemed to be on top of mummy and daddy. 'Yes,' she replied. Prior to this first weekend separation in therapy then, Georgina seemed to want to dispose of her internal parents. In the transference, at the time when she was (temporarily) to lose her contact with the psychotherapist, she would dispose of him first.

Following this weekend, Georgina came back with all kinds of stories about daddy being 'all alone'. She inverted her own experience of being all alone, so that it became her daddy, and in the transference her psychotherapist, who was all alone, not her. Over the first two months she confided to me sometimes that daddy was ill and lonely. At other times he was a powerful Superman with whom she wished to ally herself more closely by making better and better kites. Georgina time and again told me she had watched the Superman video at the weekend, giving a different version of the Superman story each time. Increasingly however, new elements crept in showing that the Superman was not all powerful. On one occasion she told me that the lady had died rather than been saved.

After this initial period Georgina came nearer to expressing her feeling of being a displaced child. While this caused her acute pain she did begin to be able to conceive of a place – her psychotherapy – for painful or messy feelings. Instead of tipping pencil shavings over her therapist or on the floor she began to use the bin or her box. Trips to the toilet became important for the expression of feelings about what she could evacuate and what she felt left with. She also seemed very concerned about there being warm water for washing, as a comfort after passing 'wee', as if in fear of losing something warm inside her. She developed an anxious preoccupation about any particles of dirt she found in the room.

Georgina was now becoming a more anxious child generally. She had become more painfully aware of the closeness of Jason to his mother in the waiting room and at the beginning of sessions stood there near them disconsolately. She would sometimes then run off to sessions with fake excitement. Her view of E.T., in the film popular at this time, was partly one of identification as the needy baby, but partly one of relief that E.T. had 'gone home', a subtle change to the famous phrase from the film 'E.T. go home'. Georgina described baby Jason as being like E.T. – without hair and holding the centre of attention.

Much of Georgina's play at this time was about 'crocodiles' or 'sharks' 'that bit the fishes'. Her drawings of people were without bodies or limbs and the faces she drew were rather scary with jagged and threatening teeth (Plate 2.3). Her phantasies seemed to be on an oral-sadistic level and her fears were predominantly of being attacked by biting creatures (Klein 1930). Georgina saw me as 'a biting crocodile', who bit into her with painful comments that sometimes made her more anxious. After I interpreted this she calmed down and began to get beyond her first scribbly drawings to draw more clearly delineated figures. At the same time, her speech, which until then had been very stilted and incoherent, became more fluent. As she struggled with feelings of persecution, it was as if the cat, the shark and the crocodile 'did not have her tongue so much'.

When she now became more used to the structure of the therapy times, there were occasional glimpses (e.g. in the new Superman story, where the lady did fall) of her beginning to think that losses and falls can occur and be survived, albeit magically. But she was still far from being able really to recognise her own need for dependence, and most of her energy went into finding ways of protecting herself. She also expected me to protect myself from her. On one of the many occasions on which she completely soaked the floor, she looked at my shoes and asked me why I was wearing those shoes. She told me she thought they were 'wellies' (Wellington boots) and that I had them on to protect myself from her and the water. She felt that I would protect myself from her and keep myself out of helpful contact with her.

During this first three months Georgina's behaviour, particularly her frequent attacks on the psychotherapist, was extremely difficult to bear. Georgina then missed a number of sessions through illness. She was clearly beset by persecutory anxiety and plagued by guilt about her attacks, so that she was confused and very fragile (Klein 1933; Rosenfeld 1964).

In the sessions after her return from being ill it was clear that she experienced her own illness in connection with her father's demise, which linked to her experience of how she had made the therapist-daddy suffer in her session. For when she came back she recounted stories to me of how 'daddy had been taken to hospital dead in an ambulance' and of how 'mummy was nagging her all the time'. I ascertained (later) from her parents that this story was not at all true, but her conviction about it strikingly illustrated the power of her omnipotent phantasies of her own destructiveness (Klein 1940; Segal 1973). Her confusion reached a new peak in the last session before the first holiday break. She was angry that the exciting daddy, the psychotherapist in the transference, was going away on holiday. She expressed this by jumping into my usual chair and urinating over it.

The internal world

After the holiday Georgina showed signs of having missed the sessions and wanting them back. Initially she also seemed more able to manage feelings of persecution about loss. But soon there was a resumption of the bitterest attacks as she showed me new depths of her despair. She now began frequently to make 'snails' with paper and plasticine. These snails were well protected from invasion by their shells and they were sticky and unpleasant, which meant they drove people and things off. Her pain was felt to be deep inside her. Sometimes at the ends of sessions, or even during sessions, she would vomit if thinking about the end became too painful. There was a volatility and changeability about her feelings, but she hung on to the idea that she could remain the inside child, however fragile she felt, or the 'butterfly inside' as she depicted it in her drawings (Plate 2.4).

At this stage Georgina's parents planned to send her to the main infant school after the end of her second term in therapy – a prospect that horrified her. Before then a series of holidays was planned, with her grandparents and then her parents, which meant she would have only sporadic periods in between back in psychotherapy before then. This theme of broken periods with parents, grandparents and psychotherapist, repetitively torn away from each in turn was reflected in a session from this time:

> Georgina began to draw a butterfly that she poked with a pencil causing a hole in the paper. She became increasingly frantic, grimaced at me saying in a raspy harsh voice, 'You cannot see where the mark comes from.' She told me the point was very sharp. Recently she had been stabbing me with just such a pencil. I said the pencil was like the outside interferences, like her holiday away, which are like scratchy points digging into her. What I said by way of interpretation itself did not alleviate her mood. I then picked out a picture she had done last time of a pointed pencil and showed this to her, saying that she had been feeling poked into by these hurtful interferences, just like being poked by a pencil. Georgina looked at me a little dazed, having just grasped my account of what was happening. I spoke of her feeling the 'butterfly baby part felt attacked'. Following these inter-pretations, Georgina became livelier. However within a short time her behaviour again deteriorated. She began taking risks by jumping about the furniture to prove that she could survive the dangers she felt threatened by.

Progressively now Georgina faced greater depths of depression and anger. She was also particularly difficult at home. In her sessions after the holiday disruptions she was often depressed and confused and at times would sit quietly engrossed, slumped in a chair and timidly sucking her thumb. One time she sat slouched on the couch and said, 'I got a father's day card; it didn't get to her.' As she said this she put the blanket on the floor near the door, all in a mess. I felt this confused statement and action indicated her feeling of being cut off from her 'daddy-therapist'. She expected something from him and did not receive it. What she really wanted was to get through to her mummy.

Sometimes her depression erupted in a violent way. I shall describe one session in detail that proved to be the nadir of her expressions of anger and despair. In retrospect it also was a turning-point in her progress and personal growth, when she began to show new capacities:

> Early on Georgina was trying to force her way into the desk drawer. When I said she was trying to get into the drawer as she wished to find something that would explain the break and find a cause for her anger, she calmed down and told me in a confidential way that her granddad had collected 'a lot of conkers'. I found this first statement very puzzling. She then pointed to the window and asked, 'What is that?' I thought she meant the dustbin outside. She did not; she meant the raindrops on the pane of glass. She did not make it any clearer. She became very manic again, covering me with a blanket and saying 'Gordon Bennett' with much laughter covering over what I felt to be acute anguish. She then hit me very hard on the nose, so that I thought my nose was bleeding. She subsided on the couch in a collapsed mood, sucking the tie on her own dress and then trying to tie it up. She said her mother normally does it. I interpreted that she wanted control but she hit my nose because she was angry with me that I controlled the time. She then turned around away from me and leaned forward sticking out her bottom and showing me her knickers. I said she felt she could find a way back to her therapist after hitting me by becoming excited and showing her bottom. Georgina now drew the blanket over on the couch and relaxed. She stayed like this for a while then wanted to go just before the end, seeming in a much calmer state. I told her when the next session was after the holiday. As she went out into the corridor she told me how, in the video, the hero had his watch broken and then stuck up his aerial and sped off in his car. As I left she went on talking to her mum in an engrossed way.

My inability early in the session to make sense of Georgina's talk about 'the conkers' and her associations about the drops on the windowpane was experienced with fury by her. This distance or gap between us could have provoked her subsequent attack on my nose, known as 'conk' by some children, because I could not prevent or really explain her despair and pain. Perhaps the raindrops connected with the tears she could not cry, and the window 'pane', also a kind of barrier, with her 'pain'. However, her phantasy was that I was not simply 'cut off' from her because she believed that I had a means of control and understanding, which I did not use, hence her later despondency after the attack on me, which was partly guilt too. When she had recovered a bit near the end, this more negative element was then idealised. Then I was like the hero who broke up her therapy time (broke the watch) and went away on holiday ('stuck up his aerial and sped off in his car'). Many themes had come together: her envy of the boys, of their supposedly superior genitals (their 'conkers'), and of the controlling nipple of the mother which has a guarding phallic function, graphically described by Klein (1961) in her concept of 'nipple-penis' and Meltzer (1967). Georgina's capacity then to express her feelings, her fury and dismay, about the psychotherapist, and at root the mother, or 'nipple', which can give access to the good milk/therapy times but also can also put obstructions in the way, allowed for more working through in sessions on these themes and proved significant to her subsequent more evident growth.

Preparation for beginning school

Georgina's parents now successfully arranged that her date for starting the main infant school would be two terms later, not after the summer but after the following Easter, giving her more time. Georgina returned from holiday looking more robust and began to build structures with the toy fences. She said in a very basic way, 'I am here now, I was away before.' She then said, 'After my birthday I go to big school.' This knowledge of having more time helped her manage subsequent separations better and for her to develop more internal structure (Winnicott 1965; Abram 1996).

Georgina also became more aware of her effect on others. She confided to me that her mother had broken the ashtray and the goldfish bowl, indicating I thought that she could acknowledge that she could drive her mother to breaking point. Indeed from this time Georgina's mother began to look more relaxed and her relationship with Georgina was less overtly fraught. She was also sympathetic to my struggles, asking me after one session if Georgina had been 'too much of a handful'.

As plans were made for a reduction in psychotherapy times from three times to once a week, Georgina began to realise that this meant a loss for her of her psychotherapist – of someone who helped her contain her feelings. Fear of this loss brought out ambivalent feelings about going to school. At times she felt that going to school meant that she was 'big'. She would be 'like daddy or Tony', her friend from playschool. At other times she felt it meant a loss of her control and she could not keep me tied down to meet her needs. She was aware of her changes of feeling, her explosive reactions to change and her underlying fear that leaving home for school would be like a complete death. To avert this at times she became more aware and angry of any possible rival and sometimes more destructive.

When one time her brother Jason had an accident and was taken to hospital in the middle of the night with a cut head, Georgina's panic and guilt were considerable. In the next session she told me that she had been very frightened and had hidden upstairs in her bedroom. We talked of her feelings of guilt, her fear that she had caused the accident and what had happened in reality. She then said she remembered a time she had slipped and fallen when she got out of the bath at the weekend. She thereby acknowledged her weaknesses in the face of loss and she sympathised with the baby who had slipped and fallen.

At times Georgina had attempted to seek an inappropriate level of physical closeness and had felt rebuffed when I told her she was not to do that. She now began to develop fears not only about her destructiveness but also about her sexual wishes. This developed into a phobia about fire of any sort related to her 'fiery' masturbatory feelings. This started on 4 November, prior to bonfire night (5 November – 'Guy Fawkes night'), when she told me she did not want to watch the fireworks and spoke of her fear of fireworks, especially in the kitchen or in someone's pocket.

I thought it was significant that when Georgina became more aware of the power of her destructive fantasies she produced her first drawing of a person with a body. I was impressed too because that day Georgina looked snotty and bedraggled as if she was carrying all her woes on her. Her capacity to develop successful ways of expressing her feelings, particularly feelings of depression, greatly increased as Christmas drew near. Some drawings were colourful, expressing pleasing situations and memories, whilst others were more composite drawings illustrating whole aspects of the dismay and alarm in her inner world, such as her drawing in her last session before the Christmas break, which illustrates a complex mix of manic excitement and dismay about the impending loss of her psychotherapist at the break (Plates 2.5 and 2.6).

Her last term at nursery

Between Christmas and Easter, after which date she was to go to school, Georgina struggled again with the options open to her: to grow up and go to school or not to grow up, cling to her mother or therapist and stay at home. In her first session back after Christmas, she said calmly, 'After this term I won't be coming because I'll be big.' She found it tolerable to say this because her feelings about growing up were that she would become triumphantly united with her mummy or daddy with equal status. Georgina then became aware that this was unrealistic and produced drawings about her bedroom at home. A change became apparent in her awareness of her position in the family. She now drew herself as one of two children in a bedroom with bunks, the older child. An amusing corollary to this were the wild stories Georgina began to tell about which children she would get married to after Easter. In the preparations the confetti was made quite soggy and hurled at the therapist. By contrast, however, Georgina was able to talk about all sorts of little squabbles and fights she was having with other children. It became noticeable from now on that Georgina was becoming more liked by the other children.

But as angry, intense feelings again came to the fore in relation to her start at school, Georgina suffered a recurrence of the croup she had had as an infant. After she had got over the illness and returned to her sessions, her drawings about a damaged daddy, attacked and then damaged by her, showed something of her preoccupations and state of mind. Also while telling me about a night-time visit to the hospital, when her parents were worried about her, Georgina's main worries were about her daddy's bad back which kept him off work and the head cuts Jason had suffered on the previous occasion. Georgina told me about her fears and seemed sick with grief about the damage she felt she had caused. As she told me her speech was again very incoherent. I thought she was in a confused identification with a poorly daddy whose back could not stand up to strain (Rosenfeld 1965).

After further work in her therapy on Georgina's confused identification with daddy, the focus of her fears shifted to the mother, who was seen as a persecuting witch. This became apparent in a dream she told in a session:

> Georgina was still very pale from her croup and had been ill over the weekend. She began to tell me about daddy's birthday coming and how she was sick over daddy's newspaper and carpet. She then said she did not like dreaming. 'Why?,' I asked. Georgina then told me the dream, 'A lady with fire on her head was chasing children under the table'. The mention of a woman's head seemed to link with hair and with mummy's hairdos, a frequent way that Georgina expressed her anguish at the mummy who goes away and leaves her. This linked with the therapist's wavy hair and his creaky shoes. The mummy figure had now been invested with the exciting quality of her masturbatory fantasies, but to a terrifying persecutory effect (Klein 1925, 1929).

As Easter came nearer the intensity of feeling in Georgina reached a peak. When she saw me in town, for the first time ever outside the clinic, she came in for her session 'bursting for a wee' and spoke of 'hating people sometimes'. She drew another bedroom but would not say whose it was. However, she spoke of daddy and mummy quarrelling at night, because mummy tickled daddy's feet. Her drawing of the room was of a deep penetrating red colour. There were strong Oedipal phantasies and she was intensely aware that if she was to go to school and reduce the number of therapy times to once a week she was being distanced further and further from the excitement of the parental relationship. At other times, though, she seemed more resigned to this fact, and expressed feelings that daddy may not be worth it after all, for as she said to me in a confiding way, 'Daddy's feet stink sometimes you know.' Also the psychotherapist was represented in drawings as a colourful man figure but with crab-like feet (Plate 2.7).

By the final week before Easter, Georgina actually used the word 'cooperate' when talking about the holiday charts we went over together. In her play with the small animal figures and family dolls she was able to map out in a more tolerable way her relations to other figures: as a child outside the parental couple who would still want to be close to mummy, and as a child who could give way to and share things with her brother Jason who was to go to the playgroup she was leaving. Although quite miserable at the end of the week, Georgina came through and was able to start school.

Initial difficulties at school

When Georgina actually started school her fears were at a height and her adaptation to the new circumstances was precarious. She arrived for her first week's session smelling strongly of urine. She was daunted by the reality of facing new tasks there. 'I have to learn to read at school, I can't do it,' she confided with some measure of alarm. She was very aware of being one of the weaker, smaller children, who had carefully to step around the older ones. She was aware too of how near she was to feeling really depressed about school and how she needed the protection of the psychotherapist and older adults.

Following this session back, Georgina's mother contacted me to talk about how upset Georgina was becoming by fires of any sort. Georgina was worried about letting her mother go into the kitchen or smoke, and would sob her heart out about it, alarming parents or grandparents. It sounded as if a mechanism similar to that seen before was in operation, where the split-off dangerous parts of Georgina were felt to be left at home, but with the consequence that they became externalised there in the form of dangerous fires which would attack her mummy, herself and others. A couple of months after this Georgina would symbolise this process in a drawing of 'the woman with fiery hair on a train' (Plate 2.8). Also a little after this session, these parts were also projected into the absent therapist then missed and experienced as the 'therapist-mummy', and indeed her real mummy, so that she became haunted by frightening figures and very guilty about the way she felt she had damaged her 'maternal' object.

Soon however Georgina began to adapt and to talk over all aspects about going to school, including her swearing, her kissing other children, and her finding it easier to get friendly with a girl from an older class, also called Georgina, than to play with children her own age. Although she had run out of school at the beginning, she now was able to stay there and mix with some of the other children. As this happened Georgina began to really take on that she had a fiery part of herself, the angry and excitable parts of herself, and moving to a new level of self-awareness.

Georgina now accepted that her reduction in her psychotherapy time did not mean a total exclusion and she could accommodate herself to the new reality. In one session, she told me there were two birds in her loft that went 'tweet, tweet, tweeting their heads off', and her 'dad was going to get them out'. Her tone was one of tolerance and it appeared that Georgina felt the two birds did not need the space in the loft – they were just 'tweeting their heads off'. I felt Georgina was aware she was making do with her one session per week, even though I was the daddy who threw her out of my mind, 'my loft', the other two times. Towards the end of this time Georgina remarked reflectively that she had taken her pinny (protective apron) to school, i.e. the one she had had in the psychotherapy, but she had not used it there yet. I felt her here expressing a hope that school would be a place where she could find some tolerance of the sort she had had in psychotherapy. I felt it significant that as Georgina was feeling more confident of finding such tolerance elsewhere I received a letter from the paediatrician saying that the symptoms of croup that Georgina had had on and off for some months had now cleared up.

From this time on Georgina produced a wealth of pictures, games and conversations to describe to me her new experiences (Plates 2.9 and 2.10). Such material showed her increased capacity for internal symbolic work on her experiences. It all was part of a pattern whereby she became emotionally stronger, she was able to go to school and achieve success in new emotional tasks, while tolerating a reasonable level of independence from her parents.

Conclusion

Georgina's experience of psychotherapy enabled her to anticipate and work through much that could later have become an obstacle to her engagement in the learning process (Wittenberg, Henry and Osbourne 1983). I have laid stress on three important areas where Georgina worked through unconscious infantile conflicts, and I have described them from a psychoanalytic point of view, following the process in her therapy. Let me now summarise the changes I saw occur.

First, changes in emotional development brought with them an enrichment of her use of symbolism. Instead of being dominated by oral-sadistic phantasies, and hence a fragmented perception of reality, frequently presented in terms of her most primitive phantasies about parts of the body, Georgina was able to work through many phases of the process of mourning, recognise the value of the lost object and maintain the wish to recreate the desired lost object (Klein 1935, 1940). This working through was most clearly seen in the transference material where Georgina experienced her object, her psychotherapist and mother too, as a guarding 'nipple-penis' which obstructs her from more contact and a better relationship. With such psychical movement in the direction of what Klein has called *the depressive position* (Klein 1935, 1940; see Segal 1973: 67–71; Hinshelwood 1991: 138–155; Liekerman 2001: 100–136), objects Georgina symbolised later on were not so much concrete 'symbolic equations' (Segal 1957), but more complex

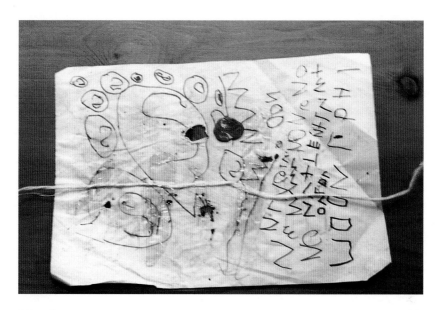

Plate 2.1 A 'kite'

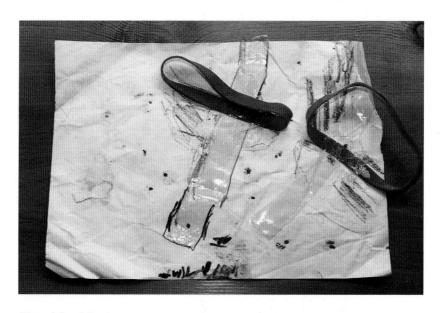

Plate 2.2 A 'kite'

Plate 2.3 'Scary people'

Plate 2.4 'A butterfly inside'

Plate 2.5 A more composite drawing

Plate 2.6 Drawing from last session before Christmas break, dismay

Plate 2.7 Therapist with 'crab-feet' and 'breaks'

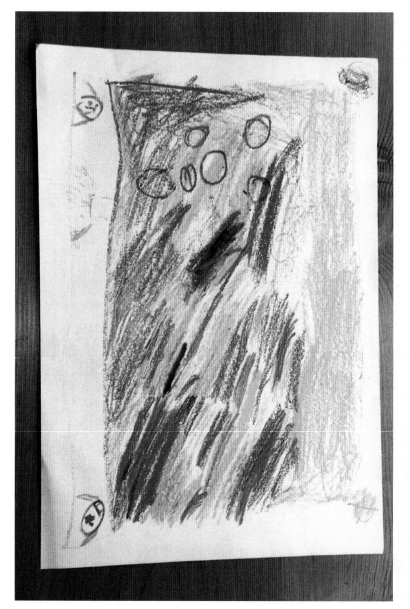

Plate 2.8 'Woman with fiery hair on a train' (second from right)

Plate 2.9 'Girls on Clapham Common holding balloons' with incursion of nobbly 'red breaks' to the right

Plate 2.10 The 'therapist-daddy'

symbolisations capable of shared meaning between people, as shown in her symbolically richer drawings and her more lucid speech, which were evidence of a more securely internalised good object.

Second, as part of this process Georgina became increasingly able, as most normally developing children can, to overcome the early domination by infantile fears and fantasies. Events were then experienced as not so severely upsetting, so that she now could avoid frequent lapses into illness, and she could get on with the real tasks in hand. There was less likelihood of psychosomatic confusions, which may have originated during Georgina's first year of life, after weaning, when she suffered from measles then croup. In her treatment the confusions began to appear again after she had made a strong attachment to her father, shown in the 'kite' material, and she had begun to have fears about her father being damaged by illness. In the transference her attacks on her psychotherapist were an acting out of her phantasy attacks on her father. What emerged then were earlier phantasies of damage to the mother and the breast.

Such phantasies lead to psychosomatic confusions because early primitive psychotic anxieties, particularly paranoid anxieties, are felt as conflicts within the body and can be experienced as physical damage to the ego (Rosenfeld 1964). Frequently for Georgina this was seen to be linked to her excessive use of projection identification, and to other complicated splitting mechanisms (Klein 1946), so that her attacks in phantasy and reality on her father or mother led to her feeling 'damaged' because she had a 'damaged' mother or 'damaged' father inside her. Anna Freud (1952a) in a study of orphan children describes a similar process in which confusion of body image contributes to an increased tendency towards hypochondriacal illnesses in small children. She found that the children tended to identify with the lost mother, while retaining a view of themselves as their body, so that the child actually deprived of the mother's care becomes like the mother and gives her care to his/her body, and thus plays 'mother and child' to his/her own body. In Georgina's psychotherapy a maternal transference had begun to replace the paternal transference and became stronger as the process deepened. The significant point in this process was that as I, the psychotherapist, worked to contain her infantile anxieties, so Georgina began increasingly to accept loss and to find again, and introject, a strong maternal object.

Third, changes in Georgina's capacity to be an independent schoolchild depended on her ability to move on from early Oedipal object relations. These were dominated by a greedy, dominant and omnipotent control of her maternal and paternal objects, denying that they are a couple. As she moved to a later stage of Oedipal relations, then, she could be content to be separate from the parental couple, as a child amongst children, and a girl with other girls and boys. Georgina's need to be a boy was rooted in her envy of the position she perceived this boy to have within the family. The change for her was achieved partly by her being more able to accept her angry and anxious feelings, her experience of being accepted and thought about in the psychotherapy, and an improvement in her relationship to her mother, with an increased possibility that she could identify with her. At root she could settle down and forgive her mother for having a baby, so she could see herself as a girl who could also become a mother.

The problems Georgina faced were to do with separation, stemming from the sudden weaning and separation from mother during her early illnesses and mother's hospitalisation (Klein 1936). The early experiences of being psychically 'cut off' from her mother perhaps dated from the Caesarean birth, and were experienced in an emotional separateness between mother and child. Before psychotherapy mother and child were unable to enjoy each other freely and improve their relationship, when mother felt there was something terribly 'stuck' between them. From early on in the psychotherapy I observed that although Georgina felt the oncoming breaks would be unbearable she did in fact progressively learn to manage.

To a degree some of the patterns of family relationships continued. For example, when Georgina made some changes in psychotherapy the parents felt relieved but then wanted her to finish or to 'cut it short'. It became necessary for a colleague in the clinic to offer work with the parents for a while, so that they could allow time for Georgina's treatment to continue and growth to happen. This also led the parents to give support to each other, so that they could have a joint approach to Georgina's difficulties, even though they were reluctant to accept ongoing psychotherapy themselves. They could however see 'preparation for school' as an acceptable reason for continuing Georgina's psychotherapy. When Georgina saw her parents more united she could now allow herself to savour more independence and not be so persecuted by guilt for splitting her parents.

Very soon after beginning treatment Georgina gave up the soiling and wetting that were symptoms of the early developmental difficulties. But she needed additional time at home with mother to develop their relationship, and further time in psychotherapy to work through internal conflicts. For many children, advances at a social and cognitive level may only be achieved as emotional change occurs. I felt this was illustrated by changes in Georgina's increased capacity for symbolisation and the improvements in her relationships with other children.

Milner's (1955) notion of the symbol as a type of illusion is helpful in understanding this process, as given time the child produces a fusion or illusion and believes that the secondary object (the thing 'symbolised') is the primary one (the 'mother', or the 'breast'). When this illusion breaks down and she is able to go back to the primary object, the child can experience again the illusion of oneness by successful use of the breast and recreation of the symbolic link. If such conditions exist there can be a fostering of psychic growth. If, however, the memory is of a too sudden breaking up of the 'illusion of oneness', the child feels intruded on from without and an emergence from primary narcissism that is tolerable to the child is hindered. Georgina, then, needed time to work through early internal conflicts, so that a successful introjection of a strong maternal object could be made. One most striking feature in this process was that her most significant advances were made at points where she found it tolerable to experience the sharpest mental pain (Joseph 1989; Abel-Hirsch 2003; see Chapter 6 ahead). The time when Georgina eventually went to school was one such point and I was struck by how intensely she prepared herself. Her time in psychotherapy before going to school enabled her to make this important social change tolerable and allowed her to get back on track with her normal development.

Chapter 3

Early identifications in the borderline child

Introduction

In this chapter there is an outline of the use of psychotherapy of a more severely disturbed child in one particular type of applied setting, a day centre for children combining psychotherapy and education at the Children's Centre at the Cassel Hospital, UK (Marsden 2003; Kennedy, Heymans and Tischler 1987). I describe the treatment of a four and a half year old girl called Anita who had suffered repeated abandonment and changes of care during her first years of life. Anita continuously expressed her acute infantile distress as she struggled to recover from trauma that had profoundly affected her ongoing emotional development, and had left her with confused and insecure attachments. I aim to show how psychotherapy, three times weekly for three years, brought out early identifications and the underlying splitting processes, and helped Anita develop as a child. The overall intensive work was part of a combined treatment model in which Anita also received continuing nurturing care from her nurse and teacher. In the discussion I shall also outline some features in the treatment that are relevant to Anita's diagnosis as a borderline child.

Our method of working allowed for the sort of modification of technique found to be necessary in borderline cases (Bleiberg 2000: 62–68; cf. too Geleerd 1946, and the similar approach of the Menninger Clinic, USA). This enabled Anita to have close personal contact with her nurse, forming a real ordinary relationship, whilst in the psychotherapy sessions as her psychotherapist I could follow the unfolding transference. This dual method allowed us both to do something to remedy the *deficit* Anita had suffered in her damaged attachments, and yet allow, in the growth of the transference relationship with her psychotherapist, the emergence of central figures in her inner life and to deal with *internal conflict*.

Anita's whole short life had been a struggle to deal with painful and intolerable experiences that limited her capacity for emotional maturation and to grow and change (Klein 1932). To understand the emotional impact of severely painful experiences for an infant or young child, we need to recognise the effects both of the trauma and of the neglect and how very strong the feelings of inner persecution can be. The child feels in constant danger of being overrun and overwhelmed by inner anxieties, so that a relationship with a good inner object, which could survive the turbulence and change, cannot be established (Klein 1932; Riesenberg Malcolm 1999).

Trauma and early identifications

There is a history of childhood trauma in many borderline children and adolescents (Herman and van der Kolk 1987; van der Kolk and Fisler 1994; Herman, Perry and van der Kolk 1989; Pynoos 1990, 1993; see also Chapters 11 and 12 below on adolescents). To understand some of the links between trauma, phantasy and unstable early identifications, I shall briefly review some theoretical issues, before going on to outline Anita's history and treatment.

Freud had a succession of theories about the determining elements in trauma. By 1918, in *Inhibitions, Symptoms and Anxiety*, he thought there were two main determinants: (a) the strength of the ego as compared to the intensity of the stimulus; (b) the power of internal as compared to the external sources of stimuli (Freud 1918). If the ego and the internal sources of stimuli are strong enough, phantasies are produced which are a form of defence and can reduce or prevent the effects of the trauma. Such phantasies will form the content of many early identifications in the child, which as partial forms of knowledge serve the purpose of reducing a full knowledge of the experience and the level of psychic pain. In *Moses and Monotheism* Freud restated his view that the traumatic event was followed by a regression to primitive modes of psychic functioning, either as 'fixations' to the trauma or in the form of a 'compulsion to repeat' (Freud 1939). Primitive phantasies embodying early identifications are part of these 'defensive reactions' to trauma.

For Freud the concept of identification comes to have a central importance not simply as one psychical mechanism amongst others in a process whereby symptoms or dream elements are formed but the operation whereby the human subject itself is constituted (Laplanche and Pontalis 1973; Sandler 1988). Identification is both a normal developmental mechanism and a mechanism of defence. Sandler and others make an important distinction between primary and secondary identification, as they are now understood. Primary identification is a state of primary identity or confusion in which the infant cannot differentiate himself from his object, which leads to a loss of 'ego boundaries'. For Mahler it involves a regression to an earlier 'capacity' (of the child being united with mother). For Klein there is similarly a regression, although the concept of primary identification is not used and the regression is seen to be not to an earlier 'capacity', but is a move away from a present painful reality under the influence of an omnipotent form of phantasy (Segal 1973). In both views more severe forms of regression will herald psychosis. At a primitive level of phantasy, objects that are similar are regarded as the same and an omnipotent form of phantasy gives rise to confusion between self and object (Tausk 1933; Freud 1923; Hinshelwood 1991).

When there is a secondary identification, the representational boundary between self and objects is not lost, but the subject comes to relate to an object on the basis of perceived similarities with the ego. Such early identifications can still give some measure of psychological stability. But where there is, as illustrated in my case study of Anita, a sliding into primary identification (the Freudian view) or a dominance of early primitive phantasies (the Kleinian view) and a great instability of secondary identifications, such stability is lost (Ekstein and Wallerstein 1954). For some this feature is the central characteristic of the borderline child (Rosenfeld and Sprince 1965). By contrast the achievement of secondary identifications presupposes the formation of an ego and the awareness of the self as a separate entity. In normal development there is a more progressive growth and development as early identifications are replaced and influenced by new levels of internal and external awareness and more mature identifications.

For Klein 'the primal internalised objects form the basis of complex processes of identification' (1955). Such inner objects are formed by the infant's own impulses, emotions and phantasies, influenced by good and bad experiences from external sources, especially the mother's attitude. The inner world influences his perception of the external world, and the good internalised object is one of the preconditions of an integrated and stable ego and for good object relations. Projective and introjective identifications need to be balanced to allow a 'securely established good object'. Klein felt that the 'fear of annihilation by the destructive forces within is the deepest fear of all'. Winnicott later wrote that it is only because of 'the survival of the object' under the subject's attacks that he/she creates the quality of externality and is able to live in the world of objects (Winnicott 1969b). I believe both aspects, survival of the subject and the object, are central, and essential to the basis of stability that the traumatised and borderline child lacks.

Winnicott distinguishes 'relating to an object' and 'using an object' (Winnicott 1969a, 1971). In object relating, the object has become meaningful, but while projective and introjective mechanisms have been working the object is still 'a bundle of projections' and there is no sense of being part of a shared reality. In object using, this stage is transcended and the subject gains a capacity to use objects: 'part of a change to the reality principle'. As a consequence early identifications are no longer an inchoate 'bundle of projections' and they can be experienced in the light of the true emotional experience of the object. But an early traumatic break-up in the mother–child relationship will hold up and prevent a development in the child of the capacity to make or sustain all future relationships, so that in effect there is a primary developmental failure, rather than simply as Freud thought in cases of trauma secondary regressions (Freud 1939; Bowlby 1971, 1973; Winnicott 1971). The intense quality of anxiety characteristic at all stages in work with borderline patients is in part due to their awareness of the fragility of this position, of knowing yet continuously wishing to escape from knowledge of the object towards a blind acting in accordance with early identifications.

Anita's personal history

Anita's personal history shows the traumatic and pathological effect upon a child of disturbed parenting and the early painful loss of both parents. As with other histories of borderline cases there is a characteristic lack of information and detail about what really happened (Kernberg 1975; Masterson and Rinsley 1976). The few details we knew were that Anita was born by Caesarean section, was bottle-fed, and had some unspecified initial feeding and sleeping difficulties. Thereafter there were no further reported problems. Her parents had married after a short courtship, when father was aged 30 and mother 19, but when Anita was just four months old the marriage broke up and mother left the marital home with her. Her father had then complained to the authorities about his separated wife's 'mad' behaviour but a health visitor who saw Anita said she was 'dirty but otherwise adequately cared for'. A lot was clearly missed and we know nothing further until Anita was six and a half months old, when her mother suddenly gave her back to father and completely 'disappeared' thereafter.

Between the age of six and a half months and 15 months, Anita's father then went out to work leaving her in the care of different friends and neighbours during the day. From 15 months, following an illness when her father found it impossible to care for her, Anita went all day to a day nursery. The staff there did not take to her and described her in a strikingly negative way as 'moody, attention-seeking, and domineering, liking her own way in everything: if she is crossed she is aggressive'. Just before she was two years old, Anita was ill again. Her father found this a problem, so she was fostered for five days a week, going back to father at weekends. The fostering started well but was not a success since the foster mother was a childminder and said Anita attacked the other children and did not mix with them. She did not eat well and began to make herself sick at meal-times, and clung to the foster father. After four months the fostering broke down, so Anita went back to live with her father, staying in a day nursery and with a child minder until father got home from work. When she was aged two and a half, her father took a new common-law wife and her son, aged 7, to live with them. For a while Anita was said to be more stable and she stayed there until she was nearly 4 years old.

From this time Anita went in and out of care and concern grew and grew about her behaviour. She began losing weight, wetting and soiling at home, but not at school, biting and scratching herself until she bled, not eating except from the waste bin and putting herself in danger by walking into things or along narrow ledges. Other behaviour was odd and disturbing. When the social worker visited, Anita would be standing like a sentry against the wall in her room quite immobile for long periods.

At referral Anita was nearly four and a half years old. She now lived in a small children's home but she spent some weekends with her father, step-mother and her son, where she was causing considerable concern by her very disturbed behaviour. She was still wetting, soiling and mutilating herself, refusing food and vomiting, and isolating herself away from the family. Her father and stepmother were in despair and could not cope with her. Anita's despair was communicated to the workers, as is evident from the social worker's final plea in her referral letter: 'Every action, including mine, taken in respect of this sad little girl, has only worsened her situation and increased her insecurity. She desperately needs very skilled help.' What I think comes over from this sketchy history is an inconsistent pattern of care and what becomes clear subsequently in Anita's treatment is a picture of a child whose parents were unable to protect her from the shocking effect of her early inconsistent and disturbed experience of life. Her consequent trauma meant persistent psychic pain and disturbed mental functioning.

Early stages of treatment: relating to an unsafe object

Anita attended the children's centre daily, mixing with other children from the adjacent inpatient family unit (cf. Chapters 4 to 8). She was brought by her social worker at first and went back to the children's home at night and at weekends. Initially Anita had difficulty joining in activities and remained isolated, standing alone away from the other children or by the side of a member of staff. Yet soon she was running up and down corridors gener-ally going wherever she liked and there was then a controlling boundaryless quality in all her contact. She would only attempt tasks that she felt she could manage on her own and could not accept direct personal help from her nurse, whom she would angrily tell to 'get lost'. She would allow no physical contact even when she was distressed. Yet if her nurse helped another child to get dressed during a swimming trip and Anita was still struggling, she would scream at her nurse, 'that's right, help them and not me'. One time when her nurse was involved helping another child, Anita, who was a non-swimmer, removed her water-wings, pirouetted along the edge of the pool, fell in and sank to the bottom. She eventually emerged looking blank and unconcerned, leaving her nurse feeling panic stricken. She dangerously tested out constantly, sometimes involving her nurse to prevent her injuring herself and at other times seeming quite prepared deliberately to injure herself with knocks, cuts and falls. Despite this lack of trust in adults, however, there were the beginnings of interactive contact with her. There were also some small improvements. Anita soiled herself only once during the first four weeks and stopped wetting herself.

In her psychotherapy Anita initially presented as a small, pale, waif-like child with a series of tics and flinches of her head and face, and underneath her fragility seemed frightened to death as if she could crack or disintegrate at any time. I thought she was shocked to have a male psychotherapist but she did not say anything about this. At first she seemed rather disappointed as she looked around the playroom for something familiar, and there was an empty, dreamlike quality to her play. I was aware of my own feeling of acute anxiety when with her and thought this may be projected from her (for intense qualities of 'free anxiety' found in borderline children, cf. Geleerd 1958: 294; Lubbe 2000a: 8).

After the first weekend away, back at her father's home, she returned with deep self-inflicted scratches on her face and her own deep anxiety erupted into the open:

> In her next session she was clearly angry and upset about the weekend break and she immediately snapped she was going to 'stab' me. Then she distractedly took some disused sellotape from her toy box, twisted and twirled it around and chewed it as if she was mimicking the bad things she had to swallow. She became even more active and energetic, then said that I was 'teasing her'. This led to her telling me how she would 'tease' other people, by which it became clear she meant attack or seduce. I started to say to her, 'You feel you have put up with a lot', but broke off because she started taking risky jumps that I needed to attend to. From the outset I felt she was showing me how she was experiencing dangers and risks in forming any kind of attachment to me, a 'teasing' person who offers something then takes it away.

I thought that this sessional material about the chewed and twisted sellotape reflected oral levels of deprivation, relating to underlying phantasies that she had lost the nipple and could only regain it in a twisted and contorted way. But she felt having emotional contact with me was a kind of provocative tease. She could easily lose it and be put more at risk, leading to further enactments in risk-taking behaviour.

Such behaviour, play and underlying phantasies with sexual and self-destructive elements took up much of the therapeutic work in the first months of treatment. Anita showed a picture of a savage internal reality that all too closely overlapped with her external experience. Like her nurse I frequently had to intervene to prevent her doing actual damage to herself. After one of the earlier sessions there was a real suicidal risk when she had run off and was trying to jump off a fire escape, so we needed to meet her to set limits to prevent her going out of control (cf. Winnicott's views on 'management' 1965; Abram 1996: 183–9; Main 1989). Progressively with this help she took less risks and although still very active and aggressive actually harmed herself for real less often.

This risk taking had various meanings. It became a way of projecting acute infantile anxiety about her insecurity. It became an enactment of an escape from an intolerable object, such as the parent who promises to protect but does not. Sometimes, such as when she took long jumps from the cupboard to the couch in the playroom, it was a kind of 'jumping into an object', a way of taking over and controlling one's mind in an intrusive way, and as such a kind of early adaptive response. Her behaviour had the effect of drawing her psychotherapist into physical contact with her (to prevent her seriously hurting herself), which she would then experience as an active caring for her body. This also became a form of seduction as she then experienced physical contact in a sexualised way. Her actions also recreated a caring and anxious couple when as nurse and psychotherapist we struggled to contain her, but this couple could be split or made useless in the face of her relentless and self-attacking behaviour.

Disturbance with her father

At the assessment meeting after the first four weeks it was decided to continue treatment, and the aim of social services was to reunite Anita with her family, that is her father and stepmother. During the next several months of treatment Anita spent some weekends at home with her father and his new family and the rest still at the children's home. But from the start these visits appeared to have a marked effect on her. She would return looking unwell and in a withdrawn and depressed state and then she would isolate herself. Her father had at first stayed at home during her visits, but appeared increasingly unable to cope with her, in particular her soiling, which had started again during the visits, and which he found disgusting. He then began to make himself less available and for some visits Anita saw him only for a few minutes, if at all.

These painful attempts to re-establish contact with her father and his family were relived in her psychotherapy sessions, in particular in her reaction to separations at weekends and her jealousy of rivals. Prior to one session, Anita fell outside on a brick and cut her head badly:

> When we talked about it, she told me, 'I hit my brother you know. . . . I smashed his head in.' I said she was angry with the child who takes her place, like the other children I see in therapy. I reminded her how she would kick the cupboard, containing the toy boxes of other children in treatment. Anita stopped and seemed to listen to me. I then spoke about how she may miss her sessions at the weekend and how she

wished to damage herself to show she was hurt. At this, she clearly felt more pain and sat slowly touching her face with a toy plate to soothe herself. For the first time the session ended calmly without the usual displays of anger and chaos.

After expressing her reactions to separation in the session Anita continued to be calm when back in the children's centre. I felt she had seemed pleased that I could see her need for protection and that I could to an extent become for her like a father who could soothe and protect.

Anita's attitude however was deeply ambivalent and she could frequently again become quite unconnected and unresponsive in a hostile way:

> During a hard session when she felt great pain, she drew in yellow what looked like an angel, with arms and wings, with buttons down the front of the angel's gown. She then said it was a 'cow'. Later on she talked of a cow 'swearing' and being 'cuddly'.

In her drawing and associations, the excitement of an angel could very quickly become a cow swearing, which could then be made to turn cuddly again. Anita was expressing how she could change between being appealing and then suddenly bitter and hostile.

Even when she found her sessions helpful she still experienced me as a superficially caring but inept father and then took over in a controlling way. This transference reflected not just her external situation but also an internalised position, dating from the time when she was an infant and her father looked after her most basic needs, including changing and feeding, but proved unequal to the task and so gave her up into care. In her psychotherapy Anita was reliving her early identifications with her father.

As it became clear to Anita that her father and stepmother could not in reality sustain any real care, her play in sessions reflected her rising concern and alarm:

> One time, she had been telling me that the water she was drinking was turning into poison. She went on to make a game of putting some water in her mouth, running to the window sill, climbing up and down, then running back and spitting out the water into the bowl, as if it were just in time. The point of the game was that she would hold onto the poison just long enough, so that she could spit it out safely and it would not seep through her mouth and into her stomach and her body.

One could see here a connection between her problem of refusing food in the children's home or the children's centre and the problem during long periods of struggle of her refusing helpful interpretations from her psychotherapist.

For she felt by accepting food or interpretations she would very easily run the risk of being contaminated.

When Anita's hopes for a home with her father were crushed, her phantasies in play centred on loss of the psychotherapist as father. Although she had by now begun to develop trust in me, it was unstable and dominated by fear. A pattern developed whereby, particularly after a series of interpretations that she had struggled against and then accepted, she would go to the toilet during the session to defecate and come back relieved not just physically but emotionally. At the level of her infantile anxiety, such actions represented evacuation of the exciting internal penis, i.e. the highly troubling relationship with the therapist as father, leaving her empty but also devoid of anxious feeling (Freud 1909a; Freud 1918a: 84; Klein 1932). One could see in this a confusion of levels, between the hard faeces trapped inside, with their associations to worries she could not process, and intrusions symbolised in terms of the father's penis, associated with his care and over-close involvement with her.

Despite the deterioration in her relationship with her father and stepmother, however, in the children's centre the staff experienced a positive change, so that her nurse no longer felt as useless, exhausted and despairing as she had in previous months. This change was reflected in one incident prior to a weekend home visit when Anita began to perform daring stunts and, despite several warnings from her nurse, tumbled to the ground. Anita recovered herself and stood still in the middle of the room fighting back the tears and unable to express any feelings, then all of a sudden she threw her arms around her nurse's neck and began crying, saying that she was sorry and that it hurt. This was the first time Anita had allowed any physical contact with her nurse, or allowed herself to cry and admit hurt, and it represented finding a maternal concern in the nurse. After this incident Anita's relationship with her began significantly to improve. She started to talk about how unbearable her visits home were and about her difficulties sharing toys or her nurse's attention.

But despite these improvements Anita was becoming more disturbed each time she went home at weekends and she began to say quite openly how much she hated the visits and wished not to go home. The painful fact was that Anita's father lacked the emotional resources to give understanding care to a disturbed daughter. It emerged too that he had himself been in care from the age of two for several years. At the next review it was decided to go ahead with plans for long-term fostering or adoption instead.

Disturbance in her feminine identifications

Following the long summer break after a year in treatment Anita had grown and looked different. Her hair, which was longer, was now decorated with ribbons and clips. But she found it difficult to settle back into the routine and appeared quiet, withdrawn and sulky. She seemed to want very little contact with her nurse to punish her and took to engaging with a male nurse instead. Anita now became continuously preoccupied with her body and openly sexually provocative, demanding kisses, showing her pants to young boys in the unit and sometimes bearing lovebites (from the children's home) on her neck. Worryingly too she began to masturbate openly. Now also the desire to have babies featured regularly in her play. Anita was aware of her changed circumstances. Her father's visits to the children's home had now stopped, but a foster home had not yet been found. As Anita saw other children from the children's home being successfully fostered she was very unsettled. Frequently Anita was in a state of panic, struggling with the strong feeling that she was so horrible nobody wanted her.

In psychotherapy, Anita tried to demonstrate my inadequacy. Again as previously just before a first session after a break she had sustained an injury, a serious cut on her chin requiring a number of stitches. As I tried to talk to her about it, my attempts were treated as just so much pretence, and Anita said that I was 'not her friend', then became even angrier and called me a 'bastard'. Deep swings that occurred in Anita's moods now reflected a change in her preoccupations, to thoughts of what kind of mother she had and to her own femininity, relating to early identifications with her mother. In one session:

> Anita flirted with the male nurse who brought her to her session and played him up. I was a little late meeting her following a confusion about the routine. Anita came down to the therapy room, but just outside she lay flat on the ground and would not come into the room. Eventually after some simple encouragement, she got up to come in and swung in a frolicsome way on my arm. When I accidentally stood on her foot whilst coming into the room, she became passionately angry, kicking me viciously and calling me a 'fucking bastard'. She was quite unresponsive to my interpretation that she was angry because she may feel that I had been unprepared to take her at the beginning. She thwacked her ruler at me, then she broke the ruler on purpose. As it shattered into fragments of shrapnel and she was caught near the eye by one of the bits, her mood switched and she burst into sobs of tears and dived for the couch. She allowed me to see if she was hurt and I found she was cut slightly on her cheek.
>
> She now began playing with the water-container and asked me calmly, 'Is this how it works?' She began to set up tea things, playing a detailed game. After a while she played the game less energetically, there was a lull and I felt her again distancing herself from me. She now began to play very carefully so that she did not make a mistake setting the things out. She now also began to serve me, taking the role of maid. I felt she was doing this to minimise the distance between us and I was

being attended to instead of her receiving the care she needed. She told me who had places and began to insist that she was mum and I was dad and she set an extra place for the dog, as she always did in such games. Towards the end of the session she created a special position for the dog under the table and then she left her place to crawl into it.

In this session, as she experienced a moment of care from me when I checked that her eye was not hurt, her play unconsciously changed to reflect what sort of care a mother gives. She could not sustain a view of a mother who cares (she begins to distance herself from me – a sign of splitting) and she switched to an identification with the mother as the woman who serves, a view of the mother and the feminine as a sort of servant. Her deep sense of hurt was that she had no place in the family or only the place of the dog.

Anita's contact with me in subsequent sessions had a hard brusque quality. She would frequently kick or hit me at the beginning and refuse to come in. Once she had agreed to come inside, I was ordered about and when I showed resistance to this, I was turned on with a fury for messing everything up. In the session after the last quoted:

> Anita began by saying she was looking for something to break up. She rummaged through her toy cupboard and when she found something she had torn up, her holiday chart, she turned on me, 'Who did that?' 'You did that.' She then tipped her toys all over the floor and muttered under her breathe 'fucking hell', 'fucking baby'. She was caught up in her fury and did not seem to respond to my interpretation that she may fear that the break had brought a disruption, a baby.
>
> She suddenly became very active and energetic and began an acting performance, rearranging everything and chanting noisily in nonsense language. One performance was 'of what little girls do'. As the game went on I was most struck by her drive and her need to show me something. I said that the little girls seemed to think they had to make a performance. Anita replied in an emphatic mocking voice, 'Of course, people like to look at little girls.' Then as she jumped she chanted several times, 'You see the scar'. Towards the end of this session when she objected to putting on her shoes again, she tried to bite me continuously and viciously, as if she had to. Anita seemed to me to be quite driven and out of control.

In this session, Anita seemed to be working on further early identifications, of mother, women and femininity, and was showing that to be female was to be a mixture of being queenly and subservient. You had to dominate or you would lose everything. Success or esteem could be gained by getting people to admire, almost like a young adolescent who has quickly to capture everyone's looks of appreciation for fear of losing a sense of what she had or who she was. Anita felt that what she had to show was her 'scar'. On one level this referred to the scar from loss and separation she had shown me last time. On another level it was the 'scar' which the highly excited girl was aware of in her jumping games, namely her vagina (Klein 1929: 217; Meltzer 1967, 1973, 1975). The oral/genital confusion in this clinical material is evident, for the genital is a scar one minute and a mouth full of teeth the next, either way a damaged place, but one which is fascinating because of the damage (Klein 1929: 204; Meltzer on autism 1975; Lubbe 2000b: 175; Rosenfeld and Sprince 1963; Szur 1983). Her confused feelings about this took the form in later sessions, and in the children's centre, of more ostentatious sexualised behaviour. It was like she was a precocious adolescent girl with adult mannerisms reminiscent of Zola's *Nana* and, just like Nana, Anita had a strong compulsion to create the myth of the happy family.

In many sessions she would make 'camps' in the middle of the playroom. Such games with camps expressed her need to have some place of care, however impermanent. Sometimes she would invite me her psychotherapist to sit close by outside the camp, 'so that I can call you when I need you'. At other times she would express quite different feelings. She would then chant from within the camp in a monotone, which brought to mind to me something eerie and inhuman, such as an evocation of a spirit in a voodoo rite. When I asked what the chanting meant, she snapped at me venomously, 'You're dead.' Then as her anger erupted again and she tried to hurt me, one could see that her feelings were violent, even sinister, and seemed rooted in her destructive masturbation phantasies (Klein 1937).

Her envy of the children from the adjacent inpatient unit whom she saw with their families was quite overwhelming. She had a deep yearning for a secure identification, to establish her identity, in a place of her own, with a family, and a sense of herself out of the infant realm. The poignant reality was that she had no mother and the only person she could recognise as a figure of dependence was her father, whom she had now lost and whom at most had been for her a protective figure rather than a nurturing figure:

> This was very striking at the end of one therapy session, when Anita noticed a set of fire regulations on a card on the back of the door. The card had always been there, but today she thought it was new. She asked me to read it to her, which I did. She was most puzzled at the bit about calling the fire brigade. She appeared to think this was unnecessary and she told me she thought that I would be able to put out all the fires.

This was a striking attribution of omnipotence to the male psychotherapist, namely that he could put out all the fires. It showed her desperate need to identify a protective masculine figure. A more nurturing feminine figure with whom to identify was absent and there was only her nurse, whom she now trusted more, but Anita was aware that she was only a temporary figure for her.

Attempts to find a family

Anita reacted to the new plan, to look for foster parents with a view to later adoption (now that she seemed more fosterable), with great relief and a dramatic improvement in her behaviour as the 'very good little girl' who could be accepted by foster parents. The implementation of the plan how-ever was to be slow and ultimately fruitless, so after several months Anita reverted to very aggressive behaviour and became once again a fragmented, uncontained child.

In her psychotherapy Anita's underlying despair was apparent. She was frequently emotionally cut off and when she did occasionally make more contact, she saw her psychotherapist as involved in a perverse game with her, in which her hopes would be aroused only for her wishes to be frus-trated and her to be punished:

> In one of her camp games, she played that a witch would put a spell on a baby to keep her quiet. If the baby was disturbed, she would wake and cry and the spell would be broken, so that another spell would be needed. Only then could the baby be quietened down.

In this play if the baby allowed herself to cry and give vent to her deepest feelings and needs, an inexhaustible amount of feelings would be unleashed. To prevent this the baby would have to be dampened down with a spell. Anita could take my interpretations of her feelings and behaviour as a form of magic, which would relieve her and calm her down. But then later this could leave her feeling bereft because her psychotherapist had become like a witch, someone who controlled her, prevented her expressing her distress fully, and then left her with more distress and anxiety.

Suddenly, in the third year of treatment, Anita's natural mother reap-peared expressing a wish to be reunited with her daughter. Anita was now aged six years and had last seen her mother when she was six months old. Anita was pleased, then upset and sad at the news. During the ensuing months she seemed torn in various ways but decided on a secret loyalty to her mother – both Anita and her mother wanted to be left alone and their growing relationship not assessed by others. The situation was precarious for Anita and when one day she hit another child on the head for no apparent reason she was terrified of what her nurse might say to her mother and hid under the table like a frightened animal with her hands clasped over her ears. When it was possible to deal with the issue without involving her mother, Anita was greatly relieved.

Anita's mother eventually did attend meetings for a while and seemed quite eager for her relationship with Anita to go well. Indeed during this time in the children's centre for a while Anita was a pleasing and delightful girl to be with. It was not until Anita was at home full time with her mother that real problems and difficulties were revealed. The social services' plan now was that Anita would leave the children's centre and attend a local school. During the two months prior to discharge, when she had left the children's home and was living with her mother, Anita again had frequent illnesses, including an infected toe and mumps. Such illnesses made one think of the illnesses she suffered in early infancy, and were a worrying sign of lack of containment. Anita's mother now became unable to keep up coming to meetings and communication was minimal. We became alarmed at Anita's own stories of her roaming round unattended in the evenings and about more direct evidence of lack of care. We now learnt that Anita's mother herself had suffered long-term deprivation and abuse. At home Anita sometimes tested her mother to the limit, who found it difficult to admit there were real problems and avail herself of help.

In the final months of the three-year treatment, the work with Anita felt very incomplete. Anita's sense of loyalty to her mother meant that she did not value her time with her psychotherapist, and now she more coldly and ruthlessly kept me out of emotional contact with her. Indeed both nurse and psychotherapist were often made to feel dispensable and irrelevant. (For a discussion of a psychotherapeutic understanding of nurse/ psychotherapist relationships and countertransference responses, see Chapter 7.)

Nevertheless at times just before discharge it appeared that Anita may have internalised a good internal object, perhaps as a result of all the work done, and could now be more capable of establishing the new attachment to her mother. There were a few times when Anita seemed calmer and in control, and she had increased capacities to make relationships with other children, to tolerate frustrations and to respond to limit setting. Her play now included elaborate games typical of a latency stage of development. Also overall since the beginning of treatment there were some noticeable changes in Anita. She had grown, was likeable, very needy of affection, but could now normally differentiate this from being sexy, and so respect more normal boundaries of personal contact. Indeed she had started for the first time to undertake some everyday activities from home, such as trips out shopping and a regular night at Brownies. She could also sometimes talk quite freely about these events and her contacts with other children in the children's centre and in her psychotherapy sessions. For a while she became less enmeshed in a frenetic struggle of infantile feelings within herself and she now seemed to have secured some separate childhood identity, however unstable. Despite so much uncertainty about her future then we felt she had gained something from her children's centre treatment.

In several psychotherapy sessions towards the end she kept making round-shaped drawings in pairs. As she did these drawings, she would also engage me in helping her to keep the coins she borrowed secure on the page. The circles she made seemed to symbolise how she could feel in contact with the good creative breast, even if she needed to control it as something that was not given but only borrowed. The final version of the drawing was one of the most impressive Anita had ever done in view of its clear outline and the range of colours. She took this drawing proudly away with her. However what she left lying on an otherwise deserted corner of the therapy room was the small crumpled little girl doll, which for a long time she had used in her play to represent herself, and which was the sole surviving figure from a set of family figures that earlier on in psychotherapy had been totally destroyed.

The aim of treatment of Anita was partly to make a permanent family placement more possible, but partly also to enable Anita to live with her strong feelings and conflicts about her damaged attachments. Sadly, a few months after treatment Anita's stay with her mother broke down. She then attended a boarding school, but managed to retain one continuous relationship from the past with the careworker from the children's home where she had lived. Although then she did not achieve a permanent placement, we hoped that her treatment in the children's centre had enabled her to feel safer in making new relationships and attachments. Whilst there she had succeeded in developing a close and meaningful attachment to her nurse and also with her psychotherapist, which had given her the opportunity to work with early identifications and to the primitive early figures of attachment.

Discussion

Lubbe has elucidated and summarised the varying perspectives and theoretical assumptions underlying the application of the diagnosis 'borderline' to children and prefers the use of the diagnosis for those children showing specific psychotic symptoms at some stage of their disturbance (Lubbe 2000a: 29, 35–8). Bleiberg distinguishes, as most other writers now do, two types or groups of borderline children: cluster A, who are more clearly psychotic at times, with a fragile reality sense and thought disorganisation; cluster B, who are mostly in the severely neurotic range, who have a 'dramatic' personality disorder, including intense dramatic affect and hunger for social response (Bleiberg 2000: 41–4). My view is that Anita had many features characteristic of a borderline child in cluster B, but in particular showed *acute and sustained levels of psychotic anxiety*. Her case illustrates four main features, which recur in the literature that are characteristic of a borderline child (Kernberg 1975, 1984). These features were:

- the lack of a sense of being safe and a continuous and unsustainable *level of anxiety* bordering on panic and characterised by primitive feelings of disintegration and annihilation
- being dominated by sexual conflicts at a pre-Oedipal level, uncertain about her sexual identity and with considerable *identity disturbance*
- a marked disturbance in *ego functioning* and lack of achievement of secondary identifications, so she appeared to change from time to time but without gaining any strong degree of self-cohesion
- a tenuous maintenance of *object relations*, with a dominance of processes of projective identification over introjective identification, with marked primitive defensive operations such as splitting.

Paulina Kernberg (1983a, 1983b) and Otto Kernberg (1994) have argued that for the borderline child (and adolescent) there is not only disturbance at a developmental level but also there is an intrinsic psychopathology and use of primitive defences, typically the mechanisms of projective identification and splitting. This follows Klein's views, where from early on she described the (borderline) psychotic child less in terms of regression of the ego to its narcissistic origins and more in terms of a blocking of development owing to the ego's over-hasty and ineffective defences against sadism. The precariousness of the ego, which is so characteristic of the infantile psychosis, is viewed not as a cause but as a consequence of the excessive use of defensive activities themselves (Lubbe 2000a: 13; Petot 1990: 218).

Anita's object relations were characterised by an intense quality of aggression, which in addition to being the result of environmental failure (Winnicott 1965) may have been in part constitutional (Klein 1957), leading to her repeated use of the repetition compulsion (Freud 1920). Her defences against trauma were therefore permeated by *an aggressive struggle*, such as in her regressive soiling, in the way she secluded herself from emotional contact, in the bizarre sentry behaviour at the beginning and in the recurrent distancing from more normal contacts with other children. Similarly her self-injuries and exposure to danger were an expression of her aggression against the self and against others and a way of blaming adults for failure. *Excessive splitting* occurred at each stage, in the splits between the mother and the father, and between her aggressive self and her libidinal self. Some of her play making camps illustrates her struggles to manage these splits: initially her camps were aimed to keep the good and the bad separate but close (a kind of wish for fusion), but under anxiety this degenerated into sharper splitting (a 'diffusion of instincts', Freud 1923: 42) with the alive inside and the dead outside. Throughout her treatment splits are created everywhere to keep positive and negative elements separate in an attempt to preserve the self. Much of the psychotherapeutic work was in effect directed to reversals in splitting. Some of the splits were between home and school; between strained weekends at home and her depressed mental state when back in the children's centre; between nurse and mother; therapist and father; nurse and therapist; male and female nurse; in her play between the 'cow mother' and the 'angel mother'; and at the end between her real mother and the children's centre workers, including nurse and psychotherapist.

I think the therapeutic gain of the psychotherapy was linked to the analysis of splitting processes and some reversals of the splitting. We can see this when the split between protective father and rejecting mother was altered in favour of an appreciation of the maternal qualities of the nurse and a search by Anita to sort out her feminine identifications, which occurs when externally the placement with the father broke down and the children's centre nurse became good. After the long summer break Anita then rejects the female nurse and reverts to the male nurse, but when the male psychotherapist stands on her toe it confirms her experience of how bad the male is. Yet however bad or ineffectual he is, she cannot let him go and even idealises him – the fire alarm all-powerful psychotherapist. The feminine identifications range from servant mother, to dominant female, to the tough cynical scar-bearing sexualised female, to the female like Nana who will rebuild her family all by herself in her imagination or fantasy. When the real mother reappears she is idealised and the nurturing nurse is rejected, as is the protective male psychotherapist, the 'bastard'. Splitting is still intense at the end of treatment and her anxiety more than ever is about the good and the bad meeting up. After treatment the question is whether integration is possible or whether unresolved ambivalence would emerge and spoil things. So Anita left treatment in the best way she could manage, by splitting and depositing the damaged self with me (the doll in the corner of the playroom) and manically taking and going off with the good (the richly coloured breast drawing).

In addition to the analysis of the splitting and the ensuing internal conflicts, it is likely that a major effective therapeutic element in the treatment was the ongoing progressive care and nurture of the child. This improved her overall pattern of experience and relationships, especially with her nurse and teacher, and helped to develop a more strengthened ego, which in part helped her deal with and cope better with intense splitting processes and inner disturbance. In most borderline cases a serious disturbance in the interaction of mother and child can be found (Rosenfeld and Sprince 1963, 1965; Masterson and Rinsley 1975). One is left with the thought that the lack of secure early identification with a mother, a good enough mother, was the most severe aspect of deficit and source of conflict for Anita (Winnicott 1960, 1965, 1969a; Abram 1996: 190–218). Mahler (1952) and others (e.g. Weil 1953a, 1953b, 1970) have singled out how there is *a damaged core* in such borderline children, produced by disharmonies in the infant's constitutional make-up coupled with the mother's struggle with her attunements. In Stern's terms (1985), Anita could not achieve a stable sense of her 'subjective self' because of her experience of severe disturbance during the emergence and formation of her core self, crucially in her first year of life and in particular in the first few months.

Bowlby and other attachment theorists, in agreement with Klein and other psychoanalytic theorists, indicate that the infant's behaviour by the end of the first year is purposeful and based on expectations generated by past experiences (Bowlby 1971, 1973, 1998; Ainsworth *et al.* 1978; Bleiberg 2000: 55). Bowlby proposed that the *aggregate* of experiences with caretakers is organised by the infant into representational systems that he called *internal working models*. These models allow infants to anticipate and develop coping strategies based on their first expectations of people's behaviour. Children can be seen broadly as secure, insecure or confused in terms of attachments and their expected responses in relationships.

The emphasis by Bowlby and attachment theorists on the broad picture rather than a detailed analysis of early identifications has been taken up and developed by Fonagy and Target (1996a), Fonagy *et al.* (1996c), Fonagy and Target (2000: 17) and Bleiberg (2000: 64). They propose that detailed interpretation of early defences may be of limited value or even counterproductive and that deep genetic (i.e. going to the earliest roots) transference interpretations may act as a kind of 'trigger language' that can precipitate acting out or regression to a symbiotic transference (Ekstein and Wallerstein 1954; Rosenfeld and Sprince 1965; Lubbe 2000a). What Target and Fonagy propose instead is a therapeutic approach that is aimed to achieve a full 'mentalisation of affect' and enhance the child's reflective processes.

My view, following the Kleinian position, is that the type of interpretation is largely governed by consideration of the child's immediate anxiety (Lubbe 2000a: 31). This does not mean diving in prematurely into an analysis of content of the underlying phantasies but, as Joseph and Alvarez stress, allowing time for the missing or disturbed feelings to be contained and explored in the psychotherapist for a period of time, long before the patient may be able to experience them as belonging to him/ herself (Joseph 1978: 112; Alvarez 1992: 105; Steiner 1994). As they then emerge or become accessible, detailed analysis of defences is required to deal with underlying severe levels of internal conflict. Our intensive three-year long day treatment work with Anita showed that these underlying levels were touched on at each stage of the work. The sort of detailed and continuous psychoanalytic work in the transference which becomes possible in this context also of course allows for the kind of enhancement of reflective processes, at both conscious and unconscious levels, that Fonagy and Target are arguing for, and may help to shift, in Bowlby's sense, insecure and confused attachments to become more secure, allowing for the development of new *internal working models*. This to my mind concurs with the real sense of Bion's concept of containment. It is the internal processing in the mind of the psychotherapist of disparate feelings and thoughts reflecting the deeper unconscious levels of conflict, with its bizarre elements, not just the broader often more conscious brush strokes, that allows for the child's experience of being understood and being contained (Bion 1961, 1963).

Alvarez's careful attention to allowing the child to move beyond early conflicts and identifications by recognising new moves forward, however small, is in closest sympathy, I believe, with Bion's emphasis (Alvarez 1992; cf. also Baker 1993 on the relation to the 'new object'; Sandler and Freud 1985: 105). It also concurs with Klein's emphasis in her earlier work on the importance of introjective identification for the development of a stable internal world. Alvarez stresses that successful work with highly disturbed children may depend as much on questions of *perspective* rather than questions of projection, and locating the perspective of the child may actually involve the beginnings of an introjective process rather than a projective one (Alvarez 1992: 79; 2000: 96–8).

There is now agreement across the spectrum of theoretical differences for a dual approach to treatment of the borderline child (Lubbe 2000a), including care for the changing and developing child, along with psychotherapeutic work with the child's affective responses stemming from the underlying sources of intra-psychic conflicts. This underlies our emphasis in the work with Anita in combining psychotherapy with the children's centre work of education and primary nurture, and in our looking separately at Anita's developing relationship with psychotherapist and nurse.

Part 2

The Child in the Family

Chapter 4

The child's experience of an inpatient therapeutic setting

Introduction

As outlined in the General Introduction, Part 2 looks at the child in the family. Chapters 4 to 7 examine some special features of work with children within an inpatient therapeutic setting – the inpatient Families Unit at the Cassel Hospital. To start, my focus here will be on the assessment of children and their conditions of treatment in this one type of applied setting. I shall outline that there are different issues for children to face and different criteria to weigh up in assessment and treatment. What is said here will have applications to other types of applied settings, both inpatient and residential.

In this particular context of assessment, the child neither simply accompanies the parent who is seeking treatment nor the converse. Instead both parents and children enter together into a specific kind of setting, which provides opportunities to examine relationships from a number of points of view. In assessments in an outpatient context, the child expresses views about the psychotherapist or the setting – his/her arrangements for times, the room, and details of a particular or personal nature – and such views will add to our understanding of the transference. So within the inpatient hospital setting the child will express views and demonstrate within their everyday life their reaction to or awareness of that setting. Such reactions and feelings can be examined in psychoanalytic psychotherapy times, in ongoing observations of ordinary interactions and in various meetings, which provide insights not simply into the child's outer life but into their inner emotional life.

The child's view is particularly valuable in the treatment of families. Typically, because they are less defended and their perception is often simple and unequivocal, children can betray what they and their parents think and feel. Children express not just their own views but sometimes those of others, especially their parents, like a kind of mouthpiece, and important insights can be gained into parent–child relationships and family dynamics. Within an inpatient therapeutic context, as I shall illustrate below, what the child says and does may also express in an important way for others the impact of events within the therapeutic community and the changing life of the community.

Here are two simple examples from family consultations prior to admission, of how a child's view of the hospital provided at the outset an understanding of the child's emotional life and place within the family.

In the first instance, a single parent could only consider inpatient treatment for her family if her daughter aged five could describe for her what the hospital was like and how it worked. While the mother sat talking to my colleague, unsure about what to do and incapable of making any decision, the child engaged me separately, asking me a number of intelligent and apposite questions about what people did in this hospital. In particular she wanted to know details about how they could get in and out, and asked, 'Is the fire escape safe?' At this point, it seemed that the child was helping her mother decide about treatment – would it be safe? Just before admission her mother was again delaying over a medical appointment for an eye defect she thought her daughter had. After a significant piece of work by the admitting nurse, her mother saw that the family admission and the child's appointment about her eyes need not conflict with each other. It eventually turned out that the issue of her daughter's eyesight was indeed symptomatic. The meaning of the symptomatic defect in the child related to the mother's reliance on her daughter, in particular her use of the daughter to decide something important for her about the family's decision whether or not to go ahead with the admission to hospital. This mother, who also was a twin, felt the admission was only possible if her daughter, like a substitute for her twin with whom she may have shared certain essential faculties, could see her way for her mother (Bion 1967: 3–22).

In the second instance an 11-year-old boy showed, in his random associations about the hospital on his first visit, his acute capacity to get to know us on the inside. This illustrated a complementary process in his relationship with his mother, whom he irritated or 'got inside'. It was a single-parent family and one of the main presenting difficulties, at the root of relationship difficulties between them, was the irritation this mother felt about the boy. As we made our way through a series of corridors to the consulting room, he chatted about how the building looked like 'mum's work' and the garden was 'like my uncle's, which has 24 acres!' His mother was irritated with him and rebuked him, correcting him on details and saying that he was being inconsistent. At first my feeling was that he was relating to the hospital and to the grounds, and telling us how it fitted with his previous experience. He had picked up that his mother wanted to be the professional with us, like at her work, and he identified me as an uncle figure. But what was soon striking was how quickly this boy made himself at home in the hospital and in his contact with me. In what followed, as we continued up the corridor to the consulting room, I now began to see why on one level his mother got so irritated with him. He told me he wished he 'had brought his compass with him today', and then insistently and actually quite accurately pointed out the direction of nearby important buildings. He thought he could soon know his way round the hospital and show me. Within the room as we talked he then produced an interesting drawing of a fire engine which had come out of a 'tunnel-road'. He told me about 'a fire near his grandmother's house, where people were looking from behind curtains, laughing and squabbling to get the best viewing position'. He told me 'a nightmare in which a boy was lost and then found again'.

Although then my first impression was that here was an excellent candidate for psychotherapy, further reflection made me question whether what he had told me was not just so much scintillating tit-bits to interest me and involve me with him. This squared with another impression I had, namely that he had embroidered the account of the fire, his manner was controlling, and he was verbose and may have a facility with lies. I then began to understand something of how his mother felt about him, when she found she could not 'think straight' because of his excitability and frequent lies. These impressions I had of the child, especially the quality of intrusiveness he conveyed, were the beginnings of a transference to me, which would develop later in treatment. Understanding his first experience of the hospital was integral to an understanding of the boy individually and some aspects of the family problems.

The place of the child within the hospital therapeutic community

Since the early 1960s children have been able to accompany their parents to hospital, to keep the family together and to allow the treatment of whole families (Main 1989; Kennedy *et al.* 1987). The rationale for this practice has evolved. At first, it was with the aim of keeping mothers and children together, in particular puerperally ill mothers and babies, to keep the bond and prevent attachments being broken. Soon children who required psychotherapy were referred, especially if psychiatric disturbance and family problems were so severe that the parents were not able to support treatment in an outpatient setting. In such cases, where for example the child suffered from phobias about school, or there were identifiable problems of family functioning, work with couples and work centred on the parent–child interaction was undertaken. Fathers were then seen to be important and also came into treatment, either in their own right with psychiatric problems or, claiming back their role, in support of their wives and children (cf. *The Importance of Fathers*, Trowell and Etchagoyen 2002). The emphasis then shifted to a full study of family interactions in all cases, including the problems of men and fathers. Since the early 1980s this capacity to study family interactions, in addition to giving individual psychotherapy to parents and children, along with community treatment, has led to the Families Unit working with child abuse, both long-term treatment with family rehabilitation and assessment for outside professionals including the courts (cf. Kennedy 1989, 1997).

How does the child fare in the transition to inpatient life? The child who becomes an inpatient will have significant adjustments to make from their outside life. He or she will have a hospital room, shared with brothers or sisters, or children of the same age from other families. Since a new purpose-built family unit was opened several years ago, the child is more likely to be in rooms with siblings close to other members of the family, as at home. The child will change school, attending for a short time or perhaps for the duration of their stay the hospital children's centre staffed by a teacher and nurses, and attended by some day patients from neighbouring areas. Some children may attend a local school, especially where they are caught up in disturbing family pathology and there is an emphasis at assessment on their special need to keep or maintain continuous educational progress and outside contacts with other 'normal' children. This can be seen as extricating them from entangling family problems whilst the children have something good for themselves. Contacts with home life may be broken, even though the child will go home most weekends. Sometimes he or she will stay in the hospital with the family if there is a particular crisis. This will mean losing contact with schoolfriends and dependable, significant people, such as relatives, teachers and family friends.

The child will be thrust into a large, changing and amorphous patient group, which will comprise a frequently imbalanced children's group. There may be other children of similar age and sex amongst the group of families there at any time, but sometimes there are not. The numbers and age of the outpatient group in the children's centre will also affect the composition of the group. The child or his/her parents may strike up friendships with older patients, in the adult or adolescent units, with whom they will share some meetings and activities. The particular impact of all of this on any one child may vary. What is clear though is that whatever benefit the children themselves get from inpatient life in a community, which I shall look at below, the presence of children can be a stimulus to growth in other members of the community, reintroducing the sanity of everyday needs to inpatient community life and focusing attention on the 'actual family'. The presence of children can bridle the regression that can occur in inpatient settings, introducing a valuable and relevant reality perimeter for parents with severely neurotic, borderline and psychotic features.

Overall, making these adjustments in the transition to inpatient family treatment will cause a strain for the child, so that great attention is needed by parents to help the children settle with the minimum of stress. This is not always easy for parents who feel under stress themselves. The child can experience further stress if their parents are unable or unwilling to recreate within the hospital a safe environment for their child. I shall look at some aspects of this here and in the next three chapters.

Two central accounts have been given of the child's place within the community by Lydia Tischler (née Folkart 1964, 1967), a co-founder of the children's unit in 1962, with Salo Tischler. It had always been a central tenet in Tom Main's thinking about therapeutic communities that patients should retain as many responsibilities and ties with their outside life as were compatible with their illness (Main 1989). This basic premise was extended to families too, so that whilst they are inpatients, parents continue to look after their children. A prime focus of work is on disturbances of 'mothering' and 'parenting' and their effect on the development of the child. Despite dangers that the parents' 'acting out' can and does precipitate too quickly inappropriate requests that staff give individual attention to them or to the child, it is still important that as far as possible decisions affecting daily life be left to the parent. Of course how parents arbitrate such decisions will become a focus of treatment, and staff will need to intervene sometimes to protect the child or provide alternative forms of nurture or care.

The contrast between the inpatient and outpatient psychiatric settings, the outpatient hospital or child guidance clinic, is important. In the inpatient setting a number of families with shared or separate disturbance are brought together, and the work of the community breaks down defences and opens up wounds. The child sees his/her parents as more exposed and will be aware of the effects of their treatment on them. The level of shared anxiety can be intense, is felt by the children, and is communicated in their individual psychotherapy and demonstrated in the community.

The parents' reaction to their children's psychotherapy can open up unusually intense feelings of guilt. The child psychotherapist may be seen as a sort of expert or even someone who can provide better alternative real care for the child and can frequently be viewed with an unusual degree of idealisation or denigration. All of this has important general implications in the inpatient setting and for how the child psychotherapist sets up individual psychotherapy times for children. It is important to realise that treatment success or failure cannot be gauged as due to the effects of psychotherapy alone, rather than the protective environment of the hospital and the work of the therapeutic community, or indeed vice versa. It is due to a composite effort and the intricate relationship between different branches of treatment.

Also, in contrast to the outpatient setting, where the transference relationship between psychotherapist and child is the way of understanding the child's emotional life, in the inpatient setting equal attention needs to be given to clarifying the relationship of the child to his or her parents and others in the community. The child psychotherapist is a member of that community, with roles and responsibilities that extend outside the consulting room. This is a complex task, especially as the child psychotherapist has to evaluate not simply the child's view of the psychotherapist as transference object, but a host of qualitatively different information from separate sources, including from the parents' psychotherapists and the family nurse.

Observations of the child's daily experience, whether in the family, the children's group, the whole inpatient group or the group of children in the children's centre, with other families, in teaching groups and outings, with the nurse, or with other nurses and in the patient community, can be evaluated at a weekly children's meeting. Views distilled from all parts of the hospital can be shared by staff and thought about here. Some children have individual psychotherapy sessions (up to three times weekly); others do not. However, the way in which all children adapt to or react to life within the community is of special concern to the child psychotherapist. It is the psychotherapist's task not only to offer assessment, but also to make observations about the progress and psychological state of the children, which will increase the therapeutic possibilities of the hospital treatment.

This function of the child psychotherapist of assimilating the inpatient experience of the child is so important. Life in a therapeutic community, with several types of therapeutic input, can be bewildering, requiring the child psychotherapist and indeed the child to be, to quote Montaigne, 'a good swimmer . . . (who is) . . . not swallowed up and drowned by the depth and weight of his learning' (Montaigne, *Essays*, 1580).

Perhaps it is because the child psychotherapist is identified with the work of the Families Unit in providing not only a therapeutic but a supportive environment for the child, that he or she comes to be seen in a parental role. Given the feelings not only of the children but of the parents, the stage is set for the idealisation and denigration I described earlier. Such views about the child psychotherapist will of course become expanded in daily contacts in the hospital. There may be a particular view of the therapist supplied by this community life which is carried by the child, but which may be distinguishable from the child's own view. However, the former view may dominate over the child's view. An example of this, culled from many sources, is the occasional fantasy which parents have that the child psychotherapist is not fit to see the child, that the psychotherapist is too lax, or too strict, or harms the child. Such group fantasies make for difficulties, not only for the child who has individual psychotherapy but for the child psychotherapist. To minimise the difficulties which may result from such fantasies and work with them in a therapeutic way, it is necessary that the child psychotherapist be, and be seen to be, flexible, accessible and unmysterious in the necessary contacts with families and staff alike.

To appreciate the currency of beliefs about various aspects of the treatment, to minimise splits in the therapeutic approach, and put splits which occur to therapeutic effect, there is a need to understand the daily life of the child in the community and examine working relationships with other staff. Such an approach alters the psychotherapist's understanding of the concepts of transference and countertransference in the inpatient psychoanalytic setting.

Briefly, for this is expanded in this and subsequent chapters (especially Chapter 6), the child psychotherapist will need to be aware, not only of the child's transference and his or her own countertransference in the psychotherapy session, but of the child's 'transference' to the hospital and individual staff members, in particular to the family nurse. In supervisions too, the psychotherapist must pay attention not only to countertransference to the child, but also feelings towards other workers with whom the child may have a significant relationship.

The experience of the child within the hospital

People outside the hospital always react with surprise at the idea that children and whole families should be in a hospital, and that they undertake such an intense therapeutic experience together. Frequently, it is asked, 'What do whole families think about going into hospital together?' and 'What does this mean for the children?' The children themselves give diverse answers that reflect changes in their inner experience of events, in addition to changes or disruptions to time-honoured patterns of personal and family life. Children are clearly concerned with the minutiae of their daily life and ask questions such as 'Why are we staying here overnight?' 'Where do we sleep?' 'What will we eat and who cooks it?' 'Who will we have to share with?' 'Who will we have as friends?' The children may form views and make adjustments before their parents, giving valuable indicators of their feelings and those of other members of the family. Such indicators are vital in our assessment as to whether the child and family's use of the inpatient setting is likely to be therapeutically successful. I shall give some examples from my initial assessment of children when they come to hospital to illustrate this.

The hospital as a place of containment

Two very young children, a boy of pre-school age and a girl in first infants' class, showed in separate ways their awareness of family events during and after the transition to hospital life. In this instance I assessed both and they were brother and sister. The assessments, which took place before a too complex level and web of transference had developed for each, meant I could see contrasting perceptions of family life and their introduction into residential life. In my first meeting with the girl, she drew a picture of a fishtank with a bullet-like frog in it, along with a vacant-looking fish. Outside, a pig looked on in the garden with fruit around. Patrolling the house was a rather shrunken looking tortoise. The tank seemed to represent her sense of confinement, with characters as follows: the frog herself, the fish her brother, the pig her mother and the tortoise her father. The passivity of the mother was represented as sloth, while the paranoid armour of the father was represented in the tired old tortoise. The family was not functioning or moving forward, and the children were captives. I had warmed to this girl in this first meeting, but as the meeting went on I found she slowed up and that her play was becoming more stilted. Overall I felt I was being drawn into becoming a captive with her, caught up like her and her family in the confinement of the fishtank.

A week later, however, her experience was changing and I found she was expressing herself more in her play. She used a Lego set to construct the family home and then the hospital, showing as the significant change a shift in perspective from a house where all the windows look *in* to one where they look *out*. This signified an opening up from the nervous defensiveness of family life and the shared fears of that family, about types of food, intruders and much else. She then developed a game with animals that were all locked in a pen, saying, 'They are so overcrowded inside . . . they can't move . . . they can't even open the door.' I felt her describing something not only about her internal world, how feelings and thoughts are locked inside, but also how she felt her family was restrictive and confining. She now ventured an admission, 'I like to eat steak', rather than the vegetarian diet that her parents required them to eat. It now came out that she experienced the restrictions on her diet at home as restrictions on her omnipotence. This had been shown in her flaunting attitude to male staff, her severe physical punishment of her younger brother and her lack of responsiveness to a caring approach. The restrictions were now being challenged in the community, as they saw other families acting differently and as a result of new open divisions in the family. Her emerging fear was about her own internal state and reaction to this, that removing the restrictions may be tantamount to giving way to unrestrained expression on her part, and she would need to face issues of her own omnipotence and her fears about self-control.

The change in perception for the boy was more marked, for as he began to develop his play (or in Winnicott's sense *playing*), his behaviour in assessment and subsequent psychotherapy sessions moved from chaos or stony withdrawal towards construction and expression (Winnicott 1971: 44–75). In our first meeting he disturbed me because he was so cut off and unresponsive. His anxiety was at first latent and he spent his time nervously moving from object to object, from toy to toy, fingering it and putting it down. Only with the play dough did he linger longer, trying fervently to wrap it up again. He emptied everything out of his cupboard as if completing a thorough search. He had a nervous way of wiping bubbles away from his mouth, as if the end of a feed were most uncomfortable. By the second week his awareness of painful psychic reality was evident. In our staff meeting it had been reported that now he spent time crying on his own. He told me he had no friends and seemed to shy away from me, like a boy before his headmaster, not giving anything away. Only when he crawled under the table did he relax and smile. I felt he responded from now on to containment without being over-close. He drew a child and a rocket, the two sides of him, mildly withdrawn and manically explosive.

In our third meeting, his drawings and sequences of play began to show signs of development. He began to experience strong feelings of anger when separating from his mother, and expressed anger to his parents at the weekend. In the fourth meeting he began to play mealtimes with me as if he had felt there was a real dialogue with me, in contrast with the counterfeit relationships within the family, without mutuality, where, for example, he and his sister were not allowed by his father to eat the same food as his mother. His drawings were now of a shaky house, showing I thought that he could find some level of containment in the hospital and in the psychotherapy which was now planned for him.

Both these children had experienced the family as a place of confinement. The girl had shown me first the fishtank drawing, whilst it was soon revealed that the boy had one night suffered the traumatic experience of getting himself locked in a trunk with water at the bottom for a considerable time. The girl's drawing, no doubt, alluded to this incident, which seemed to epitomise the child's experience of family relationships. At first in treatment the family were obsessed with views about hidden forces, but would disregard the everyday evidence of cause and effect. In such circumstances, the everyday structures of community life were of first importance in establishing a more open communication. Interestingly the family's view of themselves influenced their view of the staff, so that at first the parents expected psychotherapists and nurses to convey messages amongst themselves on issues regarding the children (thus assuming the staff to have a secret system of communication), which they, the parents, could if they had not been so secretive convey to each other. Work with this family continued for several months. The boy received individual treatment, as the parents had too, before progress faltered. The family closed ranks again as deeper secrets were being revealed.

The hospital as a dangerous place

Many of the views expressed by children at the beginning of treatment reflect fears of the hospital, of their own badness and fears of loss of control. Two boys in one family had been circumcised in another hospital shortly before admission. They had had little or no preparation for this. Their initial reaction on admission to the Families Unit was one of panic and shock. The elder boy, 6 years old, had felt betrayed by his parents and the doctors. He would only come to assessment meetings if he had fully negotiated this with me on his own terms. He seemed to feel no confidence in his parents' powers of negotiation and his initial reaction to me, of suspicion and fear, was rooted in his belief that I would not be able to offer sufficient containment for his acute feelings. A week later he felt a greater degree of safety. He built a spaceship, in which he no longer needed air bottles. These seemed to represent the dreaded oxygen cylinders of his earlier hospitalisation, his fear of what he had been subjected to unawares, and his newer sense now that he could survive in the atmosphere of this hospital. He also felt that I could probably understand what it was like for him in hospital because, as he said, 'When you were a little boy you were probably in hospital sometime.'

For his younger brother, 4 years old, the recent hospitalisation for circumcision was just one of a series of hospitalisations for adenoids, tonsillitis and grommets, which had heightened severe separation problems for him. He was wetting his bed and he seemed to me to be a confused and disorientated child. Inside the room, he flicked electric switches in an aggravating way. His play about ambulances becoming 'firebirds' and crashing into the playroom walls, damaging the plaster, clearly expressed his anxiety about being in hospital. Side by side with his attacks on the fabric of the playroom, he showed however a wish to use the therapy room as a safe place for his anger and his confused feelings. At a deeper level, his belief that the playroom could be dangerous, and his fear of entering, seemed connected with his phantasies of killing off the baby within. He seemed highly aware of his parents arguing and fighting and he was curious as to his parents' sexual behaviour. Yet his fear, common to many children, was that he was in hospital because of his 'badness'.

The hospital as a place of comfort and security to keep away conflict

Other children often see the hospital as having an interesting and varied life, where difficulties can be forgotten and denied or become diffused with the difficulties and disturbance of those around. Early relief can also lead to patterns of idealisation. Reception into hospital can then be experienced as a form of seduction, which is enjoyed and then regretted, so that deeper anxieties about intrusion are soon heralded. For one school-phobic girl, these fears about intrusion became focused on the psychotherapy, so that she became unable to communicate in the therapy room. By contrast, she banned all entry to her hospital room, to forestall any intrusion. Only when staff, after much disagreement, could share the view that this girl was using a splitting mechanism, dividing rooms into totally safe and totally unsafe, was progress made. The girl was then given a room with others her own age, at first with much protest. Work in psychotherapy sessions and in the community could then come closer together. In fact, in view of her limited concrete way of showing her feelings, it was only by concentrating on the minutiae of her daily living that progress could be made, so that the work of her individual psychotherapy was to focus on her adjustment to life within the community.

A 6-year-old girl (discussed in Chapter 3) who attended the children's centre and came for psychotherapy three times a week found the privileges of the inpatient children intolerable to bear. She was from a children's home and had not yet been found a new home. She found it insufferable that other children had their home with their school. She frequently played out her conflict about being the intruder in stories about Goldilocks and The Three Bears. She expressed strong wishes to stay in the hospital, eat with patients and sleep there. The hospital became idealised as 'the safe home' and intensified the conflict that the children's home, her natural parents' home and any possible foster home would not be good enough. In a way, this child experienced a conflict that centred round the breakdown in the child's idealised notion of a family, which other children from inpatient families also have. However, for this child, it was most concrete as she did not have a family. (For Freud's concept of the 'family romance fantasy' see (1909a) S.E. 9: 235–41 and Chapter 8 on 'The Adoptive Father'.)

The hospital as a place which allows the child his individuality in his family

The way the child is wrapped up in the conflicts of his ill parents can sometimes be observed in their views about the hospital. One boy from a large family drew airships and seemed both intrigued yet concerned about how one design of airship led to the design and production of another prototype. It struck me that his interest sounded like an account of early genealogies in the book of Genesis. He was worried about himself and his brothers and sisters being the cause of the problems within the family. The airships he drew seemed like the stream of babies that came along. He told his nurse that the family were coming into hospital because 'the children are mad'. At age 11, he was still eneuretic. He was a helpful child, whose concern for his family actually significantly contributed to them managing at all, but he lacked the individual interest in him from his parents that he needed.

All of this was reflected in his first views of the hospital. He liked the food and found the hospital very interesting, as he had discovered that there were many ways to get from the ground floor to the central rooms. I felt that here the hospital was being seen like a large body, which feeds, and has special bottom and middle passages, perhaps linked to phantasies about procreation and excretion. It was especially significant then that the family referral for inpatient treatment was made after a final attempt to resolve problems by marriage guidance. But up to this point the parents had made no mention about sexual difficulties in their relationship even though there were many. It was as if, then, the child not only cared for the other children of his parents, but in struggling with his own childhood sexual phantasies he carried the preoccupations about sexuality which his parents had disowned. Additionally the meaning of his problem of eneuresis was linked to these preoccupations. This resolved itself in once weekly psychotherapy sessions. Coming into hospital appears to have enabled him to work on his unconscious phantasies about birth, procreation and what it means to be a child in a large family. The main work in the hospital of psychotherapy and community treatment concentrated on his parents' illness and their func-tioning as a family. But he was encouraged to express his needs as a child, including his anger, to have his own interests and more attention from his parents, so that he could develop individually and not be so dominated by his parents' illness. He also attended school locally and developed outside friends and interests in his own right, not just in the family, as is appro-priate for a latency age child.

Case example

I shall now describe some features of a nine-month period of psychotherapy (three times weekly) of a boy, Mark, aged five, in the inpatient setting. This was the second half of an 18-month inpatient stay for Mark and his mother, a one-parent, one-child family. I shall lay stress on features of the treatment where the child's transference relationship to his psychotherapist illuminates the child's life in the community, and vice versa.

Briefly the history was as follows. There had been difficulties between mother and child from the start when there were problems over feeding, and breastfeeding broke down. Mark's mother had described this as a feeling that 'there was nothing for the baby to hang on to'. She was young and vulnerable and her marriage to Mark's father had not lasted long, so she returned to and became highly dependent again on her own family.

Mark's mother had taken a number of overdoses and had had frequent admissions to psychiatric hospital. Mark was separated from her, either being looked after by her parents, going into residential care or being fostered. For 18 months prior to their admission in the Families Unit, Mark spent the whole day at his mother's parents and only slept at his mother's home. Mark and his mother were admitted then to see whether they could live as a family. In the home visit just prior to admission, the nurses recall how the house was bare of furniture. In relating to each other, mother and child had numerous angry bouts. Even at the time Mark came for psychotherapy, there was a question of whether his violence could be contained, doubts about whether mother and child would be able to live together and about whether Mark would be able to attend an outside infant school. The issue of whether mother and child could connect with each other was still central, from the time of the earliest disconnections in infancy. It was now clear that mother and child would only face their biggest challenge after they had left the hospital, for until then the difficulties of being together would be mitigated by life in the community. This was especially so since Mark, though frequently unmanageable, was very well liked, and his mother was very active in taking responsibility in community affairs. This degree of adaptability to the social environment to some degree reflected previous dependence on the mother's family – she worked hard but remained very unsure of her real place within it.

There were, however, bizarre elements in the mother, such as rapid and stark changes of image and repeated periods of mental abstraction, even during the course of otherwise normal conversations. She wanted Mark to have psychotherapy, but she had mixed feelings. She and Mark strongly felt the loss of the male nurse, who had now moved to another unit, and who along with her psychotherapist had previously run play sessions, focusing on their interactions. She also seemed afraid that I, Mark's psychotherapist, would take Mark over as her family had done. She was particularly alarmed, I thought, that Mark might experience the depth of his feelings in psychotherapy. Another family with whom Mark and his mother had become friendly were just leaving, and they were worried about their own lack of preparation for life outside the hospital, as well as this family's.

My first impression of Mark was of an attractive and boisterous child, who seemed to slur over and deny his feeling that I was taking him away from his mum. Underneath I thought he did not believe that he could make an attachment to me. He did see me as having a function, as a 'wheely-mind man', who would talk to him about his 'wheelies', i.e. his losing his temper. However, he would become furious when I did not hear something he said: 'Are you deaf?' he would shout. The feeling in early sessions was that Mark enjoyed the rapport but wanted this without regard to me, in a taking over sort of way. Also, he chose safe toys and used limited forms of symbolic expression. Although very intelligent he was unimaginative, so it was not surprising that he communicated through ruthless action. It became clear that Mark's troublesome, noisy behaviour in the hospital had the function of stimulating the mother's attention. He engaged wholeheartedly in his sessions, which led to the rapid establishment of a quite intense dependence on me, his psychotherapist. But soon his main complaint was that I, the psychotherapist, 'stopped him from thinking'. I think Mark feared a kind of psychotic impingement.

Mark was a mixed race child. He sometimes mockingly spoke in an 'African' accent and coined a new name for me, 'British Beef'. As time went on, he appreciated his black relations more, particularly after painstaking work by his black nurse. But at this stage, the missing white father was idealised. When I had to be away for a short period in an unscheduled way, Mark was observed to eat no meat at all in the hospital. His wish for a father, and his fear that his aggression towards me had damaged and driven me away, may have brought out deep-rooted guilt about his oral aggression.

After the first break, Mark told me a dream in which 'I saw a man with a moustache. I walked up to the man wondering who it was. The man looked at me and said, "Oh, it's you!" The boy then turned into a batman.' The man with the moustache reminded him of his favourite uncle. The batman referred to his wish to hit out or 'bat' people. The anger behind this seemed to be because the man paid too little attention to him. I interpreted that he was angry about the break and what he saw as his psychotherapist's indifferent attention to him.

As time went on, Mark became most unsettled about the arrival of other children on the unit. He felt that his territory, both inside the therapy room and inside the hospital, was being taken over. He now began to want to go into his mother's bed at night. He also became furiously angry about the fathers in these families having any involvement with him. His mother would not accept it either, so both adopted a collusive withdrawal. At the same time, Mark would frequently create a disturbed situation before his sessions, so that various means were needed to get him there. Once there, he could begin to play, to respond and to get some relief from the irritations and angers he could not express outside. But the crises he precipitated meant bringing mother, nurse and psychotherapist into a series of arrangements that were successful not just in getting Mark to his session time but in working through some of the conflicts within the community.

Mark saw himself as involved with different combinations of couples, each time excluding a third person. Sometimes he saw the psychotherapist or nurse and mother as conspiring against him, sometimes it was Mark who was allied with mother, making the psychotherapist into an intruding father. The fact that Mark had a strong relationship with both nurse and psychotherapist meant that such combinations were deeply meaningful. Mark also attempted again and again to split the parental couple, such as his nurse and psychotherapist working with him, denying that it could be visible and effective.

As we focused on difficulties arising from such struggles with Mark, he asked about his real father and for a couple of weekends his father actually came back into the picture. It was telling that in describing his father to me Mark said he looked like one of the patients in the hospital. It was clear that life in hospital, despite its difficulties, was the only home Mark and his mum had been together in for any length of time.

A focus of work in the therapeutic community was on the difficulties which came up in the times they were together, particularly regarding the mother's unresponsiveness to him and Mark's refusal to accept his mother's authority. Mark experienced any restrictions as a fear that his relationship with his mother would end, so the searing level of his protest had the function of controlling his mother. He now did some drawings of an aeroplane that might crash. Inside this plane was another smaller plane. He also told me that he stayed up until 12 midnight watching a film 'with my mum all on her own'.

Mark then began a phase of harsh sadistic attacks on me, his psychotherapist, hitting and kicking and spitting at me repeatedly, then laughing in a gloating way at me. He also tried to prise open other children's toy boxes, to take their things. In this he was expressing his anger and disappointment that I could not be a real father just for him, and anger that I as the symbolic father was seen to be required to separate or prise apart he and his mother. Even when he had appreciated the session, being able to reconstruct some toy he feared he had destroyed or overcoming his nameless irritation, he sometimes said 'the session was crap' as he left the room.

Throughout this time there were a number of incidents in the hospital of toilets being smeared with faeces and one toilet door being smashed down, and a wider pattern of community disturbance. Some in the community, including staff, thought Mark had done these things and wanted to challenge him about it. But I think they were wrong to attribute such damage to him, for Mark's mood was more often quite calm now in between his outbursts, when he was more openly angry and admitted it, whereas this behaviour was hidden and deceitful as well as very aggressive in a crazy disturbing way. I made this point within the staff group and the matter was taken up elsewhere in the community, other than with Mark. Frequently however I think that Mark was tuned into the sadistic fantasies of those around him, just as he had tuned into his mother's more strange mental processes and actions, so that he had re-enacted what was going on in the community in his session in sadistic attacks on his psychotherapist.

In a sense, he was not just the 'barometer' of community feelings but the 'detonator' too, for Mark could own up to his destructive wishes, so that they were available for therapeutic work, when other patients could not. As so often, it is the child who expresses what others cannot or will not, who invites an immediate response to himself, who becomes of special service to the ill patient within a psychiatric hospital, and the parents in a family, as a vehicle of neurotic acting out or schizoid communications. Alongside work with the child in individual psychotherapy, an important element of the work in a therapeutic community – by doctors and nurses, psychotherapists of the parents, the parents themselves and other patients – is to identify and address community-wide destructive patterns of behaviour that are signalled by the child (see Burman 1987 on 'regressive distortions' and also Kernberg 1984, 1992).

Mark's lack of creativity came more into focus as it became apparent that if he could not recreate the same good object he would not try or attempt anything. He also felt that without magic he could not do anything himself, it was 'only shit'. This lack of creativity and his very active mode of functioning made Mark an especially useful vehicle for projections in a schizoid way. For a time, he attacked me mercilessly, particularly as he began sensing the plans for the family leaving, when he wanted to test the quality of containment. His attacks were a provocation, testing whether he was to be forced out of the hospital he considered 'home'. He got in touch more with his upset as he talked about this in psychotherapy. He now began to talk about other hospitals where his mother had gone after her overdoses. He remembered how he was sick too and how 'a chip came up with the sick', and how it was 'runny and lumpy'. The memory he had was of his fear that he had driven mother to her overdoses. For Mark, being in hospital seemed to mean there was always a fear of his mother's death around.

An important area of work with Mark, and other children whose parents had significant psychiatric disturbance, was to help him with his fears and anxieties about the impact of his mother's psychiatric illness, to deal with his guilt and to try to help him give adequate space to his own needs and development. This was not easy, particularly when the stresses of treatment and his mother's relapses seemed to create a need for mother and child to be drawn together in an over-close but highly anxious and regressive type of contact. With Mark as with other children, similar dynamic patterns occur again and again, not just with his mother, but in other relationships within the social milieu of the therapeutic community treatment. These re-enacted dynamics, as we see repeatedly in Part 2, can become opportunities for work towards therapeutic change.

So, when some younger children were admitted to hospital, Mark again began to regress, talking in a baby voice, playing with soft toys and becoming more clingy. This regressive change occurred when the nurse from his earliest time in hospital, with whom he had had play sessions, moved to the children's centre and Mark had renewed contact with him during school time. Mark's regression then was comprehensible in relation to finding contact with this previously valued person. Soon after this, Mark and his mother were able to make plans together to enjoy each other's company, and yet still be able to separate and let go, aware they could come back together again. Mark also was now able to come to his session times more easily, even though he was stirred up, upset and angry at times about the end of his psychotherapy with me. He drew a series of buggies that had brakes. They were partly 'baby buggy' and partly 'moon buggy'. The brake lights signified the capacity for some self-control. As the buggies got bigger they were to have bigger brake lights.

Both mother and child had a lot of work to do towards the ending. This was shown not just in their plans about leaving but also in their attitude towards work in the hospital. Both feared they could not retain what had been learned. Mark was particularly helpful preparing for the hospital garden party, to which staff and some former patients may come, carrying five loads of materials *from the inside* of the house *outside* to the garden.

Quite out of the blue he paused and said to a nurse standing by, 'You know, I like Mr Flynn . . . but he hasn't helped me.' He seemed infected by his mother's pessimism, but he was anxious about the new outside school he visited in preparation for his leaving. He had previously been unable to go into the school for fear of the other children. In his play it became clear he expected them to be as aggressive as he could be.

His mother too was clearly worried about how well she could make the plans for herself and Mark. This was illustrated in the following incident. After a preliminary visit to the school outside, Mark's mother provoked a dispute with the community nurse in the hospital and walked off. As Mark's mother was responsible for ordering hospital provisions for the cooking that patients do, this was delayed. Other patients talked to her about her anxieties fulfilling her responsibilities for the hospital provisions and for being Mark's mother when she may be struggling on her own outside the hospital after discharge. This helped her in a very ad hominem way so that in fact she later adjusted to the task so that the provisions were ordered. She also began to improve her confidence about managing Mark outside.

Near the very end of his stay, Mark produced some of his richest drawings. One in particular was a story about pirates on the high seas. He was showing that he could anticipate dangers and difficulties outside, so that when I asked him what he felt about seeing a child psychotherapist in an outpatient setting, he said he would like to. On leaving the hospital, the family did in fact make contact with the child guidance clinic we had put them in touch with and they proved able to negotiate a new form of therapeutic contract and a further successful period of outpatient psychotherapy to take further the work we had already done with the inpatient setting.

Conclusion

The child who comes into hospital with his family will have many adjustments to make, and inpatient psychotherapy is an opportunity to reflect on experiences as the family adjusts to inpatient life. The child's particular experience of hospital life can be a valuable indicator of his or her inner emotional life. Children with major needs and difficulties can have intensive psychotherapy within the setting, whilst due attention is also given to special nurturing help within the hospital children's centre, which for many children is a compensation after many years of being embroiled in family problems.

Chapter 5

Family rehabilitation after physical abuse

My daughter, far from weeping for her fate,
Forgives her father, nay invites me still
To bow before the hand that cleaves her heart.
(Racine, *Iphigenia*, Act 4, Scene 3)

Introduction

This chapter outlines in detail how child psychotherapy as part of a whole family treatment can use the extended possibilities of containment offered in an applied context for treatment of the most severe cases. I shall describe the assessment and psychotherapy of a 7-year-old girl who suffered serious physical abuse prior to being removed from her parents and taken into care. She was returned to her mother only during inpatient treatment at the Cassel Hospital Families Unit, a process of rehabilitation that lasted in all 18 months. Her psychotherapy was one element in the treatment arrangements offered to the family during their time there. I shall include some discussion of other selected parts of the treatment, in particular the nursing work with the family and the mother's individual psychotherapy, to fill out understanding of the child's individual treatment.

The aims of psychotherapy of severely abused children treated in this applied setting are twofold. The first is common to all psychoanalytic psychotherapy, namely to understand the inner life of the child as it becomes revealed in the transference relationship to the psychotherapist. For this one needs to establish a psychoanalytic setting, with regular place and times to see the child, with a commitment to the setting and an understanding of the individual transference. The second aim is to understand the predicament of the child. By this I mean understanding not just how the child is affected by the abuse and their view of what happened, but also any major changes in the child's life that are consequent to the abuse. This includes changes in their closest relationships and attachments, in particular to their parents and other significant figures such as foster parents and children's home staff, which can bring further losses, upset and disturbance for the child.

Freud's (1919) paper, 'A Child is Being Beaten', discusses how phantasies of being beaten are rooted in sexual fantasies towards a desired loved one. A masochistic wish to be beaten or abused develops, since in a distorted way the child who is beaten is felt to be more special and more loved. The child who wants to be loved subjects himself to abuse rather than be disdained by neglect. The child starved of adequate emotional contact with the parent may feel driven to express and experience feelings of longing in a sexual way, thereby compounding already strong hidden and repressed unconscious desires. Today, with the wealth of testified evidence about the actual occurrence of physical abuse of children, we would be chary of accepting Freud's assumption at that time that 'the relation between actual experience of beating or corporal punishment at home and the preponderance of beating-fantasies is an inverse one' (1919: 180). We are rightly more inclined to treat the child's reports about abuse as possible genuine accounts of fact (Masson 1984; Hanley 1987; Kennedy 1997; Target 1998). It is significant that Freud reinforced his initial views (1905b, 1906) of the actual seduction in some cases in later works (Introductory Lectures, 1916/17: 370; 'On Female Sexuality' 1931: 232; 'Moses and Monotheism' 1939: 75–6). What is important here is recognition *both* of the facts of what happened *and* the place of phantasy and infantile sexuality in relation to potential for pathogenesis, or development of severe disturbance (Hanley 1987).

We shall see in my case study that Freud contributed to an understanding of the depth processes in the treatment of abused children, particularly as their experience of abuse develops and undergoes internal transformation. Importantly he states:

> Beating phantasies have a historical development which is by no means simple, and in the course of which they are changed in most respects more than once – as regards their relation to the author of the phantasy, as regards their object, their content and their significance.
>
> (S.E.17, 184)

The child's suffering of abuse therefore becomes overlain with phantasy elements, which reflect the deepest struggles of the child to come to terms with what has happened. Children, when they begin to process such traumatic experiences, ask themselves different questions, and give or expect to be given different answers, about why what happened did happen, whether this was abuse, why it happened to them, who did it and what they feel about it. At any stage the accounts the child may give about abuse may reflect the internal rather than the external reality of the child and the need to rework and reinterpret the experience of abuse.

In the case study then I would like to show that psychotherapy of an abused child can help to bring to light the child's internal experience of abuse, the questions the child is asking or failing to ask, and the struggle in the child to disentangle phantasy and reality, so that the contamination and pain of the whole abuse situation, in addition to any subsequent separations and trauma, may be recognised and worked on.

I discussed in Chapter 4 a number of features of the inpatient setting with regard to child psychotherapy. To add to this, adults attend meetings and events that plan and organise most of the ongoing and day-to-day activities of the inpatient community. The patient is seen as active rather than passive, and most importantly parents retain responsibility for the daily care of their children. The emotional impact of day-to-day events is discussed with the nursing staff, who work alongside their patients – commenting, discussing and reacting in a commonsense way to the patient's life in the hospital, keeping external reality to the forefront. Individual psychotherapy is offered to all adults and parents not only to explore internal conflicts in a private and protected way, but also to elucidate phantasies involved in the current reality of the patient's daily life and in particular an individual's behaviour, progress and conflicts within the hospital community. The patient forms deep attachments to nurse as well as psychotherapist and may enact deep conflicts in their relationship to the nurse as well as psychotherapist, so that family conflicts may become enacted in everyday life in the hospital community.

Clinical material

Background

Teresa was a concern to child care agencies shortly after her birth, and became the subject of reported abuse when aged two years, when she suffered a series of lacerations, burns and fractures. Over the next three years further incidents occurred, culminating in a final serious incident at the age of five. Teresa was then taken into long-term care. The abusing family featured open violence, alcoholism and miscommunication between parents. All ill-treatment of the child was denied. The stepfather was thought to have perpetrated the violence, although there was never any proof of this, and it was clear that Mrs A had at least been neglectful. Significantly the only comment about the child at the time, by mother, was that she was now becoming naughty, after she had previously been abnormally well behaved. The care plan of long-term fostering and then adoption was reversed when Mrs A, having separated from her husband, made a determined bid for the return of the child. Inpatient family treatment was therefore suggested as a way of rehabilitating mother and child, to build up their relationship and forestall any future possible abuse.

However, it was only after several months of outpatient individual psychotherapy that Mrs A was able to show enough motivation to change for rehabilitation in an inpatient setting to seem at all feasible. Even so Mrs A came over, in the consultation and in the nursing home assessment, as impulsive and dishonest, unable to acknowledge her part in events, and instead projecting all blame and problems onto other people or other agencies. The saving features, which persuaded the social services and the courts to try rehabilitation, were Mrs A's capacity to have some insight into her own childhood deprivation and her evident wish to be with Teresa. Even so she appeared to see Teresa as satisfying her needs, rather than vice versa. Mrs A was a lady of contrasts, keeping good contact with Teresa in the foster home, yet expressing violent anger against social services and even being charged with grievous bodily assault on another in a public place in the interval before admission.

Inpatient assessment

By the beginning of their assessment period in hospital, which lasted for six weeks, there had been a long separation of 15 months since mother and child had lived together. The initial plan was that Teresa would spend the weekdays at the hospital with her mother and then spend weekends with the foster parents she had been with so far.

At first both Mrs A and Teresa appeared dull, overweight and dirty. Mrs A was constantly very angry, but out of touch with any depression in her or her daughter. Teresa, then aged six and three quarter years, was slow, quiet and deliberate about what she did, constantly watching her mother to see if she was giving the 'right' response. She seemed and looked a 'damaged' or 'battered' child.

Mrs A initially maintained there were no problems and that everything was wonderful between them. Problems emerged, not surprisingly, during the first weekend, which was spent at the hospital. Mrs A was unable to set realistic boundaries for Teresa, allowing her to stay up very late and then to share her bed, saying that both she and Teresa were lonely. During the day Mrs A had noticeably little contact with Teresa, with an exception of some times she read to her daughter, which both seemed to enjoy. In the community, Mrs A found it difficult to face any criticism or situation of conflict. She could become busy or involved if it was for herself or on her terms, but was otherwise lazy and uninvolved. She had numerous disagreements with others, patients and staff, that left others feeling angry, upset or guilty, while she appeared honest, calm and coping.

Only during the assessment did Mrs A's history become more fully known – a history of deprivation, poverty of early attachments, personal losses, lack of parenting to herself, a disrupted adolescence, early marriage, a subsequent marriage and then a series of relationships to violent men. Mrs A's underlying insecurity and depression were marked with a hardened exterior. She identified with Teresa as a lonely battered child, but her actual ambivalence about her daughter was much more difficult to face.

In my individual assessment of Teresa there were certain key questions to be answered. First, was Teresa able to develop an attachment to her mother again, and could she cope with the separations from her foster parents? Second, what sense could she make of the abuse and her present predicament? In her first individual session:

Teresa looked small and stolid, with short dark hair and a round pale face, that now and later seemed impassive. As she walked awkwardly to the playroom, she was initially chatty in a superficial way, but I thought her essentially very timid.

She wore a garish-coloured lipstick like mother's. She told me that her mother had helped her settle down on the first night by recalling warm memories of the cat she had had before the family split up. In this she began to indicate she wanted to respond to her mother and be with her.

As she talked, what she said felt broken up and there was a degree of coldness and emptiness in her description of 'where mother lives' as opposed to 'home', which described the foster home. What came through was that she had not expected anything good at the hospital, such as swimming trips. She frequently mentioned that she needed to get her costume from the foster home. This seemed her way of expressing her improved expectations that something good would come of being here.

She did some drawings, which turned out to be rather flat stereotypes of sky and earth, houses, trees and people. However, I thought there were powerful underlying motifs, centred round themes of safety and incompatible elements, such as fire and water. These drawings hinted at as yet unexpressed feelings about the renewed relationship with mother.

From the start Teresa's play also hinted that she felt that her mother's needs had priority. For example, she drew two suns, but the larger one needed a lifebelt when it fell into water. She said the smaller sun needed to be near the bigger sun when it did so.

Teresa seemed to want to make a warm contact with me, which seemed to have the purpose of keeping out more disturbing thoughts and feelings. These Teresa hinted at, as if anticipating disturbances, when she told me of various exciting outings she had been on, and of the puppet shows and fights she had seen. She also told me of an incident when she had seen a plane crashing into a wall (it sounded like a story) and something also running into and smashing glass. I acknowledged her need to let me know that she could get hurt and her fear that she might be hurt here.

In the second session, at the end of the first week, her fears about abuse were clearer. What also became clear was her use of denial and confusion to dispel these fears:

> Teresa was trying to give the impression of having settled well, but she avoided talking about her mother and spoke instead of a friend in the hospital. I asked her how her first week back with her mother had been. She told me that 'nothing like that' had happened. I asked her what she meant by 'nothing like that' and she said she had not fallen over or anything like that. When I again acknowledged her fear of getting hurt in the hospital, or in her session, she felt freer to get on with some drawing.
>
> She drew what she described as 'a ladder that was leaning against nothing and seemed to be leading nowhere, which was next to an apple tree. A girl was about to climb the ladder with a paint pot'. I could see already a tendency in Teresa to gabble on in a superficial and unrelenting way – linking to the drawing, how her words sometimes 'led nowhere'. Teresa was very literal and repetitive when asked for her associations, i.e. what she thought about the drawings, saying it was 'a ladder', 'leading nowhere' and there was 'a tree'. I thought that she was in touch with a defensive wish to deny or confuse feelings, so that her efforts would lead 'nowhere', like the ladder – a kind of Tower of Babel. Connected with this was her fear that her time at the Cassel would lead 'nowhere'.
>
> At the end Mrs A did not turn up to collect Teresa for ten minutes. Teresa told me that she was worried. I asked if she was worried about her mother. She said, 'No, I am worried about myself.'

There was an interesting development of feeling during this session. Early on Teresa hinted at her mother being partly responsible for her being hurt and how she sometimes felt unsafe. Later on she also began to feel uncertain where this renewed contact would lead, so that at times, as at the end, she felt she had to worry about herself.

Prior to the second weekend, when she was to return from Friday to Sunday to her foster parents, Teresa could say very little. With the impending loss of mother she seemed stripped of her defences, her liveliness and her chatter. She also became confused about who people were. She thought, for example, that her nurse was a social worker she had seen two years previously. Her play became increasingly slow and ponderous. In the last session before this weekend:

> Teresa divided up the animals into two groups, one of horses in a paddock and another of a mixture of all the other animals outside in another paddock. Again her associations were very literal but the group

inside the paddock seemed to represent the more protected familiar foster family and herself. Outside were the unfamiliar indeterminate faces. Even so, in the familiar group there was one horse which was hanging on the railings by its neck. (I was reminded of one of the incidents of abuse in the past, namely a laceration on her neck.) Some of the most strong animals, the elephant and the eagle and the two bulls, were left outside the paddock. As we spoke about this arrangement of the toys, the fantasy became alive for her. She made a man jump on the elephant, 'and then there was a baby' she said. She then put three men figures riding on the backs of horses. Her mood became excited.

This play seemed to indicate as yet unknown links between early infantile phantasies, her awareness of events in the past, and her views about attachments now, including phantasies about the forthcoming weekend – excited coupling and the arrival of a baby. From now on, after brief periods when she was more animated, I felt there was a slow, punch-drunk quality to all her talk, perhaps because she was overwhelmed by both fantasy and reality, neither of which she could distinguish or make coherent.

Following the weekend back with her foster parents, there was another notable shift in Teresa's feelings about being with her mother. She was freer to face difficulties, as if she had, within the security of the foster home, charged up some batteries. There was also more spontaneity in her play. I thought Teresa now had some idea that she could survive outside the close protection of the foster home.

On one occasion Mrs A prompted Teresa to tell me that she wanted to stay with her mother. When I said to her that she could tell me what she felt and wanted, Teresa felt relieved at not having the burden of simply following her mother's wishes. Progressively now in the psychotherapy sessions, Teresa began to express some minimal feelings herself, including jealousy and some partial dislike for other children. In this period Teresa had often seemed baffled by her mother, but she dealt with this by shutting off and becoming like her. Her last drawing in the assessment time was of an egg opening up with a chicken inside, which seemed like the first emergence into view of Teresa as a real child.

It had been coming out in Mrs A's own psychotherapy that there had been problems in the mother–child relationship from the earliest time. Teresa had been unwanted and unplanned – an abortion had been considered – and there had been a number of early developmental problems, particularly with feeding and sleeping. Mrs A had felt unfulfilled at home looking after a child and had returned to work when Teresa was four weeks old, leaving her with a series of childminders. The passivity and slow robotic quality in Teresa, which seemed to be the result of abuse and the subsequent separation from mother while in care, may have had its roots in the early loss of the mother's love and stimulation.

However, even at this stage there were some signs to indicate a more hopeful prognosis. Teresa did want to be with her mother in the hospital, despite the fact that their relationship was thin. One had a sense that she was preparing herself for the struggle of again living with her mother. She was making use of individual therapy, where she had begun to experience feelings of loss, neediness, fear and jealousy, and was also more in touch with her feelings of being hurt. Some of these changes in Teresa were matched by changes in her mother and most importantly there was the beginning of a true emotional contact between mother and child. Overall, both the family and the staff felt committed to treatment, which went ahead after a month when there was permission from the court (Kennedy 1997).

The beginning of inpatient family treatment

The focus of treatment was to develop the relationship of mother and child with a view to family rehabilitation. The effect of a treatment contract was the development of an infantile transference – a much deeper and more strongly affective level of emotional contact – of both mother and child to the hospital.

In her psychotherapy Teresa was aware that her previous family life had collapsed and she feared, indeed anticipated, that this would happen again. This fear soon emerged in the transference relationship in unconscious beliefs that I would be dangerous like mother's previous partners and that I would leave her as they left her mother. In one session:

> Teresa drew a gate and a dandelion, which she said 'rose up, then died, and then rose up again'. This seemed symbolic both of her relationship with her mother and her psychotherapist too, which had faded and died, and which now might grow again. She told me the story of the picture: 'The girl could not cross the gate because there was a man driving a mini.' Later she added, 'dangerously'. This led to her talking of Daddy A and Daddy B (two of her mothers previous partners) leaving her mother because they did not like her. Another picture she drew in the same session was of a 'sun in the sky and a girl'. She said, 'The sun was laughing at the girl.' I interpreted this as her feeling that I would not understand her and would just laugh at her.

Very occasionally she rather bluntly and out of the blue asked me a direct question. Why, she asked me outright, could she not stay with her mother more? But such questions (prompted I suspect by her mother) seemed rarely connected with real inner feelings and change was slow and painful. In sessions I could feel Teresa making little emotional impact on me in terms of evoking sadness or other feelings beyond a degree of frustration. I did have a sense she had experienced deep pain, but found it difficult to get to it. I found her so wrapped up and poised, almost like a dutiful robot, to take whatever I said as a cue for her next action or response that I felt out of contact with her. Perhaps now I was like the mother with whom she, as a child or a small baby, had such limited contact. Teresa said little about anything that was not immediate, and if she did it was only in a very literal way. She could not express her feelings about her mother or the hospital or anything that would give a hint of her likes and dislikes outside the playroom. When asked, she would unconsciously and with lightning speed switch the theme.

When eventually after several weeks she did express more real affect, it was because she was concerned that a small child in the hospital had been 'choking'. She was now deeply worried, about this child and about herself. I thought she feared her most infantile needs would be obliterated, and her reaction seemed to be why express them if they are going to be crushed? She would then slow up again and become a most dull child. Occasionally however some of her own infantile feelings began to break through, particularly within the hospital community. There were, for example, reports of her crying in a deep-felt way following a minor upset.

Although Teresa played down the separations at weekends from the hospital, her mother and her psychotherapist, and during the week from her foster parents, her depression began to show through. She talked of missing a girl she had known in the assessment period, and began to show she was missing her foster parents. In a session at this time, while stolidly denying my interpretations about her loss, she did a drawing of 'a leaf that was being blown away'. She began, I thought, to be aware that she was changing – but in a way which worried her more because it was so much beyond her control.

Transformations in her knowledge of abuse

As Teresa began to be more in touch with feelings of neediness, anger and loss, she began to rework what she knew or could allow herself to know about the abuse she had suffered. This was important because we knew from the history that only once since the abuse had occurred had Teresa said anything at all about it. It is significant that this reworking of events by Teresa began as Mrs A became more aware, in particular in her psychotherapy, of her fear of dependence. Mrs A experienced some depression and began to be in touch with her often violent and defensive wishes to control events.

Teresa told me in one session a story of a television programme, which sounded like a dream, of 'a man who tied up foster parents . . . I think it was foster parents . . . and now was going to go to the police to tell lies'. This story appeared to represent an attempt by Teresa to sort out her feelings, but it was a strange confabulation of events, about abuse in her and her mother's life and her current feelings about loss of the foster parents. Teresa now also told me more stories about her mother and herself, which indicated a new capacity to experience a wider range of thoughts about her mother. One of these was of her going on holiday with her mother who was 'rough with her' and 'pushed her head under the water' whilst they were swimming in the sea.

Small changes in Teresa's awareness of this sort were effected however by a pattern of continuing neglect in her mother's care of her within the hospital. This continuing neglect of Teresa was particularly apparent when Mrs A absented herself in a sudden unplanned way for a few days, so that Teresa had to go back to the foster parents. On her return, Teresa's increasing expressiveness over the last couple of months collapsed. She again became more withdrawn, noticeably taciturn and depressed.

Soon after this, as Teresa's transference deepened, I experienced her as wearing and intrusive. She seemed more in touch with her fear of me, and other men, but she often wanted to bait me. Occasionally too she wanted affection, then more sensual contact from me, sidling up and leaning against me whilst showing me drawings. At the same time some of Teresa's other relationships within the hospital also became more intense. All of this seemed connected to her bringing thoughts about abuse into her mind. As her fears grew stronger about whether or not her mother would or could care for her, other feelings came through, indicating her unconscious wish to take mother's partner away from her, or find an alternative erotic attachment. Teresa idealised her foster father, and reportedly wished to engage him in rumbustious sexualised games. She would pour scorn on one nurse for speaking slowly, as she herself did, and in sessions goaded me, saying in a repeated nagging way that I was 'Stewart' – a peculiar stupid monster character from a storybook she had read. There was a split then in her view of her psychotherapist between the idealised sexual father and the dim monstrous father.

At this time her behaviour within the hospital also became more overtly disturbed. She stirred up the children after a Halloween party and deliberately wrecked the beds of others who excluded her from their play. Like her mother, Teresa denigrated the hospital, and she told her foster parents at weekends that all she did there was 'watch television'. She also was more stirred up sexually and sometimes masturbated publicly.

As Christmas and the break from psychotherapy came nearer, Teresa began to use reading in sessions to blot out any thinking. She made me a card but instead of writing 'Happy Christmas' on it she wrote 'Happy Crime'. Loss and abuse (or crime) were still very close in her mind. About the forthcoming break and the prospect of spending time with both mother and foster parents, all she could say were a few words: 'I know I feel something about it, but I do not know what to say.'

Within the hospital, Mrs A was experienced as infuriating by her family nurse and other staff because she was unable to allow her nurse to contribute to understanding and planning regarding her Christmas arrangements. The nurse felt worn down by Mrs A's wish to escape from thinking how this time could be useful in developing her relationship with Teresa. Over the same time Mrs A's therapist and myself felt hopeful about treatment, particularly as Mrs A had proved able to help Teresa with her distress at missing her foster parents. In thinking about the work together, it became clear to us that the nurse carried an important feeling of Mrs A, reflecting her depression, and her fear, as the prospect of rehabilitation actually grew nearer, that she would be unable permanently to care for Teresa again.

In her psychotherapy sessions, Teresa was again more dull and withdrawn after the two-week break at Christmas. Her play and rambling stories showed she had missed her psychotherapist and felt kept out by him. She told a number of stories that were exciting phantasies of men or large animals who had perpetrated powerful or violent acts outside the hospital. She appeared partly to feel her psychotherapist had kept her starved of contact and partly well rid of him as a potentially violent person. When I interpreted this and she could recognise these deeper levels of feeling, it allowed her to express more about the abuse that had occurred:

> In one session she gave me the clearest account so far of being abused. She told me, 'I was pushed off the couch onto the floor and hurt my leg. My doll, Peter, was broken. It has never been mended.' In a subsequent session Teresa gave a similar account, only this time the doll was called 'Jane' not 'Peter'. I thought her first version was significant, for it appeared that the abuse meant not the loss of her mother but the loss of the desired father substitute who was the abuser – the doll 'Peter'. Only in the second version was the loss of the female figure, perhaps herself or her mother, seen to be important.

During this period Teresa made numerous complaints about minor physical ailments. Asked when she had the aches and pains, she replied, 'Only in my sessions.' Hypochondriacal fears in sessions about her body were related to the fears of abuse we were discussing, representing fears of assault on her body and an inner sense of the lack of a maternal care sufficient to protect her.

It was significant that as Teresa began to express her feelings more and talk more openly about the abuse, her educational performance improved. Her WISC intelligence test results rose from 68 to 100 after the first five months of treatment. When she had first gone into the children's centre her reading skills had deteriorated slightly, for as she became less mechanical she made more errors, though she now had a better grasp of the meaning of what she was reading. She was also less robotic, though occasionally depressed and unhappy. She became more creative, her drawing and painting improved considerably, and she showed a remarkable capacity to remember details, especially in stories she had heard or seen on TV. Her number work remained problematic. At times too she got into a confused state and resorted to endless repetition. Then she would prefer to go back to safer, more concrete, ways of working.

Rehabilitation and inclusion of stepfather in family treatment

After five months of treatment a decision was made for Teresa to leave the foster home and spend weekends with her mother. After some weeks of graded visits Mrs A and Teresa would go to Mrs A's house each weekend. The clinical support for this decision lay in Mrs A's increased capacity to be in touch both with Teresa's needs, her strong wish to be with Teresa, and Teresa's own increasingly firm wish to be with her mother.

These first steps towards rehabilitation outside the hospital were tense and anxious for both mother and daughter. Mrs A provoked feelings of outrage in the staff by planning that her boyfriend, David, would visit on Teresa's first visit home. This seemed highly insensitive in view of the history of abuse of Teresa by a stepfather (though not this man). It seemed that such manoeuvres were Mrs A's attempt to rid herself of anxiety about the main problem she would face, namely how she and Teresa would get on. For her part, Teresa was becoming extremely anxious about the visits to mother's house. She talked of missing her foster mother. Impressively she was able to be open about this and was able to talk of her problem in telling her mother of this. Conversely she confided her problem about telling her foster mother about her wish to be with her mother. At one point Teresa tumbled downstairs and began a long wailing which gathered the attention of patients and nursing staff. This seemed to indicate her anxiety about such mixed feelings and show her fear that everything would collapse, or that she would be abused again.

There were sometimes elements of unreality in Teresa's hopes about how it would all work out. In her session after the first midweek visit:

> Teresa talked of watching a Mary Poppins video, and of having a 'nice bedspread'. (By contrast we knew from the nurse's home visit that the house was not ready and even the walls were not painted.) As she spoke she scribbled 'all about a kind lady and a nice man'. Clearly, she had a wish that she would be looked after by a couple in harmony together.

The reality for her after the first weekend home proved more disappointing. She could talk little about it and clearly had suffered from lack of care. She smelled slightly, and in her sessions became a dull child again.

The build-up of tension in Teresa was observable in her relationships with patients within the community. An incident occurred within the hospital which was worrying. Teresa pestered one of the adult male patients, and this man allowed her to sit on his lap while she played and talked to him, in an increasingly intrusive way. Teresa then began leaning backwards over to the floor so that her knickers were showing. At the same time she poked and goaded the man. Those around at the time described how uncomfortable the man felt. But instead of telling her to stop and get down, he was driven to slap her. No serious violence occurred but the pair broke up in distress, amidst anger and recrimination all round, including from Mrs A (who had not been present at the time) towards the man.

This worrying incident may have been indicative of shifts in Teresa's awareness of Oedipal relationships. It suggested that her developing Oedipal and sexual awareness could become manifest in an enactment aimed at sexualised affection from a man, bringing in turn a retaliatory slap from the man. I was reminded that Teresa had suffered physical abuse when nearly five years old, when she would have become increasingly fully aware of her mother's sexual relationship with her partner, and her changes of partner, and perhaps wished to break in on such relationships. As such, one level of understanding of the physical abuse of the child was that it occurred in the context of distorted Oedipal relationships. This incident may have occurred now because currently there were particular stresses on Teresa: she was losing her close contact with her foster father and felt her psychotherapist rebut or ignore her affectionate approaches to him. Most significantly she was aware that plans were being made to introduce Mrs A's current boyfriend, David, into treatment. These plans were a hopeful but stressful change, one that allowed treatment of the whole reconstituted family.

After David had come into the hospital and shortly before the Easter break, when Teresa's previous excitement had subsided, she again became dull and depressed. A session from this time helps to illustrate the complex phantasies underlying her depression and withdrawal, and in particular her fears about weekends at home with her mother and stepfather:

> Teresa came looking disheveled and wearing an old, small and mis-fitting sweater with a pink paper rosette with the words 'First Prize' on the front. She also wore a football club sweatband given to her by David.
>
> She sat silently at the table, but instead of getting out toys or starting to play or talk, she quietly and slowly fingered the three sheets of paper I had put out.
>
> (Usually she had a drawing book, or more sheets of paper. I began to feel guilty that she had so few sheets today.)

Teresa got out pens and paper and drew a duck inside what looked like an egg. I asked her what it was and she said 'stuck' ('it's a duck'). I said I thought she was letting me know she felt hemmed in here at the moment, not knowing how to move on, and she felt something similar about home too. Teresa did not answer but drew a very phallic shape, which turned into a rather spiky cactus figure that she described as having 'arms, two back legs and claws'. 'It's a monster,' she said. Below it she drew what she called a 'nest, which was empty and had soil in it'.

I spoke of her fear that I may be the monster, or she may find one outside, who would attack her. I thought that at a primitive level she was referring to the inside of her that was faecally damaged (the soil) having been attacked by the monster.

She now added that the monster 'ate the chicks'.

I said that she seemed to feel that anything new she had would be squeezed out. I thought she feared that her new thoughts, or 'chicks', indeed her own babies inside, were to be destroyed.

She did another drawing of a nest, covering it broadly in crayon. She asked me to feel how smooth it was. This seemed like setting up new defences around the nest.

When I tried to find out more, about her rosette or the armband, I felt her blocking me out. She seemed to be holding herself together by hanging on to bits and pieces: the rosette that she had won in a game with the other children, as a sign of hope that she might be seen as best, and the sweatband, which Dave had given her, as a token of her wish for contact and support from him.

Just before the end, when clearing up, this holding of herself together seemed to break down, for whilst putting the toys away she quite uncharacteristically spilt the crayons across the floor.

In this material Teresa showed how she feared attack and its consequences – that what was new in her would be destroyed. She would defend herself from further attack by building a defensive wall, but at points of stress this would break down and leave her defenceless again, like the sticks that spilt out at the end. It became clear too that Teresa (like her mother) feared the exposure that inviting a new person into their relationship in hospital would bring. From this session one can see that Teresa experienced this exposure at a very primitive level as a fear of attack on the inside and outside of her body. At another level one can see her identification with the monster who attacks the mother, who gives so little (like the psychotherapist who gives so little paper), or who attacks the mother's inside to empty it of the faecal baby created by this new couple. Understood this way the sweatband and the rosette are trophies taken away from the coveted father or the other children. Anxieties stemming from such phantasies paralysed her frequently in her sessions, although there were other periods when she could be both creative and responsive.

As the Easter break approached, when both family nurse and her psychotherapist would be away, Teresa struggled with deep feelings of loss. Her thoughts had gone back again to the foster parents. But most powerfully she was aware that her mother had someone in the hospital while she did not. She struggled with feelings of being left out and hurt. Feelings of 'hurting, 'killing' and 'being hurt' came up frequently in her therapy material – but now as less shocking and more tolerable themes that were mentionable and could be worked on.

This was a most crucial phase of treatment; with the family constituted in the same way it had been when the abuse occurred with mother, daughter and a stepfather. Despite some continued family instability, Teresa became more active and warm with her mother and Dave, as well as with the other children. Changes also occurred in the approach of Mrs A and her partner to the child, including better physical care and some capacity to pay attention to her feelings.

Recovery of a capacity to think

I shall now select some material from the last period of treatment to illustrate further a central theme in Teresa's individual psychotherapy, namely the recovery of her capacity to think. The dullness that I had seen in Teresa from the beginning would return frequently. In some sessions she experienced me, her psychotherapist, as the dull, depressed or neglecting mother who prevented her from being lively. She became in projective identification with this dull object, thereby becoming dull herself. But there were signs she could change. In one session:

> I varied my routine a little and did not put her toy box in its usual place on the table but on an adjacent table. Teresa looked at me anxiously then wanted me to say that what I had done was wrong and stupid. When I had agreed to acknowledge that what I had done she felt to be an act of stupidity on my part, she relaxed.
>
> She now began drawing most imaginatively about 'blocks' that she felt were 'being put up to prevent help getting through to her'. The help she wanted was from a strong 'Tarzan' figure, who was hidden behind a very phallic-looking tree, which in turn was completely surrounded and obscured by massive walls of blocks. A plane had to 'fly in over the top and drop a message', much like a bomb.
>
> Now practised at telling me more about her drawings, Teresa told me what was in effect another story in relation to the picture: 'Once upon a time, there lived a bad monster and he ate little children. One day one

of the children had a little walk in the woods, then the monster jumped out in front of him and said I am going to eat you up.'

Teresa then began to do a drawing of a woman who was very adorned. She called this a 'woman monster'. After finishing the drawing she put the pen down and remained static, repeating again and again in a monotone a phrase, which seemed to be about herself, 'What it is to be 6 years old.'

In this sequence from a session, Teresa began to be less tense and withdrawn and more relaxed after I had acknowledged her view that it was my mistake over something (accepting her projection that the stupidity was in me), so she did not have to be the 'damaged stupid child' herself. She thereby begins to see, because I accept her projection to think about it, that I am not the same as her projection of me, i.e. dull and stupid, and that I allow her capacity to express her thoughts and feelings about me: this lessens the grip of her identification with the dull depressed object. But her play indicates that she is still afraid of attack (perhaps as retaliation for her 'attack' on me) and wants me to defend her from it. Her ambivalence to the father (the strong Tarzan figure, her psychotherapist in the transference) is strong, for she expected help yet she was not sure she would get the help she waited for, perhaps because he is obscured from her (by the blocks) or the tree (the phallic mother), so felt angry with him (the bombing). Her next account of the picture, of little children being attacked and eaten by the bad monster, seemed to link the theme with abuse again. As the session went on, while the fear she experienced in relation to father remained intense, her thoughts about mother became more paranoid. In her second drawing, Teresa appeared to be realising just how frighteningly distant her mother could be, not concerned with her but with her own adornments, leaving her in her childhood plight (the 6 year old) all on her own: 'What it is to be 6 years old! What it is to be 6 years old!'

In a session near the end of treatment, we can see still further how Teresa could lose and then regain her capacity to think and express her feelings:

In recent sessions she had been quite alert and talkative, but today she sat sullenly, kicking her legs under her chair in a taunting and irritating way. She picked a hair from her head, smoothed her fringe from her forehead and looked at me quite blankly.

I began to feel increasingly anxious. I tried to make some contact about what she might feel, but she looked at me and said, 'No . . . nothing'. At last she got up and crossed off some days on her chart, which showed the number of days left in treatment.

I made a link saying she may feel left by me as treatment was ending. Teresa still just sat quietly, as if something else was on her mind. I then realised that it had been David's birthday last night and said so. Teresa looked at me expectantly. I suggested she had felt left out by David because he and her mother had gone out and she had been left out. I said that she may feel near the end of treatment that I would be leaving her out, and may prefer to be with others.

Teresa now drew an angel-like figure, in a colourful and accomplished way. Her associations indicated her curiosity about me, perhaps because I had unusually used some information from last night told me by a nurse. I now interpreted that my having this information meant that I too may be in a couple with someone, to go away on holiday and leave her when she left, like her mother left her and went off with Dave last night. In silence she drew another picture of a man whom she called 'Prince Murray'. As we talked about her drawings, she took on a childlike warmth and natural curiosity. She now drew a car with large knob-like wheels and lights, which became a police car. I spoke of how she felt that I was like a parent, and a kind of policeman, who kept her out of my important relationships. Teresa drew a comic-like circle coming from the police car and printed the words 'knee-knaw' inside, then chuckled to herself. I thought this police siren noise was like the childish sound of 'knee-knaw' when a child wants to flaunt or laugh at another.

Teresa went on to draw a 'redhood robin', starting with the prominent breast. The drawing itself was impressive, measured with a lightness of touch, but the level of complex phantasies that appeared to be expressed by it was even more impressive. I felt the red indicative of her excitement. I spoke of her feeling that if I did come together with a woman, there may be a baby, and she may fear this with mum and Dave too.

Teresa now told me how it had snowed today for the first time. She told me she found snow interesting and exciting. It was nearly time as she finished the drawing.

I added that 'redhood robin' seemed a mix of 'robin redbreast' and 'red riding hood', who was nearly eaten by the wolf. I said I thought she had a deeper fear, she could not express, of her daddy if her mum and a daddy came together. She laughed thoughtfully at my comment, handed me back the key to her cupboard and we then returned to her mother.

I shall not go further into the detailed and complex phantasies that Teresa expressed, which showed a greater degree of acceptance than before of the Oedipal couple in a way which allowed some growth of trust. Instead I wish to point out that the change from dullness to lively and pleasurable expression of feelings and ideas in this session illustrates how Teresa was able to recover her capacity to think. The central stumbling blocks were repression of strong unsatisfied Oedipal longings towards the father (the psychotherapist or David currently, and perhaps her stepfather previously), and a deep sense of loss in her relationship with mother, compounded by the injuries she suffered in reality to her body. This led to her regressive withdrawal and dullness. When her capacity to think was recovered, however, her associations flowed, she was able to explore more openly her phantasies about the Oedipal couple and a freedom entered her contacts with others.

Conclusion

I shall make two points, first about the trauma of the whole experience of abuse for the child and second about the pattern of Oedipal relationships relevant to the child's experience of abuse. Both of these aspects could be worked with more fully in this type of family rehabilitation in an inpatient setting, especially in keeping the child safe and carefully gauging the child's best interests, whilst understanding in depth the emerging dynamics.

First, the trauma suffered by Teresa, an abused child, resulted in a loss of capacity to think and feel. Shengold (1979) describes how the trauma of abuse can be so overwhelming that the mind is flooded with feeling. This terrifying 'too-muchness' requires massive and mind-distorting defensive operations in order for the child to continue to think and feel. What is happening is so terrible that it must not be felt and cannot be registered, so a massive isolation of feeling with confusion and denial is preferred. Shengold calls this phenomenon 'soul murder'. In one type of mind splitting the child must keep in one part of his or her mind the delusion of good parents. There may be a compulsion to provoke the parental abuse to test whether the next time the contact will bring love rather than hate. The child can have the greatest difficulty in seeing the parents as bad in any way, thus making it impossible to get over the trauma of the abuse, or even to allow ambivalence towards the parents, thereby hindering normal healthy emotional development. It is this inhibition of the ego's power to remember and to test reality that makes soul murder so effective as a continuous force. The child's defensive need to 'keep', even to merge with, the parent is often complemented by the disturbed parent's need to prevent individuation, and to hold on to the child who is regarded as part of the parent's self-image. Such children sometimes present as being 'damaged', and can even be labelled as mentally retarded, on account of the severity of their withdrawal, as indeed we saw happen in respect to Teresa at the beginning of treatment.

What had been most striking in Teresa was her dullness and the robotic quality of her relating. Her capacity to adapt to reality was impaired because of the loss of her capacity 'to think', to formulate her own thoughts and to recognise and accept some feelings as her own. This meant that her ability to contribute to any change in her predicament was lost. She was effectively then 'damaged' until she could regain this capacity, with the help of intensive psychotherapy (cf. Bion 1962a, 'A Theory of Thinking').

In the early stages of treatment her phantasies of projective identification were dominated by the need to merge with her maternal object and to rid herself of thought. As the 'thought' of a neglectful and depressed mother became more tolerable to her, and as she could bear fantasies, dreams and thoughts about an impassive or attacking mother and brutalising father, she could begin to re-experience and struggle with conflicts within herself. As she could begin again to think and feel, the trauma of the abuse could be left behind and she could begin to get on with her life and rebuild relationships within her family.

Second, Teresa's experience of her psychotherapist as an exciting but potentially hurtful father enabled us to understand some of the dynamics underlying her readjustment within her new family. We could see both from her sessions and from observations of the development of her relationship with her new stepfather that similar dynamic patterns, of fear and excitement, could be set up in her newly constituted family. This enabled us to understand a vital link between the inner life of the child and the life of the family as a whole, and retrospectively to see a possible link between Oedipal and sexual phantasies of the child and the occurrence of physical abuse. This idea of the tension and conflict between fathers and daughters is a central theme of some classics in world literature, such as Shakespeare's *King Lear* and Racine's *Iphigenia* (cf. initial chapter quote). There is an intolerable build-up of tension between the father (or stepfather) and the child, so that an incestuous act is prevented by the occurrence of an act of violence by the parent to the child.

The French psychoanalyst Laplanche (1987) has emphasised that there is always a degree of seduction by the adult of the child, as the child is relatively helpless and immature at first and has to confront the adult's mind. But this notion of 'primary seduction' has nothing to do with sexual assault. Primary seduction describes a situation 'in which an adult proffers to a child verbal, non-verbal and even behavioural signifiers which are pregnant with unconscious sexual signification' (Kennedy 1997: 126). If there is an actual sexual seduction of the child, as I shall describe in cases in the next chapter, damage is done to the child's subsequent relating and the child's capacity to deal with the significance of the environment and to use symbolism.

The child who has not negotiated a loving relationship with the parent of the opposite sex – the positive Oedipus Complex (Freud 1905b; Pincus and Dare 1978) – may be restricted to a kind of deficiency state in which only two objects exist, the individual and his primary object, usually his mother. It is during attempts to 'overcome' this deficiency state, i.e. in developing relationships further, that child and parents alike face the most challenging emotional tasks. In this case example we see that Teresa had to struggle with her mother as their relationship became more differentiated and less dependent in a parasitic way. The transference to the psychotherapist as the mother who neglects or pays scant attention to her could develop to a point where Teresa could feel more cared for and thought about for her own wishes and needs, and such work could translate itself into improvement in the actual mother–child relationship, increasing the prospect of successful family rehabilitation.

Inpatient treatment appears to have been essential, with its close links between psychotherapy and daily life in the community, in order to produce some change in such a narcissistic and highly regressed character such as Mrs A, and to allow Teresa a sufficiently contained structure in which to change internally. It is now some time since Teresa, her mother and David finished inpatient treatment. They went back into the outside community to normal jobs for Mrs A and David, to school for Teresa, and as far as we know to date progress is good.

Chapter 6

Challenges in work with emotional and sexual abuse

Introduction

This chapter looks at the impact of therapeutic work with emotional and sexual abuse, in particular work with parents and problems encountered by abused children undergoing rehabilitation with their family. Having looked at a case of successful rehabilitation in Chapter 5, I shall here look further at some of the family dynamics in other abuse cases, including issues of parenting and the 'meaning of the child' in such abusing families. I shall describe briefly two cases where the work was successful showing some of the painful realities of such cases. Then I shall illustrate two further cases, one of emotional abuse and the other of sexual abuse where family rehabilitation failed. The experience was very painful for the child, but in important ways allowed something to be resolved, both internally in the child and with their family and natural parents, so that the children could make a new beginning in a new family.

In this applied setting, as outlined in the last two chapters, both adult and child psychotherapists and nurses work closely and intensively together. Although starting from different theoretical backgrounds and using different methods of intervention, the work of each discipline can inform and enrich the other (see Chapter 7). There is some sharing of information and of thinking, so that in terms of overall aim and purpose there is a coming together to treat very difficult patients who may not be treatable elsewhere. This is especially so since severe cases of abuse can only be treated with a view to family rehabilitation in a setting that can protect the child while important psychotherapeutic work is taking place separately with both parent and child. In the work it is especially important to listen to the feelings of the other staff and to patients within the therapeutic community. Only then is it possible to work to keep the child safe during treatment. It is important to appreciate tensions about roles between workers and to tolerate severe infantile projections, often of hostility and despair, as they affect individual staff personally. Such efforts by the staff to tolerate primitive psychological processes parallels the efforts of severely disturbed and traumatised patients to tolerate and to work through their problems.

One of the central ideas of the therapeutic community movement of thinking is that individuals, groups and organisations, if given the freedom and responsibility for organising and undertaking work in their own environment, would respond, have more human purpose and fulfilment, and individual problems, including formerly debilitating psychological problems, would be seen in a new light or indeed lose much of their debilitating effect. There are many telling continuities over this time; in how a type of hospital treatment originally developed (in 1919) as a 'tool' to help 'shell-shocked' civilians with breakdowns in their lives similar in their effects to the devastation of war is now used with our current problems of the devastating breakdown of family life and relationships following serious problems of abuse and mental illness; in how rehabilitation of soldiers after war to their homes, jobs and civic communities leads to new thinking about the rehabilitation of families after family breakdown; in how problems of morale facing the terrors of conflict in war give way now to problems of morale amongst the staff and patients in a therapeutic community facing the pain, tensions and fears of those suffering severe borderline conditions, which affect all aspects of daily functioning and routine.

In this applied context, besides psychoanalytic understanding and insight and the taking on of responsible roles in a therapeutic community, patients also receive a range of other types of care. These include some quite tangible benefits for body and mind, such as food, and overnight bed, spare time, opportunities for pleasures including recreational time and activities, and the company of other patients in a shared communal living and treatment space. Despite, perhaps partly because of the presence of these aspects – a far cry from the conditions of abstinence usual in outpatient psychoanalytic psychotherapy – treatment of the severely disturbed patient in an inpatient setting provides not only particular opportunities for supportive containment of the patient but also particular dangers of severe regression and intensified disturbance. Apart then from what is specifically psychoanalytic, inpatient treatment includes some of the following:

- real bodily care
- levels of protection, from total exposure to the reality pressures of outside life and, within the hospital itself, from harmful and abusive attacks by others
- real sanctions to be invoked to prevent or reduce self-abusive attacks
- supervisions and appraisals of child-care issues and individual psychiatric mental state assessments, as appropriate.

Usually psychoanalytic psychotherapy can only take place when the patient's ego is strong enough and the level of motivation sufficient for the patient to accept the limitations of the psychoanalytic setting, to attend the same place at agreed times, to accept rules of abstinence from actual libidinal relationships with the therapist and rules of restraint from aggressive attacks upon the therapist. For the borderline patient who has failed in treatment elsewhere, who may be caught in a chronic cycle of suicidal or self-abusive attacks, or for the abusing parent who primarily wants the child returned to them from foster care, or for the abused child who is showing disturbance when placed back with the family, such preconditions are rarely there from the outset. However, as a result of treatment some adults and children can make more use of community outpatient treatments, including ongoing intensive psychotherapy (cf. Zetzel 1970; Flynn 1998; Chiesa and Fonagy 2000; Fonagy and Target 2000: 69).

'Tolerance or survival' in the child during family rehabilitation

Within the hospital there are a number of elements of treatment for the family as a whole and for each member of it, but essentially relationships are tested not just with others in the therapeutic community but within the family itself and, importantly, between parents and children. It is important to assess the impact that treatment is having on the child, not only in family meetings and mother–child work but also in the wider community, by bringing together an understanding of all aspects of the work and centrally the intensive individual psychotherapy which the child has during treatment. This is invaluable for assessing the overall impact of the therapeutic community work (Flynn 1988; and cf. Chapter 5) and, importantly, what the child can put up with or survive.

In cases that involved severe abuse children can 'survive' abuse by learning to put up with too much, causing deep emotional scars. But unless they can *tolerate* the emergence in a painful way of central issues, attempts at rehabilitation may not survive. There are painful issues about when and what to tolerate or not to tolerate, in particular when thinking about the parents' continued feelings about the child and behaviour towards the child, and about whether this furthers or hinders the child's attempts to develop emotionally and survive psychically.

We know, after the work of Bowlby (1971, 1973, 1998), that a child in a new foster or adoptive home, having left their family of origin following loss of parents or family breakdown, will face a major task of readjustment on return to the family, and that such experiences can be traumatic and disturbing. The task for an abused child coming back again to their family is that much more difficult, especially in coming to terms with how the abuse has severed family relationships and when reliving aspects of the abuse. There are then crucial questions we need to ask throughout this rehabilitative treatment:

- Is the child surviving emotionally?
- Can the family now provide enough protection and security for the child?
- Has the family survived?

The work of attachment research in the late 1970s and 1980s became increasingly concerned with child maltreatment and physical and sexual abuse. The disorganised/disoriented classification (Main and Solomon 1986) was linked to maltreatment of the child (Cichetti and Barnett 1991) and unresolved trauma in the history of the parent (Main and Hesse 1990b). The frightened/frightening behaviour of the parent, who at once signals safety and danger, undermines the child's attachment organisation and, potentially, their entire behavioural system (Fonagy and Target 2003: 240). As Jeremy Holmes puts it:

> The perverse paradox of abuse from an attachment perspective arises from the vicious circle in which an adult who is a caregiver can be both the attachment figure to whom the child turns for protection, and the source of threat which gives rise to the need for that protection. The more frightened or in pain the child becomes, the more the child clings to the perpetrator.
>
> (Holmes 2000: 41)

This is so frequently the pattern of a vicious circle of abuse in child abuse tragedies (Reder, Duncan and Gray 1993).

Rehabilitation of child and family after emotional and sexual abuse

Children in treatment are often haunted by their abuse and need considerable help to free themselves from its consequences. In ordinary terms such children often lack concentration, are over-stimulated and have poor impulse control, can be driven and aggressive, show confused and sexualised behaviour, lack basic trust in adults, and can be intrusive and irritating with their behaviour. Relationships between parents and children can be similarly distorted and disorganised. The reality is that treatment of these abused children is less concerned with sorting out (recovered) memories of the past than in confronting the current emotional impact of the abuse (Kennedy 1997: 135–7).

Issues between parents and children in the present, as the work towards rehabilitation is going on, throw up central issues for improving current relationships as well as crucial and thorny problems for the traumatic past of the child, especially disentangling and knowing what actually happened. Progress in the work is chequered and in the transference with abused children and adults the requisite empathic atmosphere may deteriorate (Kennedy 1997) and misunderstandings, mistakes, guilt and re-enactments by psychotherapist and child may take its place (Joseph 1989). It can be difficult to bear uncertainty or repeated and violent projections. In family work the abusing or former abusive parent often cannot tolerate the child who is showing his/her psychic pain in helpless and out of control behaviour (Kennedy 1997: 140). The abusing parent sometimes sees the child as destroying or taking away whatever is felt by the parent in a fragile way to be good. Vengeful attacks then occur, along with repeated neglect and emotional detachment from the child, characterised by deep denial. This feature is picked out as most significant in the research about effects of such family treatment of abused children. Those who do *not* do well are those who show 'an inhibition of reflective self-function'. Children who remain deeply disturbed by abuse are also manifest borderline pathology later, as adults or adolescents (Fonagy, Steele and Kennedy 1996c; cf. Chapter 12 below). Conversely, parents who improve during treatment show a changed capacity for self-reflection and this is matched by improved relationships with their children (Kennedy 1997: 134).

Analysis of the official inquiry reports following child abuse tragedies in the UK indicates that the 'meaning of the child' becomes distorted in abusing families (Reder *et al.* 1993). In the normal family a child carries the hopes and aspirations of the parents, and they in turn sacrifice some of their personal gratifications to further the child's development. In some cultures this can lead to the child having a highly important place in the society, often reflecting the place and prestige of the relation they are named after (Brody 2001). Yet with the vicissitudes of family life, with social difficulties and pathology in the parents, the child can acquire an undeclared 'script' (Byng-Hall 1979, 1985). The child may then become 'like an actor in someone else's play' (Ron Britton personal communication in Reder *et al.* 1993: 52). When the child takes on such undeclared 'scripts', the meaning of relationships in the present is distorted (Reder *et al.* 1993: 52). The analysis of the inquiries of these tragedies makes chilling reading and underlines how problems in the lives of parents have a deleterious effect on how they see and relate to their children.

Case illustrations

I shall now briefly outline two successful cases of family treatment towards rehabilitation following sexual and emotional abuse. The first case treated for 18 months concerned a boy, aged 6, who had been anally abused at least once by a man, and repeatedly exposed to promiscuous and perverse adult sexuality, whilst his mother worked as a prostitute. In this case I was the psychotherapist for the mother, whilst another child psychotherapist saw the boy (see Kennedy 1997: 113–15 for a fuller account of this case). The effects of abuse are repeatedly seen in 'abuse equivalents' (Kennedy 1997) in the family care system so that most of treatment is taking up with dealing with them. These 'abuse equivalents' are situations that have some similar dynamic quality, often of deceit, manipulation and enactments, but in a hidden and seemingly unrelated area. They occur importantly in the thick of an inpatient treatment process, and there are examples of them in Chapters 5, 6 and 7.

Inevitably my work in this case as the mother's psychotherapist was focused on parenting issues and how her behaviour affected her son. My knowledge from treating sexually abused children would also be important, when it was allowed to come into play. Although thoughtless and confused, this mother's determination to have her son back with her out of care was crucial. But treatment was inevitably difficult. Her behaviour was quite delinquent and within the Families Unit she was a frequent instigator of anti-therapeutic actions, allying herself with anyone who wanted to cause trouble (Kennedy 1997: 114). She was overly confident in her ability continuously to manipulate her environment and to seduce and control men, especially me, her male psychotherapist. There was little room for psychological thinking or recognition of how her behaviour affected and had traumatised her son. Initially every piece of work in her psychotherapy took on the quality of a paid-for transaction that she felt she then controlled, as she watched me and gave me just enough to keep me interested. Although she had vowed she had given up life as a prostitute, and I think she had, such transactions, even more positive bits of work, seemed influenced by her former approach to life. Emotional contact was frequently confused with sexual contact, the transference was sexualised and she constantly denigrated me as another man she would reap revenge on. There was little sign of her allowing herself to develop her individuality and little room for anything new to happen. The shock and horror of her exposure of her son to abuse was split off, projected and left with me or other workers.

Only gradually, after interpreting this and after painstaking work to expose the defensive quality of these 'abuse equivalents', especially in her repeatedly manipulative behaviour in the hospital, did her denigration of me lessen and did she develop some trust. Progressively she then got in touch with her own neediness and recognised her son's vulnerability. With this recognition there was a flood of intense guilt about what she had done and allowed to happen. The perimeter of her horizons broadened as she saw the connections between her abuse as a child, her seduction into a life of massage parlours and prostitution, and the severe and continuous sexual abuse her son had suffered.

This was the most difficult time in treatment. She could be violently angry and out of touch, and threatened to give up treatment more than once. Only when she had more trust and could feel more contained with these violent thoughts could she avoid rough and ready solutions and really own up to her own part in what had happened, and the destructiveness towards herself, her body, and towards her son and the intrusive sexual attacks on him. She then began to be more sympathetic and tolerant of his difficult behaviour, yet also could stay with problems it gave rise to in his relationships with others, especially other children, and the need to face reality tasks, such as reintegrating back into school. She seemed more secure about giving up prostitution, though not without leaving me with doubts about it, and used her considerable 'business capacities' to organise and plan for a steadier less exciting and more mundane lifestyle centred round her plans for her son's future and development. Back home in the outside community, progress has continued and been maintained and her son has had continued ongoing psychotherapy.

In the second case, James, aged 6, created great anxiety as he and his mother perpetually got into furious rows, which increased without limit and became emotionally abusive. During and after them he reacted in dangerous and uncontrolled ways, such as climbing dangerously and running out onto the road. In family treatment for 18 months, it emerged that James's mother had been severely emotionally and sexually abused as a child. James was treated in twice weekly psychotherapy with a female psychotherapist whilst I saw his mother for twice weekly psychotherapy. His mother had taken major overdoses, had cut herself and self-harmed in other ways, which particularly disturbed and disrupted any normal patterns of family life. She struggled continuously and had few coping mechanisms of her own, suffered from a poor image and was very overweight. She would remain in bed as a way of blocking out her problems and seemed in a bottomless pit of need. In community treatment she seemed unable to hang on to anything good that was given to her and needed constant confirmation from people that they cared. In the transference to me she reacted with great anger if she perceived there was any lack of care or concern. Initially she seemed cut off from feelings related to her early childhood and focused her hurt and anger on her current relationships. Her ambivalence to James was expressed by violent outbursts followed by temporary reconciliation when she became wrapt up with him in an over-close way, finding it intolerable to see him as a separate person with his own needs. She rejected him when he was separate but found his *presence* an immense pressure.

This mother's very survival as a child with needs and reasonable rights and demands was threatened, as was her son's needs with her, so her survival in my *presence* and mine in hers became a central aspect of the transference. She told me she saw me as a devil, a Mephistopheles, who could demolish, intimidate and trick her, and then laugh at her. No person knew what she had been through. As a child her mother had locked her in a cupboard and now she felt locked in a prison. Her family had been incestuous and neglectful in different ways, she had been sexually abused and subjected to being photographed in child pornography. My comments and interpretations were experienced as severely intrusive, repeating the bodily and mental intrusions of sexual abuse. She violently shouted at me, demanded expressions of care and love, feared I saw her as repulsive and cried and ranted in an exhausting way. She repeatedly marched out of psychotherapy sessions early, slamming the door so hard it created a shattering tinnitus effect in my ears. If I attempted through self-preservation to keep any distance from these intrusive attacks I became like the abusive pornographic photographer, who looks uninvolved on the sidelines but controls and manipulates. This further sexualised the contact, confused her and unbalanced the sessions.

Over time, as she struggled with these conflicts, I continued to interpret in the sessions, and she assumed productive and responsible posts in the therapeutic community and worked to improve the daily and hourly care of James, she improved. She could sometimes be immensely capable and still immensely vulnerable, and had to face the huge issue of her dependence on treatment before she could become more internally secure and independent.

In assessment James came over as sad and depressed despite a superficial liveliness. He showed marked signs of missing a father, even the abusive father who had walked out on him. In his psychotherapy James's play was highly regressive and he spent his time building houses under the table where he looked after his bear and other toys. He expressed longings to be totally cared for by his psychotherapist and his mother. These sessions alternated with sessions of fiercely controlled latency type play involving cutting paper, gluing it, making darts, sticking things together, writing and drawing, indeed all types of production, especially of objects that he could make and take away to his mother.

He then discovered water play, literally 'splashed out' and expressed himself liberally, even anarchically, doing what he liked and taking his psychotherapist's (very wide) tolerance to the limit and beyond. James's regression proved creative (Balint 1968) and, as he learnt and expressed himself more, he began to talk more and rein in his freedom, accepting and establishing limits for himself. He explored the concept of maleness by marking out some animals as 'particularly fierce because they were men' that had 'purple blobs of plasticine on their backs'. Interestingly, James's work in psychotherapy about being an independent boy went parallel with his mother's work in her psychotherapy to become more feminine and move away from a homosexuality that had been part of the abuse and partly a retreat from it. James progressively began to express more symbolically rather than through wild and detached play, became calmer and grew up more. Towards the end of treatment he was able to make extensive use of his therapeutic education in the children's centre to re-enter school and take on school tasks again. Following discharge, both James and his mother continued progress in a sustained and fuller way.

The child's experience of failure of family rehabilitation

The first case I describe is of Stefan, aged 4 years, who had suffered emotional abuse, repeated physical ill-treatment and verbal attacks, whilst in the care of his mother, a single parent. Isolated from her home environment, Stefan's mother had had postnatal depression and then drug and alcohol problems. Most seriously Stefan had fallen out of a high window, but survived. It was evident that the accident was the result of severe neglect. In three times weekly psychotherapy, Stefan presented as a dull depressed child with a speech impediment, withdrawn sometimes, but with alternating wild out of control behaviour – hitting out, hurting himself and scratching me and him – and close clingy contact. In the therapeutic community, although now off unprescribed or hard drugs, his mother seemed uncommunicative and locked in on herself as if she were drugged. She was sometimes warm and physically caring, but then hostile and lashing out verbally at Stefan as she felt he was punishing her. In a preliminary meeting with his mother present, he first drew on paper an outline of a crocodile, then played with fascination with a toy crocodile. When his mother handed it back, he flinched away with terror, as if it were a real crocodile which was going to bite him. I thought his experiences were so powerful that play could become concretely real. He seemed frightened of his mother but also now and later his capacity for symbolic communication in play and speech was very tenuous.

In psychotherapy sessions Stefan occasionally shifted out of his depressive dullness and become a lively and expressive child. He was however often painfully confused, had a speech impediment, and I almost literally had to catch the words from his mouth to understand him. It was easier to do this when he began playing, which he could now do in an energetic and increasingly meaningful way:

> In a session early on, an object was pulled out of the window of the dolls' house and fell. Then the biting crocodile pulled the tree-person out of the window. In another version it was pushed and then the building collapsed.

Stefan was pleased that I could make sense of his very bitty play. I indicated I knew he was talking about what happened when he fell. He felt guilt and bewilderment about this and the catastrophic destruction of his time with mother. This linked to earlier when his mother 'fell out of sight' during her depression. In sessions, if I was not fully attentive to him, he re-experienced this as another form of my 'falling out of sight'. Then his fear of catastrophic loss reappeared and with it all his difficulties. Usually he had a devilish streak, which was largely playful, but sometimes it gave way to frenetic repetitive activity. He then subsided into timidity and abject whininess, which I found had a very wearing effect on me. Basically however he thrived on attention to his feelings.

After some months of treatment, Stefan's mother's behaviour became increasingly more disturbed, for reasons I shall not go into but related to her unwillingness to make plans about Stefan's care. Then her active rejecting behaviour towards Stefan in the hospital was observed to increase. His behaviour now worsened. In one incident Stefan got up in the night and poured water over two other small boys. His mother was furious with him and poured a jug of water over him. She refused to change him or do anything, was quite out of control and abusive and threatening to staff. Typically she took a long time to come out of her rage. In brief this is what happened in Stefan's psychotherapy session next day:

> He and his mother had 'made up', and as I approached the waiting area he was asking his mother for a kiss and a cuddle in a whiny but playful voice. His mother did not look at me and insisted on carrying Stefan to the door of the room, supposing him not able to come. Inside the room, now his mother had left, he immediately complained there was no water in the bowl. He began impulsively hauling the water container off the shelf and knocking the side of it. I pointed out that there was water in the bowl. He took it, put it on the table and began to put pieces from the teaset in it. He then jerked and tipped the bowl forward and poured some of it over his jeans and his shirt. He started whining that he was wet. This developed into a real cry and then sad sobbing. I said he had wet himself and felt I would leave him wet and unhappy, like his mummy had done in the bedroom last night. I said I knew about the incident last night. He said that he had wet the boys because they were 'too hot'. I said I thought he may feel the boys had his hot angry feelings inside them. Stefan did not reply but stood still crying saying he wanted his mum. I was undecided what to do, phone his mother or try to help him myself. I decided on the latter. I acknowledged he did want his mother really to do the drying for him, but for the moment I would see if I could dry him, so that he could continue to stay with me for the rest of the session. After I had dried him and begun to wipe up some of the mess, he became angry with me for doing this and threw over two small chairs in a rage. He cut his box with scissors and threw the toys all over the floor. He clutched his trousers and pulled on his penis, then used the pencil sharpener damagingly on some felt tips and crayons. He tipped the rest of his toys in the bin and then tipped this on the floor. I was left scrambling around, wondering if I could stop the devastation. Stefan clambered onto a small table and managed to fall, hurting himself and

he began to cry again. I said again about how he was showing me how mixed up everything was, and how he felt I would leave him to fall and get hurt.

I had to choose in this session whether to help Stefan directly, call his mother to help him, or to continue deeper with interpreting his internal perceptions and conflicts in the transference and in relation to the current reality of life with his mother. My dilemma over this increased over the next weeks as the situation deteriorated further. Stefan then presented either as a very ideal child, quickly collapsing into acute disturbance, or as an openly depressed child, when he was passive and 'floppy', as if he did not have an effective skeleton. His relationship with his mother became increasingly impoverished and he became more self-destructive, actually cutting and hurting himself – a disturbing thing to see in such a young child. Stefan was now showing that the continued efforts at rehabilitation were intolerable. Treatment was stopped at this point after nine months. I was left wondering whether in Stefan's interests we should have acted earlier on the deterioration.

Since Stefan's treatment, we have begun to look for earlier signs and clearer criteria about whether children find continued family rehabilitation tolerable or not. These include assessing parental responsibility in relation to the capacity of the parents to keep the child in mind rather than 'turn a blind eye', to give adequate provision of physical care, to be consistent in behaviour towards the child, to empathise with the child and show capacity for trust, and importantly to have a capacity to change. Careful monitoring is needed so that the child does not become the victim of repeated abuse. This involves trying to keep a balance with a constant tension between the need to intervene and the need to foster responsibility by not taking over and see if the parent can change (cf. Kennedy 1997: 17–21, 30). When the child finds it intolerable, their psychic survival is threatened and there are open signs of deterioration. This as we saw with Stefan can lead to further reactive disturbed behaviour from the parents towards the child.

The second case about failed rehabilitation is about Stuart, aged 9, who had suffered physical and sexual abuse (anal abuse) from his father. His mother was extremely deprived, had suffered continuous abuse and humiliation as a child, and came from an horrific very large incestuous family where each child barely found a way just to survive. Crucially too in the background Stuart had a history of lack of maternal containment; his birth weight was just four pounds, he was in an incubator for several weeks, and he had a bad pneumonia during his first year.

When the psychotherapy setting was established, Stuart used it to express his vulnerability and his need to build up defences. He was sad and lonely, unsure about his mother and triggered easily into expressing violent feelings towards her. The experience of abuse had represented a physical and a mental threat and in particular was like being psychologically killed off. He tried to placate and fit in with what he thought I wanted of him, which was alarming, and expressed a deep mistrust of being himself. I felt it important to allow him to build up some of his own defences. He could use the sessions as he wanted, and only talk about the abuse if he wanted to.

Even when he knew this, his anxieties shown in his play were very much centred around anal abuse. He covered his toy box with plasticine and various types of covers so that it would be safe. Cups were thrown into a bowl of water to be tested to see if they were clean or dirty. I was tested by being given the dirty one and then observed with glee. The transference developed and he had a number of phantasies about secrets and showed fears that I would harm him. Confused sequences developed in which he would want to barter with me. I would be seen, in the play, to give him money, and he would do things for me. He did however genuinely want to develop a special affectionate relationship with me. I think he found my interpretations about his vulnerability relieving, but even 'being relieved' was a confusing experience, and he frequently had to rush to the toilet after points of anxiety or relief in our interchanges.

Clearly he was suffering a number of types of zonal and functional confusions. He attempted to rework his experience and to gain some control over it. One frequent sequence of play was to make masks that he could use to see the top half of people but not their bottom half. Outside the sessions odd behaviour occurred too, for example, when he suddenly stuck a balloon into the nursing officer's face and nose. Going back to the case record we learnt that he suffered from having his father's bottom stuck into his face.

From early on Stuart was preoccupied with why he rather than his brother or sister was being rehabilitated. He was lonely, guilty and confused about this, and behind it were the questions, 'Why was he chosen for abuse?' 'Why was he now with mother?' 'Was he special, or had he managed to push the others out?' What now came more into focus was how he could identify with the sexual aggression he had suffered. He frequently poked sharp objects into the playroom wall and damaged it. He had misgivings about his sexual identity, was he a boy or a girl and how should he act to men and to women? At times he was very confiding in me in a genuine way, telling me all sorts of details about life with his mother and father. These periods were when he was settled. But at other times the effects of the abuse showed through in difficulties with other children and staff. Some of these involved difficulties keeping to reasonable sexual boundaries with other children, and some concerned his excitable and overactive behaviour.

As time went on it was apparent that it was increasingly difficult for Stuart to sustain progress. He became ill at points of stress, and his mother's alliance with me as his psychotherapist progressively lapsed, for example in not telling me of fights he had had with his brother at the weekend, which at one point may have explained some of his upset. The accumulated impression was that he was not being thought about. As her alliance and capacity to care and nurture Stuart lapsed, it became impossible for him to talk about the abuse at all in the psychotherapy. In other words he lost all sense of trust that I would be able to think about him. His mother at this point was finding it especially difficult to face the facts of her own abuse, and broke off treatment and her attempts at rehabilitation.

After a long period of time, clinical follow-ups and the ensuing court proceedings, Stuart's mother could accept his need for another family. The work towards this had been done in the treatment. Crucially Stuart had learned to trust and understand more of his own needs, and he and mother could agree about her incapacity to meet them now. This recognition of reality allowed for a good placement in a family elsewhere to be made and for a number of years of intensive outpatient psychotherapy to be arranged for Stuart. His mother has independently made something of her life and they are still in regular contact with each other.

Conclusion

During family rehabilitation the child's capacity to distinguish internal and external reality may be affected, particularly if insufficient work is done on the trauma and abuse suffered by the child and on patterns of behaviour of the parents and their attitude to the child. As we have seen in the examples above, many of these parents may also have suffered sexual abuse or emotional abuse (vas Dias 2000: 159). The terror inflicted on the child by abuse continues to affect them internally, through continued persecution and dread. Primitive feelings and emotions connected with the earliest emotional life are stirred, primitive confusion (Rosenfeld 1964), catastrophic anxiety (Bion 1970) and fear of annihilation (Winnicott 1956). Meltzer (1973) defines terror as 'paranoid anxiety whose essential quality, paralysis, leaves no avenue of action'. A dread develops because of a loss of protection against terror, and a tyrannical internal organisation may build up. This needs to be tackled therapeutically before progress can be made to understanding depressive and dependency needs. Because of this one needs to understand both the child's repetition of abusive contact and confront the tyrannical and omnipotent element within the child, which in my experience so frequently gives the therapeutic encounter with the severely abused child the quality of a battle. Only after addressing the underlying terror can progress towards rebuilding relationships be made. In family rehabilitation the parents need help to recognise the needs of the child and to understand how the child will react and behave with difficulties after the abuse. Importantly, the parents need to acknowledge responsibility for their part in causing the abuse, whether they are the actual perpetrator, or if they have colluded in it. Intense work is necessary to build up trust. They have to recognise that they have duties and responsibilities as parents, which will determine whether the child finds the family safe enough, including the need to provide clear and safe boundaries for the child.

The child psychotherapist has a central role in an inpatient therapeutic community setting to make and maintain contact with the deepest aspects of the child's feelings and emotional responses, to work with and help the child directly and to contribute to the thinking of the other staff. He or she will also face emotional pressures and conflict in the work, as different levels of disturbance become manifest, either in a directly understandable form or as painful and irrational forms of enactment, by the patients or indeed amongst the staff struggling in the work.

Chapter 7

Mother–infant work during family rehabilitation

Introduction

As described in the last three chapters, in inpatient treatment at the Cassel Hospital, psychotherapy and psychosocial nursing work to inform and enrich each other. A bridge of understanding is built using the patients' perceptions of, adjustment to, and conflict about the inpatient setting, and the affective impact of the processes on patients and staff alike. I shall now describe this in more detail here in respect of the work with mothers and infants following severe abuse. Two clinical examples of severe child abuse family cases are given: the first of Munchausen syndrome by proxy (now often called 'fictitious illness syndrome'); the second in which a baby sibling had been killed. They show how in-depth psychoanalytic work with mother and child and individual psychotherapy of the child can be combined with psychotherapy of the parents and intensive work in the therapeutic community. Such a combination can contribute, even in cases of severe pathology, to the development of the relationship between mother and child and promote successful rehabilitation in the outside community.

The roles of nurse and psychotherapist

Psychoanalytic treatment is possible at the Cassel because the patient is held in treatment by the mutually cooperative effort of nurse and psychotherapist, and by the sustained involvement of patients and staff together in a 'culture of enquiry' within the therapeutic community. There are many areas of shared aims and focus, particularly in concentrating attention on the capacity of the patient actively to address his/her problems around what Kennedy (1987) has called the 'work of the day' – that is the emotional issues which arise in the performance of the tasks of everyday life that give a structure to the patient managing the day.

Within the therapeutic community context of the hospital, patients have responsibility for their own treatment and parents have an actual and real responsibility for their children throughout the day and night (see

Chapters 4 to 6). Nurses working alongside will help to make emotional sense of what the patients are doing; dealing not just with eruptions of disturbed behaviour, but with the patients' capacities and difficulties in taking on specific responsibilities and tasks.

There are essential differences between nursing and psychotherapy and each brings something quite distinct to treatment. Nurses use their own experience of patients as a central guide to their understanding of them individually and in community and institutional processes (Barnes 1967; Kennedy 1987; Griffiths and Pringle 1997). Nurses help the patient to relate, to confront the all-consuming aspects of personal conflict that take them away from a focus or direction in life, and can reduce the ordinary to the superficial or the irrelevant. As such it is essential to the work with the underlying narcissistic base of the patient's problems.

Nurse and psychotherapist have separate tasks and separate roles. Yet each will focus on the current processes of the patient's treatment. The psychotherapist primarily concentrates on an understanding of the patient as it becomes apparent in the individual transference. The nurse primarily seeks to elucidate the nature of the patient's capacities as manifested in their daily activities and relationships, guiding them with plans and strategies for moving forward, keeping in the forefront the emotional meaning, quality and impact of their behaviour and plans of action, using ordinary human reactions and responses. Each, nurse and psychotherapist, will be aware of the work of the other. For the psychotherapist, this provides valuable information to set alongside what is emerging in the individual transference, and may lead to an understanding of wider transferences, including split transferences, for example, to the nurse or to the hospital, or parts of it.

Patients form transferences to both nurse and psychotherapist, and to other important figures and indeed to aspects of the hospital. Nurses also draw the transference around ordinary household issues to themselves, as they work alongside the patients in the kitchen, the pantry, the linen allocation or activities groups, and can more quickly than psychotherapists become the focus of a community or institutional transference (Barnes 1967; Heymans et al. 1987; Griffiths and Pringle 1997; Flynn 1998). Some aspects of the transference may be apparent early on, but the patient's transference to psychotherapist and to the hospital, including that of the child with his family, usually only becomes apparent as time goes by, and may come from psychotherapy or nursing, or interestingly from both at once, after the importance of what each have been struggling with has been fully recognised.

In cases of primitive attacks and confusions the staff themselves can begin to lose their own identity and capacity to work in their separate ways, and their effective functioning together may break down (Rosenfeld 1964). As Tom Main outlined in 'The Ailment' (1957) and in other papers (1989), the strain of working in what becomes a hostile environment can become manifest in a decline in the health and capacities of the staff. This can lead to failure in individual cases, effective splitting of the staff team and the possibility of retaliatory attacks by the staff upon the patients, or vice versa.

Such work, with its unremitting quality at times, does have its strain. Effective working together of psychotherapist and nurse can however have a supportive and restorative effect for one another, and can produce more ongoing cooperative effort in the work. Work with the destructive, fragmented and depressed sides of the patients may move the patient out of a quagmire of regressions and regressive distortions, and may lead them back to something more lively and restored, bringing relief to patients and staff.

Nurse–therapist supervision

Both nurse and psychotherapist then have affective contact with the patient and what is most useful in nurse–therapist supervision is to understand how both nurse and psychotherapist fulfil their separate roles and deal with conflicts that come to light. As Tischler (1987) writes, nurse–therapist supervision 'pays special attention to the feelings in the countertransference which patients evoke in their treaters, and the effect these feelings have on their work'. There can be a 'proliferation of the transference to the institution, not only the transference of the patient, but also the countertransference of the staff to patients and to each other'.

Nurse–therapist supervisions are different and additional to other supervisions of clinical work. A senior psychotherapist and a senior nurse meet with a primary team of workers with a family, including the nurse, the child psychotherapist and the adult psychotherapist. One or other of the workers will elect to speak first, talking of how they find working with the family, how they are working in their role and how they are communicating or not with the other workers. Each of the workers will follow, then the supervisors will pick out themes. It is important not to make it into a formal review and to keep it to a degree experiential, so that one may feel and see if there are processes of re-enactment at work in relation to each other or one or both of the supervisors; for example, does one of the workers feel squeezed out, dropped, neglected and murderous towards the rival? This work requires a degree of freedom and trust of each other to be able to bring out in a group of workers the countertransference feelings which may show up how adequately one is working in one's role with the family and how able one is to work with other professionals. Such supervisions augment, for many nurses and therapists, their own experience of personal psychoanalysis, and are generally experienced by staff as invaluable in developing working alliances, particularly when working with families that have intense disturbance and where there may be hidden severely destructive splitting processes.

Mother–infant sessions

Mother–infant sessions take place weekly in the Families Unit when working with severe child abuse cases and involve a child psychotherapist and sometimes a nurse. They are set up so that the mother can discuss with the child psychotherapist any issues of concern about the infant. A few toys are provided and the mother is encouraged to bring some of the child's own toys. There is a freedom to talk and to play, and cover ordinary worries about contact with the child and about development. The child psychotherapist can also observe and work with the here and now of the mother–infant relationship, integrating outside observations from within the hospital or the foster home. When there is a father or stepfather involved, they sometimes also attend. Most of the infants are returning to their mothers after being in foster care.

The sessions are usually very emotionally charged, and in most cases there are contentious legal issues about whether mother and infant should be together. Often, after abuse and neglect, and having lost and indeed missed out on emotional contact with the child, the mothers need to recognise and face up to aspects of their way of relating to the child that are hindering a deepening of their bond. Mothers need to be able to accept responsibility for their part in what happened and, as treatment goes on, acknowledge further guilt, shame and painful awareness. The sessions have to work against the danger of contact with the child being lost and weak links severed. Our experience of this work indicates that this is especially so if the mother cannot accept responsibility. In effect, the mother does not bond again with the infant unless she can get beyond the abusive behaviour or her part in the abusive experience. If, as often happens, a defensive or protective shell is created around the mother–infant couple, the mother can fail to notice her own habitual responses to her child along with the infant's attempts at communication and their changing developmental needs. Mother–infant work aims to increase awareness of all this so new patterns of relating can be learnt (Bion 1962b).

Case one

There are a number of recurrent themes in the long-term mother–infant cases of severe child abuse treated over this time, especially whether the violence to the child is a reaction to stress or part of a perverse pattern, or a combination of both (Glasser 1998; Steiner 1993). Here I shall illustrate how a psychoanalytic understanding takes shape in this particular type of case in an inpatient setting and shall focus on:

- supervision of disturbed or abusing patients
- work with the parents' underlying destructiveness
- problems of intense dependence.

The case is one of Munchausen syndrome by proxy (Coombe 1995; Kennedy and Coombe 1995; Kennedy 1997: 116–28; Day and Flynn 2003: 15–81) where two children had nearly been killed through systematic poisoning by salt, for which the mother eventually accepted responsibility. The poisoning had occurred in a clandestine and murderous fashion over a period of many months. The two children who had been poisoned had now gone to an alternative placement and the mother, Mrs A, and new baby, Joan, were currently in treatment, after being under 24-hour surveillance in a mother–baby psychiatric unit for the first 11 months. Joan was aged just over one year old when inpatient treatment began and the treatment lasted for two years until she was three years old.

The view of the adult psychotherapist, who saw Mrs A for individual psychotherapy (twice weekly) and later for group psychotherapy, was that her central psychopathology involved an incapacity to bear separation or difference. This underwent some degree of modification through the Cassel experience. She characteristically avoided experience of loss by various means, including denial, reaction formation, manic flight and hostile devaluing of the object. She had a harsh and envious element that could become obscured, warded off or controlled under many circumstances. It was clear that there was a psychotic centre to her personality and there had been one previous psychotic breakdown, which occurred when she was briefly separated from her new baby after an emergency protection order.

When I began in the mother–infant sessions in this case, the quality of Mrs A's conversation about Joan was inconsequential 'coffee morning talk' about the child's development and interest in food, toys and people, delivered in a monotonous nasal drone. It was hard to get to specific emotional truths about what was going on. Mrs A was very stuck in her bizarre, unreal accounts that were full of denial. Nevertheless, at some level I felt there was a genuine attachment to Joan, who was just one year old, and some hope of change. Joan herself was not very appealing and had a way of throwing her head back and making a groaning guttural shout that sounded distressing and disconnected. She did not experience her mother as being able to cope with her discomfort and distress, and hid her hurt after small accidental hurts such as bumps and knocks, or seemed to hide her needs if she wanted something. Her mother generally did not notice.

The atmosphere in treatment was a difficult one. Mrs A's own mistrust of others was projected into people around her, so she then had to protect herself from them with an 'armour' of deviousness and pseudo-normality. She resented bitterly the supervision that was organised to keep the child safe and, as with many patients in this category, put much of her energy into thwarting the efforts of the nursing and psychotherapy staff. She felt watched in the hospital and that I was watching her and Joan in sessions, which made her more false and compliant. Work with this meant that a crucial link was made between a major conflict for Mrs A in the hospital in a wider transference, and what was then going on in the here-and-now transference of the mother–infant session. I took up her fear of being watched by me, while relating it to what was happening more widely. The result was that I saw a more fluid contact from mother to infant than I had seen so far and the possibility of something more real and flexible between them. Interpreting Mrs A's responses to supervision then, and linking them to issues of the lack of contact between mother and child, brought out transference issues in relation to the whole treatment. Following this work, she was able to acknowledge the tension of being observed, and her wish to isolate herself and cut herself off.

A lot of the nursing work at the Cassel involves working in groups, from morning work groups, to group meetings and group recreational activities. Mrs A liked to work on her own or with one other person whom she would control. At first she managed to get into solitary work groups, like the laundry work group, and to be manager of the sewing activity, and then gardening manager, each time working hard, but on her own. Her nurse then worked to steer her towards contact with other patients. Her wish to cut herself off or dominate made the therapy groups, which were introduced during her stay, particularly hard to bear (Coombe 1995).

In the ensuing months the problems had to get considerably worse before they got better. We were then seeing more of the underlying destructiveness. Her two older children were at this stage going to a permanent placement, and her relationship with her own parents had now broken down. Mrs A's way of coping with these real losses of her mother, stepfather, husband and children was to replace them with a search for her real father. This inability to deal with losses is important aetiologically, especially the inability to mourn her maternal grandmother, who died just before the birth of her first child (whom she poisoned), and the loss of her natural father as a child, which had contributed to the embittered relationship with her mother throughout childhood. It was important for her nurse, and the adult and child psychotherapists, to work continuously with her holidays and absences. Her nurse also helped her to say goodbye to the children she had previously poisoned. They met with the father and social worker and the mother spent an hour with them explaining that she wanted them to live with daddy, and that she was sorry but she was not able to keep them safe. She gave them a photograph album with pictures of their childhood. This was a moving goodbye and, after being very upset, she told her nurse that this was the first time she had felt that these were her two children.

The issue of loss became more acute when a foster home was found where Joan could go at the weekends. This was arranged to facilitate a degree of separateness between mother and child and to allow Mrs A space in her flat at weekends on her own away from the intensity of the treatment. To Mrs A this signified the unpalatable fact that Joan could be a separate person. It also underlined the fact that rehabilitation might not work out, which created a feeling in her of not being totally in control, and brought intense conflict for her. The level of Mrs A's paranoia about other people increased. Just prior to a difficult case conference, she 'accidentally' caused a moderately severe injury to her own hands. Her anger was also directed against the staff, in particular her nurse, who suffered a sustained and unmitigated barrage of attacks. Later her anger came out with Joan. An incident occurred within the hospital in which the child was put into an over-warm (though not scalding) bath. This was taken very seriously by all concerned. Paradoxically however, when the hidden murderousness began to surface and Mrs A had to acknowledge it, she became more workable.

We now began to see more of the range and depth of Mrs A's destructiveness, and some of the psychodynamic patterns. Mrs A was excessively controlling, so that Joan's independent development and play were hindered in various ways. Joan had begun to develop several traits just like mother, some areas of competence such as speech, and some unhealthy behaviour, such as bullying other children. In response to this continuous interference by her mother, bodily and psychosomatic elements appeared, such as a lengthy period of chest infections and some asthma. During the hospital tests for this, Mrs A accused others of putting poisonous substances into the child. Her nurse saw that Joan had been on six courses of antibiotics in a period of eight weeks. She was very concerned that Mrs A might be doing something to cause these illnesses. When she asked Mrs A outright if she was doing anything to Joan, Mrs A was furious with her nurse. This was a very useful piece of work, with Mrs A being faced with the reality both of what she was doing now and the reality that she had poisoned her two children. Another focus of the nurse's work was to help Mrs A voice ambivalent feelings she had about Joan. When Joan had chicken pox and was in semi-isolation on the Families Unit landing, she was able to say how trapped she felt and how difficult she found it being with her daughter all the time. Mrs A could voice her feelings and her complaint, and her nurse could hear it. The other patients could take her complaint as normal, and people responded to her needs by offering to babysit to give her a break. This was so important because before the poisoning of her children Mrs A had made repeated visits to her GP asking for help about different issues of concern about herself and her child, but the overall pattern of her behaviour was not recognised and the precipitate danger not registered. This feature of failed 'appeals' for help to primary health services is typical for other perpetrators in Munchausen syndrome by proxy cases (Kennedy 1989; Kennedy and Coombe 1995).

After several more months of painstaking work with mother and child, there were some signs of change in the child. She was happier, more relaxed and began relating directly to me on occasions. I have found in mother–infant sessions that the capacity of the child to have a separate relationship with the child psychotherapist is a good prognostic sign. This usually is indicative of some increase in security and some ego development in the child. It can show that the child feels her mother is able to make contact with the child psychotherapist, so she has permission to do so too. In this case it meant the work could go deeper to underlying issues about dependence and desperation. It became possible at last to look at Mrs A's now voiced near-psychotic fear that, if she allowed Joan to change, she would grow into an 'alien child'. Underneath this was the terrifying fear that she would personally reject Joan as she had the others, with terrifying consequences if her actions went out of control. Joan's own anxieties about separation from the symbiotic level of closeness with her mother now began to come out. When actual separations occurred, Joan began to wake at night in the hospital screaming. She reacted adversely to any strange situation which she seemed to take in an unprocessed way and which then seemed to haunt her. Both the mother and child had to cope with intense anxiety during separations. The mother–infant sessions aimed to help them understand this and adjust to changing ways of relating.

Since discharge and successful rehabilitation into the outside community, the family and the outside workers have had follow-up consultations over the last few years. The ongoing assessments are encouraging and there have been no causes for alarm that the child would be harmed. Mrs A is very successful in her area of work, and Joan now has a number of friends and is getting on well at school. Although the work was successful at one level, we are aware that much more could have been done if this patient had been able to accept further intensive psychotherapy. This had been offered in a specialist outpatient setting and recent consultations show that splitting processes and glimpses of the mother's underlying aggression become apparent from time to time.

Case two

In my second clinical example I shall look at how a psychoanalytic understanding of a mother and child, separately and together, took shape in my work, by relating it to the work of the nurse and the whole hospital treatment. It is inevitably an abbreviated account and I shall concentrate on the child's experience.

This is a family in which a four-week-old baby had been killed by horrific non-accidental injuries, with neglect and injury from the age of one week. The mother, Susan, was being rehabilitated with the older child, Ann, after the mother came out of prison. The baby's father, Ann's stepfather, had been convicted of the injuries and the killing, and was still in prison. Ann was now two years nine months old: she had been one year three months when the baby was killed. Ann had been plucked into care immediately in an emergency way, without any preparation or goodbyes, and remained in a foster home. Along with the range of other psychotherapy and nursing work, mother–infant work looked at whether the mother could rebond with her child. Later in parallel individual psychotherapy from the age of three, Ann was helped to face the break-up of the family, the broken bond with her mother and the trauma of the killing, which she had probably witnessed (Black 1993).

Whilst in prison Susan had managed eight months of once-weekly psychotherapy. Her prison psychotherapist thought of her as having 'a dangerous capacity for denial'. This period of psychotherapy proved, however, to be an important preparation for the subsequent attempts at rehabilitation, especially in bringing some recognition of the extent of her own state of disturbance and her own wish to be reunited with her child to try to become a mother again.

In Susan's psychotherapy, the mother–infant sessions with Susan and Ann, and in their work with nurses, and indeed patients in the community, prominent features from the start were evidence of trauma, flashbacks and nightmares in mother and child, a marked trait in the mother of ambivalent and oscillating attachments and persistent deviousness in her behaviour, particularly in relation to professionals. Although there was some wish to be together, at first there was no real bond between mother and child. Susan was sometimes cold and cruel to Ann and thoughtless about her needs. There was also in Susan an inner guilt and a wish to be punished, and so to lose her child. Awareness of this guilt led to further cycles of projections. The Cassel was then seen not as the prison, as it had been seen, but as the hideously depriving and longed for mother. Susan could act in quite a schizoid way, when her capabilities and functioning disintegrated. Ann learnt to develop a pseudo-closeness to her mother to deal with the painful experience of her dissociated states.

The family nurse found that when Susan was in these states of mind, Ann became more distressed, her sleeping pattern became disturbed, she was more clingy and she asked for her dummy continuously. Susan found these times even more traumatising when she realised her effect on Ann. She swung from thinking 'No, I can't look after Ann' to 'Yes, I must' with great rapidity, and with a dispersal of the previously felt immobilising anxiety that was alarming in itself. It was a reminder of her capacity to deny, to split her mental states and cut herself off from the reality of her difficulties, which her nurse was helping her to face. Threatened by these sudden changes, Ann was often very angry with her mother, biting and pinching her. This brought out how guilty and bad Ann felt. It proved immensely difficult for her nurse to help them with the painfulness of their relationship. This was particularly so since Ann could not tolerate her mother being with a third person. Her nurse found that, when she got involved, Ann desperately tried to oust her, saying 'Go away', or pretending to fall asleep or demanding attention. Ann looked intensely to her mother for her needs and cuddles, and imitated her, wearing her clothes and shoes and mimicking her smoking manner and ways of talking to people, in an attempt to keep her mother by a primitive identification.

Within a short time Susan encountered considerable difficulties accepting the supervision arrangements within the hospital, and it became apparent that she felt unsafe. Susan, however, could honestly see this and after a fortnight she requested a temporary separation, when Ann went back to foster parents for a week. This initial realism and acceptance of the depth of her problem, that she might not manage to have the child back, though disruptive for Ann, meant that we could look at the reality of the difficulties. On Ann's return to the hospital, the effects of the disruption were indeed apparent.

In the next mother–infant session a couple of days later Ann looked very tired and flustered and Susan was again in a bored and disconnected state. There was little contact or communication between them and Ann was left to her own devices and wandered round the room aimlessly. The painful experience with mother was dissociated. She ignored her mother's punitiveness to her and said to me instead 'I'm not talking to you'. I then became for her the rejected and rejecting transference figure.

The early transference of the mother to the child psychotherapist formed part of a process of splitting of the 'good motherly man' as distinct from the 'bad/fascinating man' (Welldon 1992). Usually I was seen as the former. But of particular concern was a relationship mother had with a man in the hospital who had been and could be violent, and the possibility that there could be a repetition of how the family violence had occurred.

In one session Ann took one of the duplo men figures and put it in a chair in the dolls' house watching the TV. It fell out and I asked her if she wanted me to put it back in one of the chairs. She said 'No', and insisted that I put it in the particular seat where she consistently put it, the one where the man sits and watches the TV. I felt that she was aware of me as someone watching and listening regularly and being consistent in that position. I interpreted that it was important for Ann that I could be the man to sit and watch, and help her think about being back with her mother.

From the nurse in the playgroup I now learnt that Ann was becoming preoccupied with babies, how to bath them, put them asleep and so on. She brought a huge baby-size doll to the mother–infant sessions. It was clear that this related to her awakening preoccupations with how babies were treated and what had happened to the baby in her family.

After four months, however, a serious problem developed in the mother–infant sessions; the mother was preventing the child from having more open contact with me, limiting the effectiveness of my contact with her. A change in structure was therefore needed, so that there would be one individual psychotherapy session per week, with one mother–infant session per week to run in parallel. This change of structure came sooner than usual. I would usually move directly from mother–infant sessions to individual sessions when the child had developed a capacity to relate to me separately, the need for the joint sessions was passed, and the whole process worked through with the mother and child. This time I was pressured by the courts outside to see if the mother could not just keep the child safe but allow her to be separate and express what she felt. This in turn put a pressure on me and indeed on the child to adjust very quickly to what was happening. I think this pressure reflected not just a difficult technical issue, or a particular difficulty in an applied setting, but reflected something for the child and indeed her mother, namely how a change of outlook and a deep internal change were necessary and how thinking and feelings had to be processed rapidly in a very complete way, if mother and child were to be rehabilitated together.

In her first individual session, Ann began with a game of toy trains. Then she repeatedly dropped toy animals from her head onto the floor. She spoke of mummy and daddy while playing with the small figures from the family set. I mentioned to her that she had seen daddy (at the prison) yesterday. [This was all part of the rush mentioned above, that this vulnerable child still had a relationship with her 'daddy', her stepfather who had killed her sister, and saw him once a month in prison. It was an arrangement that would eventually come to an end.] She smiled and laughed, saying she was given sweeties, and seemed pleased. When one of the animals fell off her head, a gorilla figure, she said it was 'killed', though it was not clear by whom. She now placed a woman figure in the chair looking at the TV, whereas in previous play it had been a man. The woman was then bathed and put on the toilet. Ann then became preoccupied about how the plugs and the taps worked. She involved me in a game with her of making them work. She did traces of my hand on the paper, and she wrote lists of children's names. She finally also pointed out to me that one of the chairs was mended.

My impression as the session went was that Ann felt more contained because she was being thought about and understood on her own, and she now could make more sense of what she felt and saw (Bion 1962b). Overall, I had the impression that Ann was beginning to talk about things that could be broken, that could fall away, perhaps be hurt by falling. She mentioned 'killing', but evident too was a sense of things being mended and repaired. She was perhaps only working from 'traces', as she traced the shape of my hand and hers, and she was concerned with naming new relationships and ordering her new knowledge, by means of the list of children's names.

In the following joint session, the mother told me a dream that Ann had told her which had scared her. She had woken up saying there was 'a fat man on the ceiling' and she had shown fear, even terror, talking about it. It sounded to me as if it was a dream that was so realistic that Ann had repeated it as if it were still going on after she had woken. Now, as mother spoke to me, Ann listened and then said, 'There is a fat man on the ceiling.' She soon reverted to her regressed use of the dummy and said she was not talking to me. This time I felt that the not talking to me was a way of protecting her mother from the things she might say. At the same time she ran the bottom of her shoes up her mother's leg, taunting her, getting under her skin, mirroring how her mother taunted her sometimes. I thought that this taunting was a veiled way of indicating she knew about more serious forms of hurting and being hurt, to do with her painful memories of separation from her mother and possibly with memories about the baby.

Susan, when I briefly saw her on her own to discuss her anxieties about how upset Ann was becoming, seemed herself now like Ann able to feel fear and anxiety. We discussed what Ann may be feeling, so that Susan could now tolerate to think about a possible understanding of the dream: 'the fat man on the ceiling' might refer to a composite memory of a man and a baby, a sort of screen memory of the child lying in her cot and being preoccupied with the baby (Freud 1900). It was an important part of the work with the mother that she could bear to learn something of her child's experience, of what Ann had gone through. She could see that if Ann now knew more about it, her feelings would be disturbed and she would have to adjust to these experiences emotionally. Sometimes Susan could bear this, but at other times she could not and again produced more erratic and schizoid behaviour.

Despite some periods of listlessness and despair, and other periods of manic dissociated identification with her mother's more disturbed behaviour, Ann was nevertheless developing a strength in herself. What she needed to be allowed to know and express had an urgency that went beyond her mother's disruptive behaviour and incapacity to digest what was happening emotionally for her and Ann. It was striking that, as Ann's work on mourning, for her sister and the loss of her mother (and stepfather), developed and when she felt overall more settled with her mother, her nurse could do the overdue work around potty training. Her nurse had been very aware of how Ann would regularly 'shut down' her capacity for awareness, such as at the weekends when she went back to the foster parents, going into a mindless forgetful state. Such behaviour had been very puzzling and painful. It seemed Ann's anxiety was that she was required to hold in her anger, her feelings and needs, and indeed deaden herself, in an unconscious way doing what she felt was demanded of her, in identification with the dead baby. Now after some time Ann could 'let go' in different ways, and the potty training was achieved very quickly, so that her contact with her mother was strengthened.

In another individual session Ann now played out a scene, explaining everything to me as she did it, where 'the man smashes an armchair and is very naughty for doing it'. She then threw a chair vigorously and shouted loudly. Ann spoke clearly and with possession and pride about 'her times', her individual psychotherapy times with me, as if increasingly realising her need for some privacy in her containment of her inner experience. But there were other signs of distress such as her deliberate nose-poking, which caused regular bleeding. When this was talked about in a mother–child session, Ann went to pieces and started asking in a monotone for 'dummy-mummy'. She seemed to make use of mother's own defensive attitudes, and sometimes hid behind a mother who did not or would not understand and would keep anxiety away, 'the dummy-mummy'. Later on, she continued her explorations. She took a toy Duplo diver and wrapped the string from its helmet round her leg and spoke of her leg being broken. She laughed and was then able to take the dummy out of her mouth. Ann was currently becoming upset about babies again, especially one who was leaving the hospital prematurely and without warning as rehabilitation broke down. Mother sat thinking reflectively about how Ann stroked this baby in the same way she used to stroke the baby that was killed.

Ann's anger with her mother and stepfather was emerging much more now in various ways. She would usually quickly deny her anger and anxiously tell her mother she loved her, making an open show of rejecting me instead. Susan would flaunt this in front of me, laughing flirtatiously at me, and not particularly helping the child make better contact.

The arrangement of alternating sessions did bring conflict for Ann, but she seemed more contained within the individual sessions to be able to express the most conflictual material. In one she spoke about 'a baby killing a man'. She played frantically with figures tumbling about in the dolls' house, as she gave me precise accounts of the unfolding story. This story seemed an inversion of the story I thought she knew at some level of awareness, and perhaps had witnessed, of 'a man killing a baby'. A related theme in relation to her play was her talking of the TV programme *Baywatch*. Instead of putting the male figure in the chair in the dolls' house to watch the TV, Ann had recently begun to put the 'little girl' figure in the watching position. I interpreted her 'Baby . . . watch', and her worries about what happens to babies.

This work of helping Ann to be allowed to know and experience was so intensive that it spanned each setting in which the child was seen in the hospital. She had different experiences, particularly with nurses and other children with whom she had built up a bond of trust. Some of this material was stirred up vis-à-vis Ann's continued visits to John in prison. This is the nurse's account of the next children only play session:

> Ann was quiet and subdued. She simply wanted to listen to stories most of the time, with the exception of one specific piece of play with the dolls. In this Ann put her baby to bed in the playhouse and then a few

minutes later brought the baby to the nurse, saying she had woken up, having had a nightmare, a monster had frightened the baby. Ann reassured the baby and put her back to bed. A few minutes later Ann asked the nurse urgently to come and kill a strange man who had woken the baby and frightened her. The nurse asked if it was a burglar. Ann said 'Yes', so she and the nurse phoned the police. A few minutes later the nurse asked Ann if the police had been and she said, 'Yes, the policeman killed the man. He fell down a black hole in the floor into the crocodile's mouth, he's dead now and baby's not frightened any more.' The child then stopped playing the game, and came and sat quietly, looking sad and wanting another story.

Towards the end as rehabilitation and a return to the community were being organised, Ann felt strong enough to fill in some of the missing links in the story. She asked her mother outright one day, 'Did daddy kill Helen?' and her mother answered, 'Yes, that's right.' In the joint session the mother needed some help to know how the child could have known this.

In her next individual session, Ann got out a set of teddy puppets (hand puppets) and began a game of two babies who were being looked after. The game reached a climax in which one of the babies, while being changed, was 'pinched' and 'hit' for being naughty, first by the mother and then by the father. I was clearly directed by her as to what role I should take. To begin with I had to be someone who held the baby when she was not looking after it. Then she reversed the situation, by making me the person who asks her what the baby can do and what should happen to it. The baby was dealt with somewhat roughly and was passive throughout.

A child of her own age was now leaving the hospital community. Ann was upset and beside herself, and cried continuously and 'hysterically'. She settled down only after having been able to talk to the child again on the phone a couple of days later. It sounded as if Ann needed confirmation that this other child, even though she had left the hospital, was still there. She needed a reassurance that the other child was still alive. This was another real experience of loss, at an affective level, when Ann re-experienced, through this child's leaving, the traumatic loss of a sister figure. The child had been a playmate and friend in the hospital, with whom she had had many ups and downs, in particular related to Ann's repeated biting behaviour with other children, mentioned above. The child also saw me with her mother for mother–infant sessions, and so was a 'therapy sibling' too. Thinking about this difficult experience with a sibling, in therapy and in work with her nurse, enabled Ann to move further in her ability to readjust to the traumatic loss of the killing of her baby sister.

The family made a successful discharge to the outside community. In the time since discharge, progress has been satisfactory. There has been social services support but not further treatment.

Conclusion

These are two very severe, indeed extreme, cases in which, until recently, no kind of psychotherapeutic treatment would have been tried. I have attempted to outline a few features in each case that helped to keep the work going and how we attempted to face the severe splitting and underlying destructiveness at work in the patients; how this had to be done openly; and the impact of it borne by both patients, nurses and psychotherapist, so that a better side, something new, could emerge. As far as the workers themselves were concerned, such work took its toll and demanded not just personal resources, capacities for containment and reflection, and capacities to set and redefine the boundaries of treatment, but also all the resources of supervision, including nurse–therapist supervision (Tischler 1987), to prevent splits that could make the workers enact destructive relationships or want to give up in despair. It also required us to bring our work in the hospital together with the work outside, to keep the therapeutic work with the family within a legal framework (Kennedy 1989, 1997), and integrate the views of external agencies, the social services, probation, the guardians ad litem, other expert consultants and the High Court.

To summarise the work in Case One: following the clandestine poisoning of two children, Mrs A used the mother–infant sessions, in a long treatment lasting two years, to get to know her next child Joan, aged 11 months on admission, as a real person. She needed also to use them to recognise she could unleash on a child her own disturbed feelings, and that she could be out of touch with her own dangerousness. An incident about giving the child an over-warm bath brought her hidden murderousness into view within the therapeutic community and, on a smaller scale in the mother–infant sessions, other parallel examples of potentially dangerous behaviour could be faced. Important work too was done in the mother–infant sessions about intense fears over separateness of the mother from the child. Joan was encouraged to develop more as an individual, alongside parallel work in the nursing about developing Mrs A's social and group capacities with others, and in her own psychotherapy about the early breaks in her relationship with her parents as an infant, and the false solutions she adopted to cover over her hostile and embittered relationship with her mother.

Such cases of Munchausen syndrome by proxy were previously seen as untreatable (Meadow 1977; Kennedy and Coombe 1995). The focus on the child and her mother's interactions with her, which was possible in the mother–infant sessions, and more extensively in the daily interactions of nursing staff with the family, importantly enabled us to know the possible risks to the child, the effects on her development and the progress of the mother–infant relationship, and made the work possible. I have referred only to a fraction of the work, but have tried to show how the most central aspects of this family's overall treatment came jointly into the mother–infant sessions and the work of the therapeutic community. These were the focus on what was actually happening to the child while being watched, on dangerousness and destructiveness, and on the psychotic elements behind the fears of separation.

The mother–infant work in Case Two was done with a mother who had been released from prison after serving a term for neglect following the killing by her partner of their baby girl. Her daughter aged 3 years now was being returned to her from foster care after 18 months. In the work a new bond had to be formed between them, the positive wishes to be together nurtured, alongside other passive, muddled and negative wishes in both mother and child. The erratic and disturbed behaviour of the mother had to be relived to a degree in the therapeutic community before she could more fully accept the effect it was having and had had within her family.

There were elements in this case that were typical of many cases of the treatment of abusing parents and other borderline patients at the Cassel Hospital over the years. Susan had shown a capacity to use psychoanalytic psychotherapy, but the everyday reality of her treatment was that she undermined this repeatedly in a thoughtless and destructive, almost psychopathic, way. Again and again her ambivalence about having Ann back with her, which undermined their progress together, was brought out into the open. There were difficulties, splits and strain all round at times, in the family and in the workers. Some workers in the hospital felt that Susan's behaviour was too chaotic and her treatment of Ann still thoughtless and sadistic, and that Ann should not be rehabilitated, while others felt they could see changes, that it was what Ann wanted and that she was managing.

This latter view in effect influenced the change in technique halfway through, to parallel mother–child and child psychotherapy sessions, to help mother and child adjust to each other and also to allow the child to have the fullest possible space within the circumstances to express herself. It also became more important at that point to recognise that bringing mother and child together could produce a negative response in Susan, and sometimes in Ann too, when she gave way to a muddled and passive negativity.

But overall it was Ann's tolerance of individual sessions and her wish to have her thoughts and feelings understood that showed her willingness to persevere through the painfulness of the process. Ann had to be able to know how it could have happened that her baby sister had been killed, in order to overcome her internal trauma, but importantly to know, too, how thinking in her internal world could get killed off, and would need to be known and reintegrated within her. Susan had to face her own responsibility and some of her failings. As indeed she did do this, she eventually by the end of treatment became capable of deep and genuine guilt and remorse, which she thought about and worked through in her individual psychotherapy. She also needed to be able to allow her child to express her feelings, including her anger with her mother and her acceptance of her stepfather's responsibility, indeed to allow herself to know what happened. Sufficient support and tolerance was needed in the whole inpatient treatment team to survive negative attacks and to create the space for something new to grow between Ann and Susan.

To reiterate a crucial point about this work with severe emotional disturbance in mother–infant work in this applied setting, it is the tolerance of severe infantile projections, of hostility and despair, and the struggle to maintain cooperative work together, not just the technical changes of the inpatient setting, that make work towards successful rehabilitation of such families possible, and in the end enables the workers to survive and to continue to work in a psychoanalytic way.

Chapter 8

The adoptive father

Introduction

I have so far discussed relationships between emotionally disturbed children and their parents, but my emphasis has been mainly on mother–child relationships. Here I shall focus instead on the father, and in particular on the role of the adoptive father in the new family after adoption. I shall go on to outline some important contributions that psychoanalytic psychotherapy can make in this applied field of study to the understanding of adoption.

Most accounts of adoption give very little space to the adoptive father. Whilst rightful emphasis is given to the adopted child or adoptee, to the natural or birth parents, and to the adoptive mother, even specific discussions of the adoptive parents give the father only a small mention. In short the adoptive father is a bit of a nonentity. Such an attitude has until very recently underlain our current notion of adoption in western culture, and expresses a primitive emotion and thinking, a 'myth' in Bion's sense, indicative of a limited level of growth, and certain particular preconceptions and fragmented forms of thinking (Bion 1962b: 63, 67).

This lack of emphasis on the father is markedly different from the family as understood by Freud, where the Oedipal conflict underlies all relationships, and where the role of the father is central. Also the psychoanalyst/psychotherapist experienced as the father was central to the development of the concept of transference and remains the central psychological mechanism of understanding in psychoanalytic treatments. Maternal transference came later in the history of psychoanalysis and could in fact be devalued by overemphasis of the paternal transference (Britton 2002).

The comparative neglect of the adoptive father is in part due to the absence, until very recently, of cogent and fully expressed psychoanalytically informed views about the role of the father within the family. Yet the very marginal view of the adoptive father flies in the face of the intuition and experience of many who work in the field of adoption, who see the role of adoptive father as crucial in practice to successful and unsuccessful adoptions alike.

It has been recognised now that the theory and practice of child rearing has been decidedly matricentric, with a relative lack of studies of the father and his role, which may have limited and distorted our understanding of the dynamics of development. In the last 30 years social scientists have put more emphasis on the role of fathers in families, so that the previous gap has been filled by a proliferation of studies (Jordan 1995; Lui 1997; Zelkowitz and Milet 1997; Cath and Shopper 2002, and others). Applied social sciences, linked to social work, psychology and nursing, have related this approach to adoption, including increasing mention of adoptive parents and the adoptive father as well as the adoptive mother (Derdreyn and Graves, 1998; Sharma, McGue and Benson 1998; Smith and Howard 1999). For example, Baumann reviews recent changes in adoption and how the media and literature have portrayed the birth father and the adoptive father, and the significant attitudes of each to the other (Baumann 1999). Psychoanalytic accounts of the subject of the adoptive parents, and in particular the adoptive father in the adoptive family, have tended to lag behind those in the social sciences (Quinodoz 1996, 1999a, 1999b; Hopkins 2000b; Flynn 2002; Bertram 2003; Canham 2003).

I shall outline them in this chapter, that *the adoptive father* has a key role in the development of the adopted child insofar as the following obtains:

1   *He supports the nurturing of the adoptive mother*, which focuses around the physical and emotional developing needs of the adopted child.
2   *He actively creates meaningful links for the family*, for the child and the adoptive mother, about their relationship, his part in it and with other members of the adoptive family.
3   *He actively creates meaningful links for the adoptive child about his/her personal history*, including about his/her adoption and the connections to the natural parents.

I shall look first at two widely contrasting cultural perspectives on adoption to highlight what I believe has been our modern perspective on adoption, and what has been lost and is missing. Then I shall outline some philosophical ideas from the Enlightenment, in particular calculations about needs and wants, and how these ideas have pervaded the literature on adoption until very recently. I shall fill out my own view of the adoptive father with reference to some more recent psychoanalytic studies on adoption, then give some case illustrations from psychoanalytic work with adopted children and adoptive parents.

Historical and cultural perspectives

There is no universal or singular view of adoption, so that within different historical and cultural contexts there can be widely differing philosophies of it. I believe our modern views on adoption have lost some of the richness of our cultural heritage. I shall try to bring this out by making an historical comparison with the Roman concept of adoption, which is especially important for understanding a central feature of the role of the adoptive father. In the Roman world the philosophy of adoption involved conferment of privilege and high rank, essentially of status. Interestingly much of our terminology of adoption is Latin, the words 'adoption', 'parent', 'father', 'family', 'infant' and so on. (Interesting exceptions are 'mother', from the old Norse *modar* [not the Latin *mater*], and 'child', from the old English and originally old German root *cild* – the mother–child bond is rooted in the culture of our more Northern ancestors.)

Adoption occurred in the Roman world neither because of the neediness of the child, nor because of the neediness of the adoptive family, but as a means by which very worthy individuals were sponsored by a very senior figure (for example, a senator or governor of a province), so that they could be groomed to take on the privileges and responsibilities of office. The central figures in it were all men, especially the adoptive father, whose action in adopting a boy or young man was a symbol of his substantial importance and position. One of the special features of Roman law was the principle of *patria potestas*, the power of the father, which involved the lifelong authority of the father over the person and property of his descendants, and was the outcome of the family organisation of a primitive society. (Compare here Freud's discussion of the power and authority of the father in primitive and mythology society, in *Totem and Taboo* 1913). This authority in its earliest form could be quite total, although it was modified in later centuries, and included the power of life and death, control of the marriage of son or daughter, and power of transferring them to another family or selling them.

Trajan is an example of an adoptive father in Roman times. As a successful soldier and provincial governor, he adopted another Spaniard and his great-nephew, Hadrian, who was then a very promising young man, a soldier from a lower ranking provincial family. Hadrian joined with Trajan in his military successes as he conquered the Dacians, whose territory he constituted a Roman province (modern Romania), and a large part of the Parthian empire, reaching the Persian Gulf. Trajan was Roman Emperor AD 98–117. We know something of the relationship between the two men from literary sources and interpretation of the dramatic sculptures of Trajan's column in Rome.

When Hadrian, with many successes of his own, succeeded Trajan as Emperor in AD 117, he put his main energies not into further conquests to extend the empire but into improving its internal cohesion. As a former provincial Hadrian knew of the real dangers of incursion by barbarian invasion, and the dangers of misadministration, corruption and chaotic use of power and authority in separate corners of the empire, so his energies went into creating links and connections, to strengthen the body of the empire as a whole. As part of his task he organised afresh the imperial bureaucracy, placing men of the equestrian order in high posts formerly held by freedmen. He codified the Praetor's Edict and made it the fixed law of the whole empire. He spent many tireless years travelling all the provinces, visiting amongst others Britain, where he built the famous Hadrian's Wall, from the Solway Firth to the mouth of the Tyne. This work, continued by others later, effectively ensured the survival of the Roman Empire for a further three centuries (Harvey 1937; Boardman, Griffin and Murray 1986).

What I am hoping to bring out in this historical analogy is the importance that Trajan conferred on Hadrian by his adoption. It meant a major increase in Hadrian's status during Trajan's lifetime and, after his death, his succession as Emperor. Hadrian accepted the privilege of his adoption by Trajan, and lived up to his early promise by identifying with and devoting himself tirelessly to his 'adoptive role'. Interestingly in relation to my argument about thinking and cohesion in the adoptive family (see below), he made the empire more safe and internally coherent, and promoted long-term effective good government.

Contrast this view from ancient Roman culture with a more modern view of the child who does not belong and is not wanted in Ibsen's *Little Eyolf* (1894). Halfway through act one, Eyolf, aged 9, wishing to overcome his personal defect (lameness) and become a soldier, and aware of the sterility of his parents' marriage, his father's depression and his parents' forgetful indifference to him, slips out to the garden. By the end of act one he has been seen drowned, lying on his back with his eyes open staring upwards, his crutch floating on the water, before he is swept away by the 'undercurrent' deep in the fjord. The awful truth dawns on the parents about the undercurrent of their family life, their marital difficulties, and in particular the father's failure to be a father. He has been emotionally withdrawn and falsely preoccupied getting nowhere writing his life's work – a book ironically called 'The Responsibility of Man'. In real terms, failing to act, the parents have neglected their son, whose death, a second accident, like the one that crippled him, occurred in the midst of their indifference. Eyolf left the home after the Ratwife left, and his following her is deeply symbolic of his being got rid of like the loathsome rats, who follow the Ratwife to be drowned in the fjord. The rest of the play painfully unravels the complicated reasons for their failure and neglect, including the father's near incestuous connection to his 'sister' Asta, confusions of identity between her and Eyolf, 'big' Eyolf and the poor substitute 'little' Eyolf, the hate and disowning of the child as 'only half mine', the blaming of the child for their problems – 'the evil that lies in the child's eye'. The forgetting of Eyolf is just one sign of their failure to address and find the meaning of their relationships – 'I forgot him completely', 'He slipped right out of my mind. Out of my thoughts.'

ALLMERS: . . . our child never really belonged to us.
RITA: No. We never loved him.
ALLMERS   [*quietly*]: The crutch. . . . While he lived, our cowardly, furtive
           consciences would not let us love him because we could not bear
           to look at the – thing that he carried – . . .

                                    (Ibsen, *Little Eyolf*, trans. 1968: 264–5)

And yet, powerfully, it is the crutch that is left floating on the surface of the
water after Eyolf drowns. Eyolf has a physical handicap, but he is experienced as emotionally handicapped – much as the adopted child may be
seen. The family is experienced as incomplete, and there is a pattern of
inadequate emotional relationships.

The philosophical ideas of the Enlightenment

Our modern philosophical understanding of the place of adoption in the
family and in society is tied up with issues about needs and wants. The child
who is abandoned or given up by his/her parents needs a substitute family.
Parents who have not been able to have a child of their own, whether
through infertility or some other cause that prevents the satisfaction of their
perceived needs as individuals or as a couple, want to take on a child to be
their own. Society, which sees itself responsible for looking after abandoned
or unfortunate children, needs a social provision that can best secure the
future development of children. The child without a family wants a family
like other children around have. A voluntary contract, the adoption, gives
the child a permanent place within a new family.

   This view of needs and wants, and of a voluntary legal contract, stems
from the philosophy of the Enlightenment, from Rousseau, Hobbes and
Locke, which sees rightful political authority to lie in a society whose
citizens agree upon a structure of needs and wants, where authority, and
sovereignty rests upon the agreed will of the people (Locke), and where the
agreement which underlies the structure of satisfaction of agreed needs and
wants is formulated in a social contract (Rousseau). No longer adequate
are a God-given right or an hereditary principle. The utilitarian theorists,
Bentham, Mill and Sedgewick, embedded such thinking within our social
arrangements, so that any particular social provision is deemed to be in
the interests of the people if a calculation of conflicting needs and wants
can be set up to show that the greater happiness of the greater number is
provided for.

   There are such potential conflicts of needs and wants at every level in
adoption, between the birth family and the adoptive family, between the
adoptee and the adoptive family. Up to the present, such difficulties are still
inherent in the procedures and legal provisions surrounding adoption. As
with all areas of child care law and administration in Britain the final test,

having taken into account the other parties and considerations, is the provision 'in the best interests of the child'.

There have been huge advantages that have stemmed from this modern philosophy of adoption. However, on a philosophical level there can also be serious flaws in this approach, since such calculations of needs and wants are after all not exact calculations at all. There are different and potentially conflicting human values that come into all of this, which spoil the simplicity of the calculations (cf. in particular Smart and Williams 1973 and Quinton 1973 for extensive arguments on J. S. Mill's 1863 thesis). Setting up such calculations of needs and wants on their own does not work. This utilitarian philosophy gives no guiding principle to follow in deciding issues about important basic values, e.g. honesty, integrity and procedures about establishing truth. Important values inevitably get overlooked and other important elements ignored or left out. Applied to adoption, when there are crucial elements like the relation of mother and child to consider, a sense of the adopted child's value to the family can be lost, as too can a perspective on adoption that gives the adoptive father a strong contributory role with the consequent tendency to see the role of father in the family as uninvolved or bystander.

Viewing adoption then as a calculation of needs and wants is most unsatisfactory. It lays stress on the neediness of the child, as abandoned or unwanted, or the neediness of the adoptive parents as bereft without children. It stresses mothering, fears of it or failings in it as applied to the birth mother, and the need to be or capacity for it as applied to the adoptive mother. But it neglects the father, the natural or birth father, because when it is a calculation of the child's needs he is seen as already out of the picture, having let the mother and child down. It also neglects the adoptive father because he is not deemed so central to the nurturing needs of the adoptive child.

These ideas from the Enlightenment and utilitarianism began to influence social institutions and law-making just as the first adoption laws were being introduced in western societies. In modern western civilisation an adoption law was first passed in France in the Code Napoleon, initially modelled on ancient Roman law. Other laws followed in Spain, then in the USA and Great Britain, and in them gradually there was a shift in emphasis from protection of the rights of the adoptive parents to a policy based on the supposed welfare of the child (Schechter 1967). These laws increasingly began to incorporate modern philosophical thinking about needs and wants.

The literature: defect and narcissistic disturbance

Although the adoptive father is virtually absent from the psychoanalytic literature on adoption, it includes two important relevant themes: discussions of defect and narcissistic disturbance in adoptive parents or the adoptive child, which I shall look at first, and discussions of the quality of relationship and capacity for dialogue between adoptive parents and adopted child, which I shall look at next.

For a long time the adoptive child who presented with problems was viewed as having them because of his/her adoption. The ratio of adopted to non-adopted children who presented at clinics was higher than the ratio of adopted to non-adopted children in the population. So the conclusion was drawn that adoption was a problem per se. This conclusion ignored the contributory fact that adoptive families have already had and continue to have better access to social and psychiatric agencies (Sharma *et al.* 1998). Now, we believe that no special syndrome or disturbance is associated with adoption (Blum 1983). However, there can be pathology in adoptive families, and there are inherent traumas in adoption itself that affect subsequent relationships. Also in the child's inner world, adoption may function as an organiser, a focus for various anxieties to do with feeling unloved, rejected, damaged, undervalued – all things that equally may occur in non-adopted children.

In some situations in adoptive families, problems are projected onto the adoptive child, as if he or she or their birth family are their cause. The child can be seen as coming from 'bad seed', which may refer to the abnormal sperm or eggs of the adoptive parents. The adopted child may become the black sheep of the family. This sort of aggressive and destructive phantasy can cause the irruption of difficulties and enactments at points of crisis.

All parents, and especially adoptive parents, who have a child from a different biological family have to deal with the instinctual sides of human life, and with the ambivalence of their children, at different stages of development. Unresolved instinctual conflicts in adoptive parents amplify normal developmental conflicts in the adopted child and antecedent issues of the abuse that the child may have suffered before going for adoption. Parental anxiety may lead to attempts to repress the child's expression of his/her instinctual urges and, if this fails, to reject that instinctual part and attribute it to the biological parents. A process can occur by which the 'defect' is attributed to the biological parents. This can be exacerbated by the perceived absence in adoption of the incest barrier and to the effect, real or perceived, of increased seductiveness in parent or child. Early separations and multiple placements prior to adoption, and the inherent difficulties to be experienced by the adopted child and the adoptive mother in establishing an emotional bond, cause further problems.

There is a stress in the literature on the vulnerability of the adopted child, who may view him/herself as unwanted and inevitably face a narcissistic blow. There is stress too on the adoptive parents being unable both to recognise the reality of this narcissistic blow in the child, and to come to terms with and work through the aspects of their own original difficulties that led to their adopting a child. These are in essence a narcissistic blow for the adoptive parents. This may be related to infertility, or psychosomatic conflicts affecting fertility (Landerholm 2001). Resultant confusions occur about issues of potency, self-worth and identity, sexual conflicts, guilt, etc., or 'injured family narcissism' – a concept used to describe a family which cannot accept its adoption of a child, because in not producing a child biologically the family cannot idealise itself (Blum 1983).

Compensatory phantasies can pathologically safeguard injured narcissism, in adoptive parents or the adoptive child. The latency boy whose psychotherapy Sherick (1983) describes had very ambivalent feelings about his adoptive father, and in the transference his analyst, as adoptive father, was treated as a 'dogcatcher'. When there was a shift away from the ambivalently cathected easily provoked adoptive father, as the analysis dealt with his masturbation, competitive wishes and castration anxiety, the boy began to see how his narcissistic compensatory defences were used against his sense of vulnerability. Now in the transference the analyst, as adoptive father, was seen as the 'coach' who could help the boy achieve his wish for praise and recognition, albeit for a while on a grandiose scale.

Many papers on adoption deal with the family romance fantasies (the wish for 'a better or happier family' in place of one's own family), which Freud (1909b) wrote about. Burlingham (1952) and Anna Freud (1965) have commented on family romances as being ubiquitous during the latency years, in which the latency child has to deal with the disappointment of the preceding Oedipal stage. Typically, in the phantasy of natural children the biological parents are denigrated and the wished for parents are idealised. For adopted children matters are less straightforward. For the adopted child, the issue of his or her discovery of and knowledge about their adoptive status, including when and what they know about their birth parents is crucial. Children react differently and idiosyncratically to the knowledge of adoption, but it comes to be associated with some defect or stain. In latency or younger children the apparent lack of interest can belie the inner existence of intense curiosity and speculation. The full impact may not be felt until later, at school or in adolescence with the emergence of new or different instinctual sexuality, individualised aggression, and issues about identity, especially personal identity. There are a number of different transformations throughout the life cycle, and at these times the adopted child may need special attention or help from the adoptive parents, and there is a particular and ongoing role for the adoptive father (Smith and Howard 1999).

The quality of relationships and dialogue in the adoptive family

The more recent psychoanalytic literature on adoption sees the quality of relationships and dialogue in adoptive families as crucial and of foremost importance for the success of adoptions. Anna Freud in her study of adoption crucially links:

- the need for *affection*, for the unfolding and centring of the infant's own feelings,
- the need for *stimulation*, to elicit inherent functions and potentialities, and with,
- the need for *unbroken continuity*, to prevent damage done to the personality by the loss of function and destruction of capacities that follow invariably on the emotional upheavals brought about by separation by death or disappearance of the child from his first love objects.

(Yale Law School seminar, quoted in Schecter 1967)

Yet it is very difficult for adopted children and adoptive parents to talk about adoption, and rather as with theories about sex and childbirth, children arrive at their own version of events (Hodges *et al.* 1984). They do not publicly disclose their thoughts about such matters, or at least not in any elaborated way. Several surveys of adult adoptees reveal a wish on their part to have known more about their origins (e.g. Jaffe and Fanshel 1970; Triseliotis 1973; McWhinnie 1976; ABAFA 1980). Most studies indicate how a circle of silence is set up by the reluctance of parent and child to raise the question of adoption.

The most commonly cited etiological factors in adoption-related disturbances are the child's learning about his/her adoption and the adoptive parents' ambivalence (Frankel 1991). After that the important factors are the quality of the disturbing anxiety in the adopted child and their sense of the level of investment in them by the adoptive parents. Learning about adoption is itself a kind of mourning process in which the child progressively modifies his conviction that he unequivocally belongs to his/her adoptive parents (Brinich 1980). All adopted children have to negotiate this and those who succeed do so by engaging in a finely tuned cooperative effort with their adoptive parents. Nickman (1985: 365) sets a different tone from that in most psychoanalytic studies in his opening sentence: 'Adoption is acknowledged as a vitally important institution in our society.' He refers to studies such as Hodges *et al.* (1984), which highlight the issue of non-communication, including passing over what the child thinks, causing resentment towards the adoptive parents (Triseliotis 1973; McWhinnie 1976; Raynor 1980). Most of the literature is still about loss and problems of bonding.

But Nickman (1985) has highlighted that little has been written on the topic of parent–child dialogues, about their meaning and feelings at any point in time about adoption, in the school years and later. Yet a child's understanding of adoption does not grow by gradual accretion beginning in the earliest years; rather, children commonly display an apparent early acceptance and understanding of the situation. This 'understanding' shifts between 6 and 8 years of age to a more complex attitude characterised by worry and questioning, in accordance with the cognitive growth which has occurred in the intervening years. Adoptive parents often make the mistaken assumption that 'telling' automatically leads to 'understanding' on the part of the child (Brodzinsky *et al.* 1990).

Natural children in a family can also suffer from the same failures of dialogue (Jacobs 1988). Jacobs describes the impact on a natural sibling of his having three adopted siblings, how he tended to play down any differences, and how his phantasies about adoption reduced his confidence in the truthfulness and reliability of his parents. Nickman argues that the major intervention, which can help an adopted child grieve for these various losses, is dialogue and discourse about adoption. It should begin at an appropriate age and continue intermittently throughout the various stages of development. Parents who cannot 'connect' with their children about adoption, in particular those who deny difference, fail to help in important ways and thereby add another dimension of loss to the child's experience. The dialogue should be ongoing in an open communicative atmosphere, and not terminated at some arbitrary point when parents, uncomfortable with the subject, decide that their job is done. In addition some adopted children and the adoptive parents can be helped by appropriate psychotherapy (Nickman and Lewis 1995; Bertram 2003; Canham 2003; plus see clinical examples below).

A new psychoanalytic view of the adoptive father

To reiterate from above then, I believe that the adoptive father has a key role in the development of the adopted child:

1   *He supports the nurturing of the adoptive mother*, which focuses around the physical and emotional developing needs of the adopted child.
2   *He actively creates meaningful links for the family*, for the child and the adoptive mother, about their relationship, his part in it and with other members of the adoptive family.
3   *He actively creates meaningful links for the adoptive child about his/her personal history*, including about his/her adoption and the connections to the natural parents.

Underpinning my view of the role of the adoptive father are Bion's view of the intrapsychic functions of linking (1959), his theory of containment (1962b), and Britton's (1989) view of the linking function of the father, in relation to the primitive formation of the Oedipus complex.

Bion describes how powerful and destructive early processes of projective identification can be employed by the psyche to attack objects that serve as a link. I believe that the early broken links in attachment for the adoptive child can at times reach this level of primitive fragmentation, and that there can be an interplay between developmental issues, external events including the fact of adoption, and primitive intrapsychic processes. Britton, like Bion, argues that if 'the third position' is not possible (i.e. for the child to be able to think about a relationship with both parents, as a couple), then for the child to 'bring his parental objects together in his mind would be result in explosion and disintegration' (Britton 1989: 97). For adopted children this is crucial, as sooner or later they attempt to bring together in their minds a sense of themselves, their knowledge of their natural parents and their adoptive parents. For there are two or more sets of parents and actual fragmented relationships to integrate, making the possibility of an 'explosion' or 'disintegration' in the mind of the adopted child more likely and progression to a thoughtful, more depressive, position harder.

The role of the adoptive father in creating links to assist the adoptive child has to happen at every level. The adoptive mother concentrates on creating a bond and seeing to the nurturing needs of the adoptive child. In the course of this nurturing process, the father should have the task of being a third object, providing at times a different way of thinking, which becomes a boundary to limit the intensity of contact between mother and child. He has to facilitate a period of 'primary maternal preoccupation', in Winnicott's terms (1956). He has to protect the mother by realistic observation and intervention. He has to foster the processes of bonding and attachment of mother and child, otherwise attachment problems will arise within the new relationship for adoptive child and parents alike.

At another level the adoptive father is in a special position to keep some continuous focus upon the adoptive child's connection to the natural family. His task is to handle a dialogue with the adoptive child at appropriate points in the child's development, to create a necessary space for the adoptive child so as to sustain links to the natural family, in thinking or in reality. It is important that the adoptive father can deal with his own envy of the adoptive mother's special position with the child and with his own narcissistic hurt since this child is not his natural child. Like all fathers, he needs to resist the wish to intrude between mother and child, and at times, when nurturing and bonding issues are foremost, to wait to fulfil his own role. His knowledge of his own narcissistic hurt may enable him to be in touch with that of the adoptive child. Something needs to be continuous and emotionally alive between the adoptive father and the adoptive child, and indeed with the adoptive mother and the rest of the adoptive family, so that a kind of emotional deadness does not proliferate, which can lead to the formation of what Quinodoz calls a 'hole-object' inside the adoptive child.

Danielle Quinodoz's paper (1996), 'An Adopted Analysand's Transference of a "Hole-Object"', looks at how an adopted person experienced a 'hole-object', in respect of what was missing in her experience of life about her adoption. Her analyst became aware of this unknown element of experience through awareness of her countertransference, and an appreciation of the true nature of the patient's transference. Similarly, with regard to the adoptive family my view is that the adoptive father needs to work in relation to the adopted child to know not just what may be known by the child and experienced by him, but also what may *not* be known and the child's reactions and experience of that. Some have recognised that this task in adoptive parents in some ways resembles the task of knowing and understanding like in psychotherapy (Noy-Sharav 2002).

Quinodoz's more recent paper (1999a) looks further at these issues. She draws attention to the obscurity of Oedipus's adoptive parents, Polybus and Merope, rulers of Corinth. Oedipus loved his adoptive parents and missed them but, importantly, he did not know they were *not* his natural parents. Quinodoz found, in analysis of adopted and non-adopted patients, that there can be psychically both natural and adoptive parents, but a failure to work through affective relations to each can bring a severe conflict of ambivalence. Elsewhere, Quinodoz (1999b) notes that this doubling of the parental imago goes hand in hand with a doubling of affects. Quinodoz sees three possible consequences of ambivalence:

- affects of love and hate are *fused*;
- the adoptive child might *link them while distinguishing them*,
- the adoptive child might *distinguish the affects but not yet be capable of linking them*.

(Quinodoz's italics)

This third occurrence can bring severe consequences such as vertigo, accidents or suicide, which Quinodoz sees as a failure of 'dichotomisation' (French: *dedoublement*), that is, of separating out psychically natural parents and adoptive parents.

My view is that there also is a *fourth type* of conflict, which is pre-ambivalent and originates out of more primitive processes of splitting (as described by Klein 1946): where *there is a not knowing, or additionally in Bion's terms a –K (minus K), or a confusion and disintegrative diffusion of affects, and an inability to link* natural and adoptive parents.

The adoptive father will need to help the adoptive child with the task of making sense of these deepest confusions.

Case illustrations

I shall now look at the linking role of the adoptive father in my psychoanalytic work with two adopted children and their adoptive parents.

Although I shall give two clinical examples of boys below, my argument here is not gender specific and applies to both adopted boys and girls. In my first illustration, the adoptive father was a white professional man who with his wife adopted two black children, Andrew and Virginia, into their family. I saw Andrew for twice-weekly psychotherapy for seven years, from the age of 9 until the age of 16, and had regular meetings with his adoptive parents throughout this time.

In psychotherapy, at home and at school, Andrew had shown an early false compliance, which hid severe early neglect and deprivation. There was a known about but unknown and off the scene black natural father, and a white natural mother who now was elsewhere. (For 'transracial adoptions' see Derdeyn and Graves 1998; Goldstein and Goldstein 1998.) The consistency of the adoptive mother's usual capacity for caring for Andrew was sometimes interrupted at times when there were intense problems, when she could become somewhat abrupt and harsh with him. This was perhaps because of unworked through issues about childlessness. There was a double difficulty for the adoptive father in that he felt a sense of not being accepted in his own family, having himself as a child for a time been fostered nearby but separately from the family of his natural father. In a sense the adoptive father experienced being excluded and *not* being adopted himself.

It was a long and difficult psychotherapy. What came through in my work, both with the boy and his adoptive parents, was that the adoptive father, despite his natural personal warmth and intellectual ability, continuously struggled to think and help his adoptive son and his wife to think and, in particular during times of crisis, to make meaningful emotional links about the boy's experience, especially about the changing emotional impact of his adoption.

At 9 years old, Andrew was an atypical latency child, more verbally able than most, but at first without a capacity to use the toys available to play. He was described as intelligent, witty and personable, but he had a distressingly depressive view of himself: 'I'm rubbish', 'I belong in a bin'. He had suffered considerable trauma and was referred because of rages at home and at school. He was haunted by fears of insects, killer bees and tarantulas, and of many ordinary situations, and by beliefs about his underlying destructiveness, encapsulated in a story from his family of origin, whereby he saw himself as responsible for a fire in the family house before he was taken into care. This reportedly had happened when he was three and he was adopted at five.

His adoptive father described something that showed how Andrew himself broke the links that could make sense of his experience. He described Andrew's 'ability to cocoon himself from past events in his life both recent and distant, and refuse to discuss them at all, as if they had no impact upon him'. This persisted to a smaller or greater extent throughout the time I saw Andrew, even as he also actively sought to find out information and understand what had happened to him. There was an ongoing conflict at a primitive level and, in a contradictory way, of continuously linking and unlinking his experiences. His younger sister, Virginia, with whom he was adopted, was highly disturbed at first, but thereafter was more secure than Andrew, despite some difficulties at times.

In some ways the adoptive father and mother could make links that helped Andrew make sense of his past, in particular his feelings about the children's home he had been in, his normality as an adopted child with other children locally who were not adopted, and 'minor' incidents of racial abuse, his feelings about his natural mother, and his natural sister adopted elsewhere. However, conflicts could erupt from misunderstanding and intolerance, and incidents between Andrew and his adoptive parents could all too readily assume a concreteness that seemed to make thinking impossible, and frequently resulted in violent disruptions of family life. At such times the adoptive father and mother increasingly saw Andrew as 'strange' and were hopeless about their ability to care for him. They then became dependent on me for out-of-hours thinking and support in such a way that I became a surrogate for the adoptive father. There were particular problems, about Andrew's feelings about his natural father and when the adoptive mother had an hysterectomy, which created special difficulties for the adoptive father.

Nine months into treatment Andrew could express his anger at my attempts to think and make links with him. He wrote to me after a disturbing outburst before and during the previous session: 'I felt very angry on Friday. It all started when we got there. I felt angry that this man was spoiling my week for me and taking out my feelings from the boxes that are arranged in shelves inside me.' He enclosed a poem:

Mr Flynn

He makes me mad when I feel bad,
I think it's Friday time to die,
but why does this man say to me,
Now what happened on that day?
I feel I could say bug off go away,
and he'd say,
Can you tell me something about,
the ruddy week?
I think what a cheek,
I'd tear down all the houses
if I could get away, and
not hear him say now,
what happened on that day?

This trait in Andrew of wishing to withdraw completely into himself remained, although he slowly learned to open up more. Two years later when he broke his arm, he told me with irritation how he was sick of the children at school (and me in the session) asking him about it. He wished he just had a notice to say he had broken his arm. Yet such things as a broken arm, which gave others the opportunity to initiate and create contact, temporarily opened Andrew up more. The day after his plaster came off and he was less noticeable, Andrew told me that his teacher had said his face mask had gone on again.

As he made progress in the psychotherapy he could be very in touch with me, secure and confiding, aware he could have a favourite place, like the place in the picture on my wall that he took to be my favourite place. He could talk about racist taunts at school, him being called 'pooface'. I thought and interpreted he could think about differences and, importantly when Andrew brought it up, about his natural mother and his origins. Some of the time he could glorify his own phallic rivalry and competitiveness. Once he heard children in the background and he was wistful. I asked him what he felt. Andrew said he wondered if 'he was like that'. As he explained, I understood him to mean, 'as a child who would cry out and may not be heard or responded to'. The issue of being heard was a very alive one for him. Andrew now confided that he had eaten cornflake packets sometimes as a child (because of hunger and not being heard).

His adoptive mother's forthcoming hysterectomy brought out anxiety and fear in Andrew. In the transference he tried to ensconce himself in the room and the house, like trying to get back into the womb, but his puzzled and confused feeling was how could he as a black boy get back into a white womb. It seemed hard to remember that Andrew's natural mother was in fact white. He also wanted to have a white father, like his adoptive father and me. When he was able to talk about his hurt, such as when he was upset when he had a tooth-break and pierced his brace, he did so in an open and more direct way. He spoke about his dad having nervous problems from bottling up his feelings about his family. He thought that his adoptive mother and father did not want him to contact his first mother and father. He talked about how what happened to him was his first father's fault. He searched for and got more information about his past, but felt overwhelmed by the information he received from the children's home. As he was more expansive with me, and trusted me as the adoptive father in the transference to help him make the links, his guilt lessened about his own part in events and he became more confident and imaginative in his play, discussion and associations.

However when his anxieties about his mother's hysterectomy increased and his parents cancelled or changed around some sessions with me, he became increasingly alarmed. This tended to bring out a kind of compulsive materialism in him, which had a wearing down effect on his parents: wanting this bike, that pair of trainers, another fishing rod, and so on, as if he had regressed to a non-parental, pre-care anarchic state. I found that as the adoptive mother herself became more preoccupied with her health and with herself, the adoptive couple could not contain Andrew's increasing distress together. The adoptive father became literally dependent on every aspect of my thinking, rather than continuing his own attempts to keep talking to Andrew and helping him through the crisis. In many ways I had been like the adoptive father to Andrew, making links and establishing emotional connections, which until now had paralleled what he, the adoptive father, had been doing and trying to do.

We all struggled on for another two years after this before Andrew's actions again involved a wider range of services such as psychiatry, the police and social services. His psychotherapy ended at this time. This seemed to mark the temporary breakdown of the adoptive family as a unit to contain the problems and the substitution of a wider more institutional non-personal framework around Andrew. It was a repetition of the breakdown in his natural family, when he went into institutional care.

In my second clinical illustration I shall describe a different outcome despite the odds against it. This is a child, Brian, who suffered not just deprivation and emotional abuse but also severe physical abuse in early infancy. On being adopted, and for some years afterwards, his behaviour was severely disturbed, getting him expelled from school and taxing everyone's capacities, especially his adoptive parents' and his psychotherapist's, to the limits. I saw this boy mainly twice weekly for five years, between the ages of 5 and 10, and met his parents periodically at two to three monthly intervals. I found in the psychotherapy that again and again I became the abusing natural father in the transference, or the weak and distancing mother, reflecting aspects of both his natural and adoptive mother as his work in psychotherapy differentiated each of these more. His natural mother had been complicit and collusive with her abusing partner and locked in a narcissistic trap of contemplation of her own beauty, which her son had inherited. His adoptive mother could become bewildered and fogged out in response to this child's very disturbed behaviour, but a determined and strongly loving inner self, with support from her husband and good communication between them, meant that he steadily improved. All this happened despite the adoptive mother developing and being treated for a major cancer, which hospitalised her at times. The adoptive father gently questioned whether his adopted son was being affected by the past or by the present. He talked to and guided his son, whose improvement meant an inner change and a capacity to think and feel, with considerably more self-control, which represented an internal capacity to link together fragmented aspects of his past and present experience.

The adoption had happened very quickly, and the adoptive family only had three days' notice before placement of Brian at 18 months. Brian's adoptive father felt Brian looked odd with his big lips and thought he would never be able to love him. They felt Brian attached to them too easily, shallowly or adhesively. His adoptive mother returned to full-time work six months after his placement. Brian did not talk until he was 3 years old. Despite the adoptive father's initial response to Brian, and I think perhaps because he reacted to looks, and something about his seductiveness and narcissistic processes and conflicts, he in time became more tolerant than his wife and more aware of Brian's inner anxieties.

In psychotherapy with Brian, contradictory harsh and affectionate interchanges alternated with baffling rapidity, reflecting his internal state and the confused and abusive treatment he had received. A recurring theme in his play was the rhino versus the crocodile, in which the crocodile (me) was pushed, mauled and crushed. He got under my skin, pierced my tough professional (crocodile) hide, and provoked near-abusive anger and retaliation from me, and guilt in me about holding him too tightly when he hit me or tried to touch me seductively. At such fraught times Brian could not accept any reasonable boundaries of conduct. We each struggled with the guilt of what happened. All of this occurred in the adoptive family too.

One session he brought a brightly coloured umbrella, using it to fly 'as free as a bird'. He hurt his finger and wanted (inappropriately) a cuddle from me. Then he found a large roll of sellotape, and put it in his pocket wanting to keep it. There were tears of severe hurt as he was not allowed to. Eventually I decided to allow him to keep it, so that we could talk about it, which we did. He told me there were frogs in the pool at school and so it was closed. His dad had got rid of a frog in a pool. Much of what he said was confused and puzzling. I interpreted that I thought he felt not wanted here, and at home sometimes, and saw himself like the frog intruder that his adoptive father and I tried to keep out.

Such understandings of his deep sense of hurt at rejection and abuse helped him make sense of why he found himself feeling and acting as he did, and to bring it under more control. Brian could then talk about his natural mother, his memories of her, and say he did not understand why she did not love him. Later too, as this was worked over and over again in the psychotherapy, with immense strain both inside and at home, he could differentiate me and his adoptive father from the abusing natural father. Brian told me of his first dad leaving when he was one, because he needed someone to look after Brian. It all sounded rational and sad, some of it borrowed from information from records that Brian knew. Much of this work his adoptive father did in his caring personal contacts with Brian, in a way that paralleled and fitted with the work of the psychotherapy, so that Brian now improved and settled down at home and at school.

Conclusion

I have outlined in this chapter how the adoptive father has a distinctive role to help provide a thinking space about adoption, which includes thinking about issues to do with adoption throughout the development of the adoptive child, in a way that gives the adoptive child an experience of consistency and continuity. It allows the child to bring together complex areas of their experience, about their natural family and their adoptive family, and it enables them to view their natural and adoptive parents separately and, in a singular way, to view themselves and their adoptive status in a full and positive light. When problems arise in adoptions there can be a feeling, whether in a therapeutic situation or in the family, that 'nothing makes any sense'. Important links cannot be made and instead there is a 'hole-object' in Quinodoz's sense.

As in my first case example, violent enactments by the adopted child against the adoptive parents can have many levels. They may be rooted in previously fragmented Oedipal relationships that cannot be recognised, especially by the adoptive father, who can feel deskilled and out of role, leaving the adoptive mother and the family exposed. Conversely, the anger that meets the adoptive child's outbursts can have a vengeful quality, showing the adoptive parents' own problems and disappointments. They may want revenge on the natural parents and, at a deeper level, on the Oedipal couple, thereby creating more destructive confusion. The adoptive father can feel deskilled and there can be a carry over of negativism towards the natural father onto him, as having no real place or role. Such attacks on the Oedipal couple weaken the possibility of acquiring more meaning in the adoptive family and the adopted child's intrapsychic functioning.

For the adopted child to grow psychically in the new adopted family, the family has to communicate to the child his/her value and real place within the family, and communicate the real value of the family to the child. The stress should not be upon the neediness of the adopted child or of the adopted parents or family, though the deeper consequences of these needs, especially unmet needs, have to be remembered. The growth in status for the adopted child in the adoptive family is not necessarily or simply social, intellectual or material. It centrally includes emotional sharing and understanding, and involves the ongoing work of developing a capacity to help the adopted child to know their psychic reality, including the fact of adoption and its consequences.

Viewing the adoption as a positive increase in status for the adoptive child and the adoptive parents, and a status that involves an enriched capacity for emotional understanding, is what is important (Auestad 1992). The standing of adoption and the position and role the adoptive father takes are crucial. The adoptive father has an active role to make meaningful links for the adoptive child and the rest of the adoptive family, and also a symbolic function to represent the value and status of the family to the adoptive child – in essence of an intact Oedipal couple – and thereby to allow for the consistent growth of meaning in the child's mind.

Part 3

The Adolescent

Chapter 9

A group for adolescent inpatients with spina bifida

Introduction

This chapter describes an adolescent group on a surgical ward in a children's hospital and its dynamic functioning over a period of four years. I shall discuss some of the group and institutional processes, the relationships between the staff, and the concerns and preoccupations of the adolescents who participated in the group. I shall touch on their thoughts and feelings about their treatment, their prospects for health, and their fears of pain and death. Adolescents express much of their social and psychic life in groups, rather than the family, so the therapeutic group is a setting that is appropriate for a first approach to understanding the life of adolescents. I shall then go on to a general psychoanalytic description of adolescence in the next chapter. The specific principles of adolescent group work are extensively examined by Evans (1998), who traces links with the work of the major group theorists Foulkes (1948, 1986) and Bion (1961), as modified by Ezriel (1950, 1952) and Sutherland (1952, 1965).

In group work specific attention must be given to the particular needs and problems of adolescents when creating the group setting, defining the group's purpose and exercising the limits and boundaries. Attention is also given to accepting the adolescents' need for free association, personal expression, play and work, and taking seriously, indeed valuing, the adolescent's own contributions. My own theoretical approach follows Bion (1961) and, as with any psychoanalytic model, in the psychoanalytic adolescent group, the aim is not just to develop adolescents' experience of life in the group, but to use interpretations of deeper levels of unconscious forces to enhance the group, thereby recognising it as a real life force for self-expression, and at times preventing it from 'deteriorating into non-therapeutic chaos' (Evans 1998: 6, 162).

In an adolescent group it is appropriate that there is an accessible, involved and caring rather than remote style of leadership. Many adolescents who come to therapeutic groups have been abused or deprived, and have a history of struggling for survival with life's difficulties without adequate parental support (Evans 1998). Contacts with new adults, as group leaders, provide the adolescent with new intermediate understanding models of adults, as well as objects for transference of deeper aspects of relationships.

The group setting

The group I describe took place on an eight-bedded adolescent surgical ward where the patients were mainly severely disabled adolescents, with conditions such as spina bifida, hydrocephalus and nephrotic syndrome. There were also some teenagers with primary enuresis and encopresis, a number with complex orthopaedic problems who were less disabled, some general accident and emergency cases, a number for specialist dental care, and later on occasionally a few psychiatric admissions usually with eating problems. The age range was from 13 to 18 years, though many of the spina bifida patients were older, some as old as 23. The ward was served by a number of consultants to cover the different specialisms involved. There was a ward sister, three or four qualified nurses, and a large turnover of nurses in training and junior medical staff. A number of other professional and ancillary staff had contact with the ward. The ward had a diffuse set of systems of responsibility and power, and generally it fell to the ward sister to provide some cohesion.

A weekly group for patients had been started three years before by the consultant child psychiatrist in response to increasing demand from ward staff for emotional help (not necessarily psychiatric intervention) for adolescents on the ward. It was initially formed as a response to the presented multivariety of individual patient's needs. This early group had been led by a child psychiatrist and a teacher, and the aim was to encourage the patients to express their feelings in the group and appreciate together common concerns. Over time new staff extended the aim to include offering patients help to gain more psychological understanding of their medical conditions. When I was asked to take over the group it was as a complex going concern. I would work with the teacher who had worked with the previous child psychiatrist and had been there all along.

When we took over we developed the structure of the ward group. It met weekly at a specified early afternoon time and lasted an hour. We spent about three-quarters of an hour before this on the ward, getting an update on patients from the staff and talking to the patients and their parents about the group. After the group we would spend another half an hour talking with the staff involved in the group about the themes that day.

The membership of the group was open and its composition depended on the patients there that particular week. This was quite variable: it could be a predominantly older group, or conversely predominantly younger, with more or less disabled patients, or more or fewer very short term patients.

Usually, however, there were spells of several weeks when there would be a largely stable group on the ward, with just a few short-stay patients coming through.

We sometimes had the group in the small dayroom but more usually on the ward itself, straddled in a circle of chairs and wheelchairs across the room between the beds of those patients who were confined to bed. The patients had the choice whether to attend or not. Some exercised this choice, even those confined to bed or acutely ill, but others complied or felt they had no choice. All issues about the running of the group, in particular the very question about how much choice they had to attend the group, could be brought into the discussion within the group. We asked parents and visitors to leave the patients free for the group hour and to remain outside the ward during the group. Exceptionally some medical interventions could not wait. For certain periods a nurse was present as a staff member and co-leader of the group, and could see to minor adjustments and procedures.

Generally we took a determined stance to protect the boundaries of the group for the hour that it ran. We talked to each patient beforehand about the group, saying that it was a setting in which they could talk about matters of interest or concern to them individually or as a group, and it was confidential. We tried to refrain from explanations that might pre-empt their experience of the group itself. Exceptionally we gave simplified initial explanations to a few severely mentally disabled patients and to those who were just admitted that day.

Adolescent spina bifida patients

Usually at least half the group members were patients with spina bifida, which is a genetic condition caused by a malformation and exposure of the spine that seriously affects motor control and bodily functions. Sufferers are liable to a range of disabilities that can vary in seriousness. Some are mobile and can live relatively normal lives, but for others paralysis can be almost total with double incontinence. Many sufferers are confined to wheelchairs at adolescence even if they were walking as children. An additional complication is hydrocephalus, where spinal fluid is unable to drain off and gathers in the brain, causing enlargement of the skull, impairment to intellectual functioning or brain damage. This can be corrected by a Spitz-Holter (or similar) valve that drains the fluid from the brain. A frequent problem for adolescents is that the valve needs lengthening because they are growing, or the valve becomes blocked causing immense pain and requiring immediate corrective surgery. Patients need a wide range of interventions – orthopaedic, renal, colostomy, treatment of sores, and for depression. Many interventions impose a continuous suffering on the adolescent and a massive effort of adjustment to do with issues of personal survival and change in the direction of independence. There are often setbacks and difficulties in diagnosis, treatments sometimes do not succeed or are only partially successful, and some individuals suffer continuously for long periods of time.

There probably will not be another whole generation of young people in the UK with spina bifida with the advent of amniocentesis and legalised abortion. There is no generation of older adults who can serve as role models from whose experience the young can learn, for until the development of the Spitz-Holter valve (in the 1950s and early 1960s) most babies with spina bifida died (Tew *et al*. 1985). Survival is now more possible, but the prognosis of reaching adulthood and an adult style of life, through years of treatment, is for many quite uncertain. The core of spina bifida patients is a beleaguered group, exposed in many senses to an often unfathomable level of personal feelings and pressures. This sense of being beleaguered added doubly to their difficulties as adolescents.

These and other patients on the ward also had little opportunity for privacy, both because of the physical structure of the surroundings (no cubicles) and the non-stop presence of visiting parents. Sometimes by trying to give non-stop care and attention to their adolescent son or daughter the parents could be enacting in their care of the adolescent a form of self-denial and retribution for having created a disabled child (Dorner and Atwell 1985). The arrested development of the parent, usually the mother, complicates the arrested development of the adolescent. Many parents do not leave their adolescent even in hospital and daily sit out the time on the ward. Sometimes the situation is dire. The mother who is still changing the nappy of a 20-year-old son would have difficulty in accepting him as a grown man. The wishes, habits and lifestyles of this close-knit mother–adolescent entity could become inextricably bound (Kazak and Clark 1987).

Illness dominated every aspect of their lives and their sense of self. Such adolescents could view illness as retaliation against striving for independence, making it extremely difficult for nurses and parents to get the balance of care right (Judd 1989). The disability could be used, by themselves or others, as a handicap and a defence against further emotional experience (Sinason 1988). At a fundamental level of mental and emotional development there could be a lack of normal development of the psyche-soma. Some studies suggest that there is little difference at a cognitive level in the body schema of the spina bifida and the non-disabled child (Robinson *et al*. 1986). But if the infant with spina bifida has a distorted view of its bodily processes, then psychological processes of projection and introjection are affected, so that good and bad objects are not differentiated, an adequate capacity for symbolisation is not developed, and events will be experienced through concrete thinking rather than symbolic thinking (Judd 1990). This further prolongs a state of malignant parasitic dependence on parental figures.

Some severely disabled patients, when faced with a testing or anxious situation and expected to express even simple personal feelings, could resort to methods of mechanical control of their behaviour and emotions. Sometimes all that one had to go on, to understand or make contact as they sat passively with intense near psychotic levels of anxiety, would be a kind of surreal play with a watch or calculator in a distracted way. Bland noises and obsequious passivity could be frequently characteristic of the adolescent with severe forms of spina bifida, which were used to interrupt or totally prevent genuine emotional contact with other people.

The group experience: themes and psychodynamics

In the groups we learnt that patients had continuously to face and relive a horrifying level of anxiety about impending operations, alterations of their body image, and painful separations from family. Despair about the impossibility of personal growth and the lack of relief from pain, the frequency of medical and daily bodily care procedures that were intrusive and caused a further sense of self-degradation, and unacknowledged fears of death, affected every aspect of ward life. Some deaths occurred on the ward over the four years of the group and even within the group. Some of these patients were living daily with the fear of death, and a fear they may not survive psychically, in some degree able to think, feel and express themselves and be adjusted to reality. In such circumstances early infantile confusions about damage to the body would come into play and could activate severe psychological reactions (Rosenfeld 1964). What became apparent, from the earliest months of the group, was that such feelings had affected the patients not just individually but as a group. The group raised issues very directly and had a huge impact on the patients, but it also did something to lift the despair and facilitate a more reality orientated mentality in the culture of the ward.

The contrasts between the two distinct categories of patient – the ones undergoing routine or specific surgery and those with severe disabilities – became more apparent in the group. Some had at least average expectations of life, with reasonable prospects for education and work, intact relationships with friends and family, and the possibility of normal sexual development. Others, particularly the spina bifida group, had much shorter expectations of life, with fewer prospects for education and work beyond a highly structured remedial college education or sheltered accommodation. Often their home life had been fractured by divorce, they had few friends outside hospital and school, and there were fewer possibilities of meaningful sexual relationships (Thomas, Bax and Smyth 1987). There were of course exceptions in each category.

The short-term patients formed an interesting category in themselves, who needed the group just as much as the others. They contributed most to the adolescent culture of the ward. They could be lively, talk about their outside friends and lives, bring visitors of their own age into the ward, flirt with or have crushes on doctors and nurses, and generally brighten up the ward. Not surprisingly, however, when brought up against the immediacy of their feelings, in the context of the group, it was as much a struggle for the 'relatively healthy' group as it was for those with severe disabilities, whose fortitude and stamina in the face of fearful protracted illnesses was often truly remarkable. Differences between the groups were at first frequently expressed rather defensively or apologetically in the group. Although then it proved shocking to most people some of the time, it was evidently good medical and nursing policy that brought these separate categories together for treatment. It provided a challenge towards growth for both. The short-term patients often received solicitous care and empathy from their fellow patients with much more incapacitating conditions, although they in turn were often willing to be quite critical and challenging of the hypochondriacal and self-destructive behaviour of some of the disabled patients.

The group became a focus for a multiplicity of feelings – anger, greed, competitiveness, pity, hate, sorrow, affection, love and sexual feelings. Phantasies about the leaders were expressed such as 'What sort of a couple were the male psychotherapist and the female teacher?' 'Did you meet in a pub?' one adolescent asked us. This could lead to discussion of their own feelings and relationships in sexual matters, their thoughts about couples including about their parents, and the direction of their own friendships.

For periods we felt we could see, understand and even affect the overall dynamic processes in their life as a group on the ward. We often discussed quite ordinary adolescent issues on the ward, such as the choice of video, when bedtime should be, what levels of noise should be permitted, and how much personal privacy they should be allowed from staff. Sometimes there was a too rigid imposition of rules by the sister and nurses and at other times ward staff acquiesced out of a sense of false liberality that could lead to a confused lack of structure and at times an abandonment of parenting. The work of the group in thinking about ordinary structures and in refocusing on the deeper feelings of the patients could help to change the atmosphere on the ward and was received at times with gratitude by the patients, the staff and their parents. There were however other times when gaining any understanding was extremely difficult and there could be, for example, periods of dullness and depression or of quite manic behaviour and boundarylessness.

Some patients were extremely inhibited from expressing their feelings strongly, being too aware of the staff and their parents. Others not so inhibited stood out in sharp contrast. One 19 year old, Andrew, was angry for a number of reasons: he was not allowed to watch '18' films on the ward; his doctor had told him his operation had been a success, but he knew this was not so and he wanted help with the uncertainty. He succeeded in stirring up a considerable amount of resentment amongst the nursing staff in expressing this anger, and he created an embarrassed silence amongst the other patients. What was striking however was how effective a group member he could be. He began to be seen as someone who could put into words and express with feeling experiences that other patients preferred to ignore or deny. Attitudes in other patients changed as they began to see that there could be another side to this young man's rage. They could see that he could be angry because he felt confident and knew what he felt. It was significant that Andrew had a strong relationship with his foster parents and was one of the few young adult spina bifida patients to be living independently outside.

The following is a description of the week's group, shortly after Andrew had another serious operation. I think it shows the level of tension amongst the patients and what the group contributed to enabling an atmosphere of trust to evolve on the ward. Our interventions in the group were aimed to encourage the patients to have a better sense of their way of relating as a group. We would direct our attention to the main experience of the group, waiting for the pattern to emerge from individual thoughts, preoccupations and responses, the manner of formation of the group, plus use of individual understanding of conscious and unconscious behaviour. All the eight patients whom I shall simply denote by names beginning with the initials A–H suffered from spina bifida:

> Andrew had just had his operation. His head was shaven, he looked very small, and from the start of the group until nearly halfway through he was in considerable pain. Nurses and a doctor were attending him from time to time. But he wanted to be part of the group. He knew from last week when we sat fairly near Ben's bed that the group does include those who may be drugged and unable to listen much, but who could still in a physical and emotional sense be part of the company. Andrew therefore asked me at the beginning if we could have the group near his bed so he could hear and ask one of us to say things for him. Fairly early on Claire went over and held his hand. At various points one or other of us would hold a drink for him. In the next bed along from Andrew was Derrick, aged 14, who was severely mentally disabled and paraplegic. He lay on his bed and took no practical part in the group. At the beginning he was having physiotherapy. He seemed bewildered by the group and the staff nurse had told us that he really belonged in another ward that took younger children. The teacher gave him a few toys and a cuddly lion to hold, which seemed to comfort him. Eleanor and Helen were in beds on the opposite side of the ward. The rest of us were in a small circle in between. Eleanor said that she did not want to join the group today because she was sleepy. We

accepted this but said that she could listen from her bed and begin to join in if she wanted to later. I think she did not want to be really involved, though she did listen occasionally in between dozing. The arrangement and atmosphere of the group reflected a deep wish to make contact but with fears and reservations about how this would be possible.

For much of the time the whole group was silent. It seemed that it was incredibly difficult to know what to say while Andrew was in so much pain. I offered this as an interpretation to the group. There were now a few brief interchanges between people, but the sombre mood continued. A little later I spoke of how the group had formed this week, and how important it had felt for the group that we had formed ourselves in the way Andrew had wanted. Ben, the young man whose bed we had been around last week, wholeheartedly and with relief agreed. This was the strongest statement within the group today. Ben looked much better than last week, but was worried about Andrew, remembering his own operation and difficult recovery. Ben now talked about how he had felt alone but had appreciated the involvement of the others from the group. It was striking today, as on other occasions, that important points of emotional contact between patients were made in, indeed kept for, the group. I acknowledged that although it had been difficult to be together in the group today, it could be equally difficult at other times on the ward during the week for them to express feelings that allowed the degree of closeness they wanted. A number of people agreed and there was a deep sense of them wanting to stay together.

People now began talking with each other, but as groups of individuals, rather than generally within the group or across the group. Ben talked to Claire or to me; Fritha and Gwen to each other or to the female teacher. It seemed easier to do this, rather than address the whole group. Also people seemed to be looking for confiding alliances. Fritha and Gwen began to talk to the group about a teacher from Helen's school who had come to visit and spent a long time by her bedside. As the group continued, some visits from outside staff were necessary to Helen, who was lying on her bed. The hurried medical attention being given to Helen appeared to have an impact on the group. Glances indicated that this was recognised as serious by the other patients.

Fritha, whose disability included partial brain damage, made it clear that she was in the group today partly because she wanted to see what I, the psychotherapist, was like. She remembered the previous male leader, a child psychiatrist, and said how he panicked when someone had gone quiet in the group and had got up and rushed over to their bedside, thinking the patient had died. She said she expected me to do something equally ridiculous like that. A few titters ensued. Fritha then kept trying to get my attention, but when I looked over she would look the other way, turning her nose up. Rather than take up her ridicule and fear about the group's concern about pain and suffering, the teacher and I commented on the pattern in the group whereby each person tended to talk to just one or two others. Fritha now began to look downcast, disappointed that I had not risen to the bait in her attempt to goad me or distract the group. Some of her chatting had a quality of mockery, and she seemed to disassociate herself from the other members of the group. It felt as though she now had few defences left and her fear of death and her anxious mocking behaviour seemed closely linked here. She continued to fiddle feverishly with the stopper of her wheelchair, pulling it in and out all the time. I now talked of their hopes that they could manage with their fears about their operations and illnesses or would be left on their own and to their own devices. Fritha left off her solitary activity and joined in again into a conversation of gentle relaxed friendliness.

Claire, the girl holding Andrew's hand, was very kind to Andrew throughout the group. We felt she was now coming into her own as a person. She had previously been very isolated, distraught, bolshy and anti-authority. She contributed some thoughtful comments in the group and said she expected to be in for another two weeks. In a way she seemed to be able to stand aside from the stress she was helping to alleviate. But as she was talking she kept putting all her rings onto the strap of her watch. It looked like preconsciously she was preparing for her operation, or for death, getting her valuables all tidy in one place. In fact on this admission she had had her operation, and was recuperating well.

I have emphasised how patients increasingly began to see their experience on the ward as part of a group. I shall now give an example of how a brief spell in a changing group had an impact and a personal significance for one individual. This account takes up observations from a teacher who herself later on in the group participated for a brief period as a co-leader, and it partly also traces the teacher's own growing awareness of the group's usefulness:

Salma was a 16-year-old girl being treated for pressure sores and suffering from hydrocephalus and spina bifida. She was an inpatient for two months and attended all seven consecutive group weekly sessions during this period. She was an Arab national resident in the Middle East and arrangements had been made for her to come to the UK to attend a school, but less than a week before going there was admitted to hospital. She was excited about starting school and most disappointed by her admission. She had very little contact with her family during her stay in hospital.

Initially Salma spent the sessions sitting in bed. She was a heavy girl, and she used to sit and watch impassively. At first her sole contribution to the session was to give her name and country of origin at the beginning in response to a request, and again at the end, in response to our usual question to everyone in the group, she would say that she expected to be present the following week. The teacher felt very worried about the propriety of including Salma in the group as she spoke very little English and seemed to be an isolated observer, yet the teacher felt acutely aware of her presence. Her non-participation seemed to underline her foreignness and the teacher felt uncomfortable that Salma seemed so excluded from the group. She worried that the effect of the group might be merely to increase the difficulties of her situation.

Gradually Salma unfolded and she began participating in the discussions, first by attentive listening, then more actively. Although she had remained in bed initially, she was able to transfer to a wheelchair for the final sessions. In the discussions many of her contributions related to the cultural differences she experienced between the UK and her own country. Salma now began to speak for longer periods with more confidence and clarity. She would compete for space to talk in, interrupt other patients, ask for explanations and stop them to sort out misunderstandings – in short, she really engaged as a person. In her penultimate session Salma shared with the group the violence within her family, to her as a disabled young woman, and the inability of the males within the family, especially her father, to protect her. She had the opportunity between groups and also in the last group to think through these revelations, to see some of the effects on her development and her educational progress, and to face more knowingly her prospects on her return to school and later her native country. In effect for Salma, 'foreignness' could be seen to be not just foreignness in society, but foreignness of illness, in particular spina bifida in a young woman. Others in the group had experienced this and could relate to Salma through her experiences. She left the hospital a stronger and more confident person and in retrospect the teacher now felt the group had been really valuable for her.

At times complex themes would be reworked in different ways from week to week. An example of this was the theme of the inescapable quality of terror about immobilising illness. The antecedents to these next brief selections from successive groups were as follows. There had been a suicidal patient on the ward who had first run away with another patient from the hospital and later had attempted to jump out of the window on the ward, nearly pulling one of the nurses with her. The girl was transferred elsewhere but following her discharge the levels of excitement and tension on the ward remained. An irrational mood of excitement and manic hilarity had been growing over the week as the disturbance this girl had expressed remained largely unaddressed. The ward and the group itself were felt to be very unsafe places:

> The next group began simply enough when a girl was expressing upset that a visitor, her aunt, had left too early on a visit for her birthday. There was not much direct contact with her or response, but there was clearly an atmosphere of vulnerability. One member, a very overweight 16-year-old boy with spina bifida, who was terrified of his own illness, suddenly rolled over in a dramatic action and hid himself away covering his head and refusing to turn or take any other part within the group. This reaction typified the terror that many felt and the group became noticeably more disturbed. But as the group progressed the other members of the group were able to disengage from this flight reaction (Bion 1961). They were able to recoup their powers to think and discuss, and there ensued a long discussion about losses, feelings about illness and death, and breaks in relationships with important people. Many patients, with help from the connections we made and having been enabled to talk of deeply personal fears, could see how their anxieties and feelings about losses were similar to the fears and terrors of the suicidal girl, especially the fears of losing one's mind. This made some sense of their current mood of depression, now the atmosphere of dangerous hilarity had gone, and it helped to reduce the level of anxiety on the ward.
>
> A similar theme continued the following week, after a girl was admitted who had had heart failure and who was still very ill and close to death. The girl was not in the group but was being attended on the ward. The group was extremely tense, particularly as there were another two patients admitted following serious local road traffic accidents. One of these, a teenage boy, was extremely upset and guilty about his own responsibility in getting knocked down. The teenage girl involved in the other accident was very confused and gave accounts of her accident that were in fact copies of the account the boy had just given on his admission to hospital. It is significant that they had been involved in different accidents and had been hurt in quite separate ways, but their experiences had become elided and mixed up together, perhaps because their feelings about the accidents were re-experienced and expressed in the intense emotional setting on the ward where a number of adolescents had experienced separate traumatic events. The two patients had in fact known one another from outside, so that the external bond became a source of support to share together their different pains and trauma as if they were the same pain (Rosenfeld 1964).

In subsequent weeks the main theme of the ward group, the inescapable terror of immobilising illness, continued. In one group each patient, in a typically teenage way, began in turn to tell stories about gory events, such as people being chopped up and murdered by gangs with chainsaws. But deep underlying anxieties and phantasies had been touched and brought out in the group. The experience of having the suicidal 13-year-old girl on the ward had been like being part of an exciting but out of control gang, which had mobilised angry feelings against the staff. Intense angry feelings had been stirred within the adolescents, the 'internal gang' (Meltzer 1973; Steiner 1982). But within these group discussions something else began to take its place, namely a growing sense of fear of their own power, and with this a lessening of the manic mood, and then the emergence of a mood of depression within the group. The stories had been one way in which the adolescents could be in touch with some of the horror that underlay their fears, yet could control the horror to be outside them, keeping it in stories and videos, and not feeling oppressed by seeing it in them or as part of or dominating their lives. The wish to include accounts about chainsaws that reflected horror films then in vogue (viz. *The Texas Chainsaw Massacre*) had another level of significance. There were three orthopaedic patients on the ward who had just had metal pins or wires inserted in their limbs. In an oblique way such stories were evidence of powerful processes of splitting and projection at work within the group.

A repeated theme in groups of adolescents is a movement from manic triumph to talk of failure and even suicide or accidental death (Evans 1998: 164). Problems encountered by adolescents, and their parents and carers, often centre round anxiety about aggression. These stir up deep unconscious phantasies concerned with human aggression, and the damage done in phantasy by that aggression (Klein 1932/1975; Likierman 2001; Segal 1973, 1979). Where there is a real unconscious level of such phantasies and the real existence of damaged and dying people in beds in hospital, these phantasies can be confirmed as real (Hinshelwood and Skogstad 2000).

Our repeated experience in the group was that different types of pain, for example, of a misfitting Spitz-Holter valve, or painful injuries from a road accident, or a missed visitor or forgotten birthday present from a relative, were experienced by the group as the 'same' (Bion 1963, 1965). When however an adolescent in the group could recognise the particular nature of the pain, it enabled other patients to differentiate and try to face different types of pain. This made individual pain and experience both more real and equally more limited. Conversely, one type of upset could set off another within the group. Such fluency in the spread of feeling, what Bion called 'valency', occurred in the continuous movement between 'basic assumption groups', namely dependence, fight/flight, and pairing, whereby individuals protected themselves from primitive anxieties which would otherwise be evoked for them in the group. Such group mechanisms are typical of the earliest most uncontained phases of mental life for, as Bion reminds us, the patient's relation to the group is as precarious as the infant's relation to the breast (Bion 1961: 141–2).

In adolescence, raw feelings and the convergence of good and bad mental and physical experiences are again as in infancy more accessible for expression and change. The peer group becomes for the adolescent what the family is in infancy, namely the group within which they can learn to contain primitive feelings. One of the most central emotional experiences of adolescence is the development of heightened processes of projection and introjection within the individual (see next chapter). These processes constantly become manifest too within the adolescent group. Work with such processes is essential to the delicate balance between disturbance and growth, which is the major focus of development in adolescence. What happens to one patient, such as the suicidal girl or the girl with heart failure, can within a ward setting crystallise what everyone feels. Repeatedly our work in the group would be to help the patients to see the impact of such events upon them and to appreciate that it could and did affect all of them as a group.

Deaths on the ward

Three patients with spina bifida died on the ward over a period of nine months. Of all the issues affecting the ward group, this had the most profound and long-lasting consequences. Unlike the other wards within the children's hospital that are recognised as being places where children may be terminally ill, the adolescent ward was not prepared for death. We found that there were no structures for dealing with it except for the ward group, which in an open-structured way gave time to the patients to express emotions and feelings, and which had regular contacts with parents and staff too. We found however that although the ward group fulfilled this important task, it was never openly identified by participants or staff that this was one of its functions. It was too painful to acknowledge that adolescents did die on the ward. So the issue of death was kept relatively apart within the discrete confines of the group. Yet it could not remain so, for the ward was physically quite open, so the adolescents died as they had lived – in the middle of everything.

Mary died in August, the one month when the group did not run. When the group reopened in September the group leaders were seen as neglectful parents who had abandoned them. This paralleled and fulfilled the phantasy of the mothers on the ward, many of whom believed their sons or daughters would die if it were not for their round-the-clock attention. Mary had been a stable group member, attending regularly and quietly stating her views. Everyone was disappointed that the leaders by their absence had failed her and them. The nurses avoided us and refused to talk to us. Some of the patients refused to come to the group when it restarted. There was also a mood of depression within the group, with patients bemoaning how long they needed to be on the ward. When individuals were absent for routine reasons such as for tests, or if anyone interesting or charismatic was missing from the group, an intense mood of depression could descend. It took months for the group members to risk valuing the group again.

All of this showed the fragmentation that could occur in the group process. Separate individuals or parts of groups, through the successive weeks and months, experienced anger, sadness and grief, loss, appreciation and restitution, all distinct stages or elements in a normal mourning process, separately within the group (Parkes 1972). The task of the group was to bring together these split and fragmented elements and give some meaning to the turbulent shifts of mood experienced there, to interpret the impact of the fact of death on the group. This was done by a process of helping members of the group recognise elements of their own feelings and appreciate those being experienced by others, so that each could assimilate them as part of their own experience.

Natalie, another girl of 18, died four months later. She attended the ward group weekly for three months until her death. She knew that she was going to die and she used the group to prepare. She was thoughtful and over this time became noticeably more openly expressive and aware. Her parents were distraught and she was pleased that we could also talk to them. They were worried that we might either say falsely reassuring things to her or talk too directly about death. One nurse felt we should abandon groups and talk to people individually, saying, 'How does Natalie feel being a guinea pig?' Patients still remembered Mary in the group and were aware of what was now happening to Natalie. Not all of the patients felt able to attend these groups. The movement between ward and dayroom, where those not joining the group usually stayed, reflected the simultaneous moving towards and moving away from the dying girl.

In the last two weeks, Natalie asked if we could all sit closer together, which we did. She talked of her understanding of what had happened to her, and how the doctors could do no more to help her condition – nephrotic syndrome, with associated kidney failure. She saw the pain her parents felt and talked of her worries about them. She accepted her own death with calm matter of factness. Occasionally in the midst of these last groups she would go off into a dream state, then rejoin the discussion later on, seeming pleased to come in at whatever point we had got to without her.

When Natalie died an hour before the next week's group, we held a different kind of group, talking to patients on the ward but individually by their bedside. Again it was striking how each patient's reaction represented some incomplete aspect of the sorrow and loss. The group became a focus to talk about their feelings and reactions and from which to extend discussion to the family and the staff. We also talked to senior nursing staff and the consultants about the impact of death on the patients and the staff. For a time extra nurses were allocated to the ward to help to deal with emotional aspects of the losses through death.

Some institutional dynamics

Powerful feelings aroused in the group reverberated on the ward during the week, both openly and secretively, and the group became the object of both appreciation and hate. To provide such an object for ambivalent feelings for adolescents seemed an achievement in itself. I was aware from my own countertransference of the level of my own ambivalence about the group. Repeatedly for months as I was about to go along to the ward to prepare for the group, I was aware of a deep feeling of depression and ennui. Neither talking to staff nor patients beforehand relieved this. Only when getting started within the group itself could I face up to what I was experiencing within myself. I was aware that others, patients and staff, felt similarly, and important personal themes needed identifying and interpreting. I would take this phenomenon to be part of what Bion called the 'work group function', as the group tried to work on, adapt itself and modify itself to the struggles the patients were having on the ward (Bion 1961).

Maintaining the structure and boundaries of the group at times seemed like an end in itself, so that the work which went into that seemed almost more important than the work with the patients within the group. Whether we were able to set up and run the group on any particular day, or in the long term, seemed to depend on how well we as leaders could adapt to the complexity of the problems we faced. Our survival then in running the group, in attempting to create a space for discussion about the concerns and interests of the patients in a group setting together, was in close parallel with the central prevailing anxiety on the ward about physical survival.

Sometimes it felt like we needed to prise apart a mother and son or daughter at the beginning of the group, and hurt, anger and resentment were caused. Nurses and doctors too could become resentful and sometimes expressed their anger by interrupting the group needlessly. At one stage however the nurses used the group time to do useful seminar and preparation work amongst themselves and to discuss how the work on the ward was going. Parents too often came to see the time of the group with relief as a time they could go out to the shops, go home, have a bath or read a magazine, and take a much needed break from being with their youngster. Indeed not only did the group create a space for the adolescents themselves, but it spawned the spontaneous growth of a host of other groups – a nurses' group, a parents' group, a visitors' group, and at one stage a grandparents' group. One week because of the shortage of space the grandparents' group was at one end of the ward around the bed of a girl who did not want to separate from her grandmother, whilst the adolescent group was at the other end, each preoccupied with what was going on for them. At a lull in our group we became aware that we could scarcely hear ourselves because of the intense conversation of the grandparents and the continuous clatter of their knitting needles – a more calming and containing group of *tricoteuses* than in revolutionary France. One consequence we found then of taking the group needs of the adolescents seriously was that others took their group needs seriously.

The adolescents could express their anger about aspects of their treatment more openly to a psychotherapist and a teacher rather than to a doctor or nurse. This sometimes made other professional staff outside the group see us as subversive. Conversely the adolescents sometimes felt the medical staff were making arbitrary plans about their treatment and expressed how they felt in a power struggle. At times patients complained that the doctors were addressing themselves to an injured foot or arm rather than talking to them directly as a person. One adolescent complained that a medical student greeted her with 'Hello dear', treating her as if she were a little girl of eight. In working with this we needed to recognise the patients' right to criticise, which all too often they failed to do, but also their sensitivity about their self-image.

Student doctors and nurses were at times criticised harshly for being less than fully competent and ordinary failures were not tolerated even within the learning context of the teaching hospital. Sometimes such criticisms represented projections of feelings of helplessness and failure from the patients. It could also be particularly hard in an atmosphere of tension for younger and more junior staff to be aware that complex dynamics and powerful projections were at play. Where sexual impotence and sterility were facts of life for some adolescents and hard to acknowledge or adjust to, it could be difficult to deal with such projections, especially if they were partly based on envy. We did spend time talking with the junior nurses and doctors outside the group and thinking over these issues.

Some of this criticism of doctors may have been deflected from the parents. Parents of adolescents need to have some tolerance of being seen temporarily as useless and 'out of date', while quietly maintaining the strength of their own parental position on their adolescent's needs. Many parents of severely disabled adolescents remain especially vulnerable to any expressions of strong emotion or any such criticism from them. Indeed the strain on the families is enormous and the statistics for marital breakdown and divorce for such parents are exceptionally high (Thomas, Bax and Smyth 1987).

Many of the adolescent spina bifida patients had been repeatedly hospitalised throughout their lives and were dependent on the hospital, especially upon particular consultants who had been responsible for them since a few hours or days after birth. The consultants were almost invariably seen as all-powerful father figures, in a primitive mould, with power over every aspect of their patients' lives. To confront them, or even exercise a degree of Oedipal rivalry with them, would be virtually like confronting a taboo and a host of unrecognised primitive emotions (Freud 1913). One patient referred to his consultant as 'the big white chief' and our groups, gathered together in a small circle for discussion, felt like the gathering for conference of a tribe. The anxieties about operations, often about being cut open, and the fear of death, of being 'cut to pieces', reflected the primitive fear of the father, central to Freud's concept of the Oedipus complex.

Freud thought that primitive societies encapsulated in their myths and taboos central features of universal significance regarding the position of authority and the Oedipal struggles between parents and children. The totem meal, as the dead father was cut to pieces and eaten, was the triumphal climax of the process of overcoming his authority and the only way of reversing the pattern of Oedipal relations. Until this point of revolt the father retains awesome and total power over all members of the tribe. At times other doctors shared in the consultants' power. When on one occasion I confronted a doctor for walking across the ward during the group time, my intervention was met with stunned silence, then horror within the group, as if I had broken a taboo. The patients began attacking me saying that what I had done was not 'right'. This theme awkwardly permeated the group meetings for weeks, in relation to the consultants and other powerful figures of authority. It sometimes meant crossing a huge invisible barrier to recognise the adolescents' emergent feelings and accepting that their feelings could and should be heard, and that they had rights, especially in deciding about operations.

Inevitably too sometimes doctors and nurses were used conversely as objects of positive projections, yet the ways it happened often meant a subtle devaluation of the patients themselves, which could lead to further passivity and could deepen their depression. Young nurses would be seen as clever or beautiful, while patients saw themselves as stupid and ugly. Again this was often seen in little ways, for example, in how some severely ill patients would keep special chocolates, or small presents to them, for the nurse. The nurses were esteemed, revered and their fresh youthful vigour idealised as part of a process whereby their beauty and value were to be preserved at all costs. In this way the potentially good or beautiful aspect of the patient was preserved, but split off and at the same time lost by the patient to the nurse, in projective identification (Klein 1946).

In psychiatric hospitals there can be processes whereby disturbance or 'madness' is kept in patients and sanity in staff, and rigid barriers are created to prevent contamination (Main 1975; Hinshelwood 1987a; Bott-Spillius 1990). This leads to severe problems in restoring patients to a degree of health in which they can own again some 'sane' part of themselves (Roberts 1994; Hinshelwood and Skogstad 2000). Similar processes occur in general hospitals, this adolescent ward and other settings, where the good and beautiful are located in staff, and patients find it so hard to identify with and own the good or beautiful parts of themselves (Sinason 1988).

Discussion

Progressively over the four years of the group we modified the structure to include the participation of more staff, with the explicit aim of facilitating better communication about the emotional life of the adolescents. We knew that the group could arouse a high level of hostility and suspicion as being too secret. Some criticisms were voiced but at different times the message was also conveyed indirectly, by increasingly frequent but unacknowledged interruptions, such as crossing the ward during the group or delaying drug rounds and other activities so that we could not start the group on time. There could be a reluctance to spend the usual time with the leaders discussing the progress of the patients, themes and events affecting the ward, or receiving the usual feedback about the group. The underlying strain of the work was shown in that nurses on the ward would show initial interest in the group but then drift away, because many found close contact with the emotional expressions of patients in the group very distressing.

The group had evolved to become distant from the workers who had the most direct contact with the patients on the ward, and we were getting out of touch with their ideas and capacities and as such diminished their capacities. We therefore made changes to involve nurses more in leadership roles in the group and I spent more time talking to every member of staff who came into contact with the patients. In effect this became an informal survey of everyday staff. There was now noticeably better involvement by all the nursing staff in issues to do with the group, better attendances by patients and fewer boundary disturbances within the group. Some of the values for which the group stood became more integrated into the general nursing practice of the ward: a system of named first nurses for patients was introduced; there was a careful monitoring by staff nurse and sister of the patient's overall care plan that included medical, social and psychological issues; arrangements were set up around specific tasks relevant in the adolescents' steps towards independence, such as cooking, home care and hygiene classes. Staff outside the ward group were now more consistently kept abreast of important themes on the ward by the staff themselves, independent of us, and this increased the standing of the group with staff and patients alike.

Because my involvement had extended to include discussions with the most senior staff involved in the management of the ward, including consultants, nursing tutors, nursing officers, lecturers, hospital managers and so on, my function became additionally in effect that of an institutional consultant to the senior hospital staff about the adolescent ward, rather than simply psychotherapist to the ward group. The hospital set up and asked me to be involved in an interdisciplinary meeting to discuss developments on the ward. Consultation within the whole interdisciplinary group helped to broaden everyone's perspective about the ward and patients including plans for the moves to a new hospital.

Menzies Lyth stated the proposition that 'the success and viability of a social institution are intimately connected with the techniques it uses to contain anxiety' (Menzies Lyth 1988: 78). If personal and social anxieties are not faced in an institution or organisation, a 'social defence system' develops as a result of collusive interaction and agreement, often unconscious, between members of the organisation. The socially structured defence mechanisms then tend to become an aspect of external reality with which old and new members of the institution must come to terms. The group we ran could be viewed as a way of confronting distorted and collusive elements of the external reality of life and work on the adolescent ward. It became, I believe, a force for change in a new direction and a technique to contribute to containment of the anxieties of the patients and to assist some of the staff with their concerns and anxieties in relation to the care and treatment of the patients.

The primary task on the adolescent ward was to help the patients deal with serious physical illness, through appropriate medical treatment. But as Menzies Lyth has maintained 'in the functioning of a social organisation . . . the importance of the primary task has been exaggerated' (1988: 46–50). We saw in our work running the group that psychological work with their emotions, in particular personal feelings about survival and their adolescent development, was equally important. In this respect such work represented what Obholtzer describes as a 'contested primary task' (2002). Consultants working with institutions (in the UK, at the Tavistock Institute of Human Relations, Opus and the Grubb Institute, and in the USA, at the A. K. Rice Institute) have concentrated thinking on defining competing conceptions of the primary task as a prelude to work to effect institutional change (Rice 1963, 1965; Miller 1993; Obholtzer and Roberts 1994).

There is also clearly a link between following the primary task and promoting the overall health of the patients and the morale of the staff. Menzies Lyth quotes Revans (1959) who found that successful medical treatment is significantly related to positive morale amongst the nursing staff. Main (1989), especially in his pivotal paper 'The Ailment' (1957), also linked successful treatment to a capacity to address psychological problems, especially unconscious splits in the staff groups, and that recognition of these splits and work with them could help to avert suicides and contribute directly to the morale of the nursing staff.

What Menzies Lyth has centrally underlined in her work is the link between the individual and personal anxieties of staff about the 'objective situation' on the ward and its resonance with underlying phantasy situations (1988: 47–8). An inability to face anxiety contributes to building up, maintaining and reinforcing the social defence system, where *evasion of anxiety* is attempted 'to give protection from the full experience of anxieties which are derived from the most primitive defence mechanisms' (Klein 1946; Menzies Lyth 1983; Joseph 1989).

Hinshelwood and Skogstad (2000: 4) emphasise that in any work enterprise individuals will experience anxieties from various sources: some will be work specific and some individual specific and in most organisations these tend to combine (Obholtzer and Roberts 1994). Also the practical requirements of a particular type of work have a strong determining effect on how the social defence grows up (Trist *et al.* 1963). Individuals may be drawn into particular work in particular organisations because their defences match aspects of the social system of the organisation (Dartington 1994; Roberts 1994). Social defences, however, can prevent the individual from realising to the full their capacity for concern, compassion and sympathy, and strike directly at the roots of sublimatory activities in which infantile anxieties are reworked in symbolic form and modified (Menzies Lyth 1975). Such social defences frequently deprive nurses and other staff of necessary reassurance and satisfactions, and itself arouses a good deal of secondary anxiety as well as failing to alleviate primary anxiety (Menzies Lyth 1988).

Our recurrent struggles in running the group were partly a result of being a sort of dustbin for feelings and anxieties not dealt with elsewhere, in view of the inevitable splits being created and the spill-over of various types of anxieties. I believe however that it was useful for a psychotherapist to run a ward group, particularly in the reformed way, for such a complex set of adolescent patients, including the spina bifida patients. Exposure firsthand to the experience of the patients meant personal and psychodynamic insights could be given directly to patients, and our regular discussions with the staff before and after the groups helped their work in contact with the patients. Indeed the group worked best when there were continuous parallel consultations with staff, so that it was integral to the other aspects of care and treatment being offered on the ward. Such firsthand group work with patients and the close contacts which were built up with staff put me in a position to contribute to thinking with senior staff and administrators about the ward within the wider institution of the hospital and the medical and nursing schools, on issues of staffing, plans for the new hospital adolescent ward, research and inter-agency relationships. My brief, then, which was initially clinical, as a member of the hospital's clinical staff, extended to become partly a consultative brief within the wider institution.

The experience of the adolescent ward group was that due attention to individual needs and feelings and their expression in the group, with appropriate consultations within the wider institution, including reaffirming and consolidating the authority of the ward group, enabled staff and patients to face better some of the doubts, anxieties and uncertainties of life on the ward. The inpatient adolescent group not only helped individual patients and groups of patients, but also contributed to an understanding of how adolescents, brought together both for serious or less severe treatments, would relate to and comprehend their life on the ward as a group, and would express primitive anxieties individually and in terms of their group behaviour.

Chapter 10

Psychoanalytic theories of adolescence

Introduction

In this chapter I shall look at some central psychoanalytic contributions to the understanding of adolescence and outline some theories that I have found useful in psychotherapy of severely emotionally disturbed adolescents. I shall develop these ideas in the last two chapters, looking at understanding and containment in an applied inpatient setting – an adolescent unit, and issues about assessment. Here I give short vignettes as examples of the use of these theories in two specific areas. First, I shall illustrate the continued relevance of Freud's developmental theory and the reworking of early Oedipal relationships from early adolescence onwards. Second, I shall look at the development of psychological structures in adolescence, which can lead to specific adolescent states of mind, and I shall illustrate how the adolescent's use of their mind and sense of their body can be affected in severe disturbances.

I define adolescence, understood psychoanalytically, as a developmental process in which the boy or girl, or young man or woman, develops new sexual and aggressive powers, including a powerful and sexual body, as they rework Oedipal relationships in the light of new tasks in life. Young people acquire a new sense of themselves and their physical, mental and emotional capacity, including a sense of their individuality and their personal value. If very severe disturbance takes hold of the adolescent during this developmental process, then the entire process will be affected, and may even be halted.

Adolescence is normally a time of change, of unpredictable and powerful reactions and responses, with the loss of childhood and movement towards adulthood. It is a time when there is a new awareness of the body, a new sense of the personal, experiences of new impulses, an increased awareness of inner feelings and an increased capacity for reflection. There is a changing relationship to groups, to other people including parents and relatives, to authority figures and institutional structures, and a wider sense of society. A normal transition through adolescence involves some measure of disturbance, both of inner feelings and attitudes within oneself, and also in relation to others. These changes occur in adolescence as part of a process of detachment from the parents and the family, and, as with earlier detachment processes in infancy, are accompanied by equally major changes in awareness of the emotional states of others (Stern 1985) and involve alternating periods of integration and lack of integration. Sometimes the adolescent appears static, behind a wall of powerful resistances or defences, and sometimes he or she surges forwards in what seems a haphazard and contradictory way. In adolescence, change can occur at any time.

Disturbance in adolescence can be such that it can be hard to give adolescents sufficient thought and attention. It is not uncommon for adults, especially parents, to wish that adolescence would just go away. Shakespeare wrote in *The Winter's Tale* (lll. iii. 59–63, quoted in Copley 1993: 100–101):

> I would there were no age between ten and three-and-twenty, or that youth would sleep out the rest; for there is nothing in the between but getting wenches with child, wronging the ancientry, stealing, fighting.

Even Winnicott (1963c) seemed to be saying this:

> There is only one cure for adolescence and that is the passage of time and the passing on of the adolescent into the adult state.

Winnicott was saying something much more subtle though; that each individual needs to experience their own adolescence, and live through it, for no outsiders can cure an individual's problems in adolescence.

Our psychoanalytic understanding of adolescence has only really moved forward in the last 50 years. Freud, in his *Three Essays on the Theory of Sexuality* (1905b) and elsewhere, wrote of the changes that occur at *puberty*, specifically noting the reworking of infantile conflicts after major biological changes. There are just six references to 'adolescence' in the index of Freud's work, which refer not so much to his specific psychoanalytic theories of changes at puberty, but to what he called a wider, more generally understood 'normal process of adolescence' (Freud 1893: 125–34), which he never explained or defined. Before Freud, adolescence had a special significance because it was seen as the time when sexual life began. With Freud's introduction of his theory of infantile sexuality, shifting the beginning of sexual life to a period long before adolescence, one could well ask was adolescence itself demoted or relegated?

Overall, in Freud's writing, there is little mention of what we would now regard as essential parts of adolescence: emotional growth, major restructuring of the personality and, particularly, adolescent states of mind. Aichhorn (1931) wrote of work with adolescents in residential settings (cf. Freud's 1925 review), and there was some work by the early child psychoanalysts. But Anna Freud herself, in 1936, described adolescence as a 'neglected period'. It was only after World War II, with widespread changes in society, that adolescence became widely recognised as a phenomenon in itself, worthy of study. Not surprisingly, some of the most enduring and expressive literature about adolescence dates from this time, notably Salinger's *The Catcher in the Rye* (1945/6), and Steinbeck's *East of Eden* (1952). There were also many films about adolescence made at this time and a recognisable culture of adolescence began to develop.

Despite this, our psychoanalytic understanding of adolescence is still based in Freud's developmental model set out in *Three Essays on the Theory of Sexuality*. Accordingly, psychological changes at puberty are based on, and derive their power from, physical (i.e. biological) changes that alter and re-evoke the already powerful but by now largely dormant infantile sexuality, which produces changes that 'give infantile sexual life its final, normal shape' (1905b: 207). There is at this time a convergence of the affectionate current (i.e. the emotional residue of infantile sexuality that still has an open existence, so long as an inhibition is interposed between the infantile sexuality and its natural goal; cf. Jones 1922: 397), and the sensual current (the fully developed genital sexual feelings) under the primacy of genital feelings.

Freud's views about changes in puberty are consistent with his views on infancy and latency, in that he thought problems occurred in puberty because of 'pathological disorders of sexual life', which become manifest as inhibitions in development, for example, in a fixation on the pregenital stages, and especially because of unresolved, early and unconscious incestuous phantasies. He saw phallic identifications and castration anxiety as occurring in this way. Puberty brings a search for a new sexual object, normally of the opposite sex. Changes of object choice in puberty do not occur clearly or straightaway, and there are periods of trial action where adolescents indulge in phantasies and live in a world of ideas, delaying any action on the basis of their object choices or trying a same-sex object choice before someone of the opposite sex. The changes in libidinal object and aim at puberty involve a progressive development of infantile Oedipal relationships, and the changes protect individuals and society against incest. There is normally a loosening of the connection with the family, both from the incestuous object and phantasies towards the mother or father, and from parental authority. The life force driving these powerful sexual, emotional and relationship changes is the libido, which for Freud is a positive force that moves out from the ego towards objects, creating emotional connections to things and to other people, and then back again into the ego. Problems therefore occur when there is a lack of libido, or there is a disturbance by a recurrence of aspects of infantile sexuality. The libido stored within the ego is described as 'narcissistic libido', and for Freud is the source of deeper psychotic disturbance (1905b: 218). In Figure 10.1 – about ego libido and object libido – one can see, in terms of opposite poles of a flow, the way in which deeper narcissistic disturbance and the capacity for contact with external objects and reality correspond, and are related, to each other.

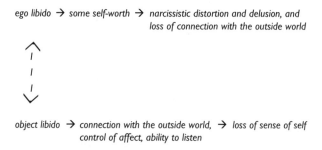

ego libido → some self-worth → narcissistic distortion and delusion, and
loss of connection with the outside world

object libido → connection with the outside world, → loss of sense of self
control of affect, ability to listen

Figure 10.1   Ego libido and object libido

Anna Freud extended and developed her father's theory. She reframed the theory of changes at puberty within his structural theory (1923) of id, ego and super-ego. She emphasised similarities between the early infant period and puberty, in that a relatively strong id confronts a relatively weak ego, albeit an ego that in adolescence commands a greater capacity for transformation. This allowed her and other Freudian psychoanalysts, notably Erik Erikson (1968, 1977) and Peter Blos (1962, 1972), to see adolescence as a new period characterised by a distinctive adolescent type of experience, with new defences of a primitive nature (such as asceticism and intellectualisation) that operate against the intensity of the new id impulses. Anna Freud gave one of the first succinct psychoanalytic descriptions of adolescence, as follows:

> Adolescents are excessively egoistic, regarding themselves as the centre of the universe and the sole object of interest, and yet at no time in later life are they capable of so much self-sacrifice and devotion. They form the most passionate love relations, only to break them off as abruptly as they began them. On the one hand, they throw themselves enthusiastically into the life of the community and, on the other, they have an over-powering longing for solitude. They oscillate between blind submission to some self-chosen leader and defiant rebellion against any and every authority. They are selfish and materially minded and at the same time full of lofty idealism. They are ascetic but suddenly plunge into instinc-tual indulgence of the most primitive character. At times their behaviour to other people is rough and inconsiderate, yet they themselves are extremely touchy. Their moods veer between light-hearted optimism and the blackest pessimism. Sometimes they will work with indefatigable enthusiasm and at other times they are sluggish and apathetic.
>
> (Freud 1936: 137–8)

Melanie Klein's early emphasis (1932) is on the intensity of feelings of anxiety in puberty, 'a kind of recrudescence of anxiety which is characteristic of small children'. Adolescents are seen to be more able to ward off anxiety with a more successfully developed ego, through interests, activities or sports, and at the same time more likely to succumb very quickly to anxiety. Because of this, psychoanalytic treatment must interpret at the immediate point of anxiety or affect in the immediate transference, linking minute signs of anxiety to get in touch with the adolescent's general affective state. Whilst Anna Freud had stressed how, in adolescence as in infancy, the ego is weaker (than in latency or adulthood), Klein stresses the strength of the super-ego in adolescence (and infancy):

> The superego determines a compulsive instigation of sexual activities, just as it determines a complete suppression of them, that is to say, that anxiety and a sense of guilt reinforce libidinal fixations and heighten libidinal desires.
>
> (Klein 1932: 115)

The same could be said, I think, about aggressive desires and feelings during adolescence – that anxiety and guilt can both increase the aggressive feelings and the acute internal reactions against those feelings. Consequently the adolescent both experiences more negative feelings and hides them more, and readily splits people and things into good and bad. Klein, like Freud, recognised the adolescent's need for action and for the expression of phantasy, and the way in which the adolescent can avoid reality and action by living in a phantasy world. She also recognised how repression of the now highly developed sexual and aggressive affect can, in some adolescents, lead to complete passivity.

Case illustrations

I would now like to give some case studies of young adolescents to illustrate the conflicts they were experiencing as they reached puberty.

Case one

The first case study concerns the changes occurring in a young girl approaching menarche.

> Fiona was 12, and her parents had divorced when she was 3 years old, when her father 'became' gay. In many ways a self-possessed girl, she was referred because she cried frequently and was very unhappy. She saw her problem as how to deal with Dad being gay and Mum always being angry with her. As a child she had struggled and searched for

reasons why her parents were not together, but at the age of 8 she 'knew' – her father had a man living with him and there was only one place to sleep. Fiona said she could only tell her mother she knew when she was 11, 'asking her not to shout at her if she said it'.

My impression in psychotherapy was that Fiona experienced anger towards her mother and blamed her because she had allowed her father to become gay and leave her. Her parents denied or played down acknowledgement of overt disagreement and disappointment between them, so Fiona was left with a sense that her anger was just something irrational inside her. I think that also, at an infantile level, her blaming of her mother was related to and based on her own self-blame and self-reproaches, which were the root of much of her unhappiness.

Within psychotherapy, which began a few months prior to her entry into puberty, Fiona was desperately sorting out and putting into place her feelings and conflicts about her parents as a couple. There was an intense and driven quality to the whole process, as week by week she changed emotionally and physically in front of me. She struggled with feelings of loss – of friends if she moved house, of her father – and, as she got to know and trust me, in the transference, her fear of losing me, related to her underlying feeling of her own lack of worth. She was often quick with direct questions, needing to take the initiative, and eager to be able to trust what she found in her work with me. Fiona soon developed a close and intense contact with me, unusual for a girl her age with a male psychotherapist, but I felt that unconsciously I was viewed like a gay Dad, so that some of the inhibitions against seductive closeness were not there. Like other girls, however, there was fear and confusion about orifices and their products, the messes from the anus and the messy expected discharges from her vagina.

There were in all of this transference connections with early Oedipal attachments to her father, her pre-Oedipal sexuality, and her current knowledge of her father's homosexuality. This was largely unconscious and came out in the transference, for example, in the way she recoiled with horror at some sores I then had around my mouth. This linked, I thought, to unconscious knowledge and confusion about her father's sexuality, and her own oral neediness. She also expressed horror at some relatives who were married 'even though they were very closely related'. In this the perils and the excitement of possible incestuous contact were apparent.

Her mixed feelings about being a boy or a girl came through. She asked if I had a daughter, wishing, I thought, to become a special girl for me. But she enjoyed, too, being centre stage in the musical as 'Bugsy Malone', and partly wanted to be a kind of tomboy. A tumult of feelings about ugliness or prettiness, and her fears of being weak rather than strong, emerged in the week or two before menarche. She talked openly about how her mother had had to have an abortion after an accident, showing her anxiety about her new procreative capacities, and the 'accidents' at periods, which she 'knew all about', and indicating her fears about her own self-worth. Her anger now emerged, in the transference at me and 'the woman outside' (i.e. outside the consulting room), and then at her mother and stepfather for being a couple. When I interpreted this she became babyish again. I thought this moved away, regressed, from her real current feelings and interpreted it as defensive, out of her fear of her aggression at her exclusion by the couple.

During the session after her periods began Fiona spoke in terms of colours, exciting roundabouts and slides. She was relieved and became remarkably calm for the remainder of her sessions as she matured and grew, before she eventually moved house and therefore finished treatment.

I thought the work she had done on her view of her developing sexuality and her Oedipal relationships, caught up in complex feelings on different levels about her parents, was deeply important in helping her deal with her anxieties during her transition into puberty.

Four young adolescent boys I treated over the same period had quite different patterns of defence (delinquent, phobic, obsessional and psychotic), although the striking similarities in the underlying pathology highlight Freud's central thesis about changes at puberty (see Blos 1962, 1972). In each case there was the problem of a continuous overly close relationship with the mother, based in different ways on incestuous patterns. The beginning of a separate adolescent development was therefore not possible for each boy; similarly, no clear separate sexual aim could emerge, nor could a new identity. After psychotherapy, which focused around unconscious sexual wishes, infantile regressions and conflicts, particularly in relation to the 'archaic mother', adolescent development could continue. All the boys did well, except for the one who used psychotic defences. I shall briefly outline two further cases, those with phobic and obsessional symptoms.

Case two

Brian had been school phobic for over a year. He was an only child whose father had died, and he had become increasingly wrapped up in a couple-type relationship with his anxious and fearful mother. In psychotherapy, he developed a close attachment to me as a father substitute, but he also progressively brought out his feelings about his unmourned father and his sense of his own Oedipal triumph. He steered his way into his early adolescent experience very slowly and gradually by reluctantly relinquishing his latency pursuits and preoccupations. These included maddeningly abstruse games and procedures he would devise, and ways of talking and thinking that could be shared with practically no one except his mother, who seemed to be the sole initiate in Brian's one-person cult.

Slowly, as his trust towards me grew and he could acknowledge his homosexual transference to his psychotherapist, Brian became able to accept interpretations about his masturbation phantasies, and acknowledge his own masturbation. He could then acknowledge the complex underlying incestuous phantasies affecting his behaviour, including his inability to separate psychically from his mother by exerting subtle emotional control of her, including physical and social over-closeness. He then experienced strong relief at having, and being allowed to have, new and interesting feelings of his own. Brian would react with excitement and bewilderment, like a toddler or small child, at every new experience. In time he got back to school and extended somewhat his social capacities and friendships.

Now, several years later, he is finishing a physics degree at university and interestingly has been able to move away from what was at root a sole preoccupation with his mother's body to a detailed scientific study of the nature of things (literally 'bodies'), a study of external reality.

Case three

Colin came from a very troubled family, and had obsessional defences. Colin's brother, two years older, suffered from haemophilia, but he was aggressive and his behaviour was constantly disruptive, leaving the family and the services around them incapacitated. Colin's father was an ineffective man. He had been made redundant from his work and acted as if he had irrevocably retired from life. Colin's mother was perceptive at times, hard working and long suffering. Although she strove to keep the family together, they were nevertheless paralysed. She tended to babify Colin, who was timid, stuttered very badly, and was frightened of any social situation. Although much smaller and slighter in build than his brother, and having a pleasant, non-confrontational way of relating, Colin was stricken with guilt, anxiety and despair that he had somehow caused his brother's life-threatening haemophilia. His brother made accusations that Colin was trying to kill him, and tried to provoke him into fights. Colin's solution was to lower his head and keep a low profile.

In his psychotherapy, Colin was continuously preoccupied with obsessional activity, which was orderly and painfully slow. For hours on end he constructed crudely formed plasticine figures, which he handled and showed with pride. In evidence was a regression to a pre-

Oedipal level of anal fixation, like the toddler at potty training, whose greatest source of pride and satisfaction is to produce and show his own bodily products, and defend and sustain attacks on them.

In his transference to me, Colin experienced his timidity and fear that I would restrict him, like a limiting mother. He also exhibited identification with a depressed and withdrawn father. Slowly, over a considerable time, through the psychoanalytic work Colin learnt that he was capable of understanding and producing something worthwhile, and that his own thoughts and feelings were valuable, and could be expressed. He began to realise that he could define his own boundaries with his parents and others, more in terms of what others his age might do, rather than in terms of the guilt and fear that racked him persistently. Subsequently this development continued with the help of a small, caring boarding school, so that now as a young adult Colin is doing well (he is working happily, independently and productively as a care assistant), despite recently experiencing, and weathering, the very aggressive and destructive suicide of his elder brother in his later adolescence.

To return to psychoanalytic theory, I shall now look at some mechanisms that are crucial both to the radical development of personality in adolescence and to the development of particular adolescent states of mind. Melanie Klein's pivotal (1946) paper, 'Notes on some Schizoid Mechanisms', introduced the mechanisms of primitive splitting and projective identification. Klein defined projective identification as the prototype of the aggressive object relationship, representing an anal attack on an object by means of forcing parts of the ego into it in order to take over its contents or control it. Since then, projective identification has acquired a range of meanings and is a cluster concept (Hinshelwood 1991: 179–208). Klein is describing, essentially, processes in early infancy, when projective and introjective mechanisms enable the infant to deal with primitive fears about survival. Extending Klein's view, I think that in adolescence, as in infancy, continuous processes of projection and introjection are also strongly in action, when there is again the need to learn to survive as a more independent individual in a new world. As part of this, continuous processes of splitting and fragmentation of internal and external objects occur internally, which alter the boundaries of internal and external reality and the shape of the personality in a fundamentally new way. As mentioned earlier, the adolescent becomes aware of, and relates in a new way to, the nature of external objects and his or her own bodily and emotional states, and begins to know more fully the nature of the emotional states of others (Klein 1932, 1946; Stern 1985).

Bion (1962a, 1962b) extends Klein's theory in terms of the value of containment of positive projective identification. This means, in essence, inducing and affecting in the other person a state of mind as a means of communicating one's mental state. It is an essential part of containment from early infancy onwards (Hinshelwood 1991: 184). To apply this concept from infancy to adolescence one needs to remember that throughout adolescence, and indeed in any adolescent's day, there are constant shifts backwards and forwards, and there occur frequent changes of emotional state and mood. This is because there are continuous and rapid shifts in processes of projection and introjection in adolescence occurring as a result of bodily and mental changes. In understanding the adolescent, one also needs to take on that there are processes of both positive *and* negative projective identification and a process of differentiating between the two. This will mean consenting to experience the feelings and thoughts of the adolescent in their split and fragmented state in order to contain his/her own state of mind until some pattern of understanding emerges. Over time, adolescents then learn to contain in their mind the thoughts and feelings that lead to progressive splitting and cycles of projection. They then come to feel that their own mind, and body, can contain what's going on, and they build a new structure in their inner (internal) world. Importantly, too, this process teaches the adolescent a fuller sense of personal value, that is based not simply in the Freudian sense on a new awareness of their sexual body and worked through Oedipal relations, but on their capacity to develop, change and contain themselves. This is what lies behind Winnicott's assertion, quoted earlier, that 'the only cure for adolescence is the passage of time', for each individual has to have his or her own experiences and live through their own adolescence. In this process, we become aware, as do adolescents, of the quality of their emotionality and their own changeability as difficult life choices are faced.

Very severe adolescent disturbance accompanied by what Klein and Bion call 'excessive projective identification' leads to a continued confusion and distortion of internal and external reality. Such disturbance can be recognised by paying close attention to one's own countertransference and assessing the quality of the adolescent's projections. It occurs when there is a fundamental hatred of life and emotional knowledge, rather than a love of life and knowing, which the normally disturbed adolescent feels. Severe self-harm, such as cutting, burning and suicide attempts, occurs in adolescents who cannot accept the value of a new sexual body and a new inner self. Body-mind confusions and splits occur at the deepest levels, so that hatred and a wish to kill can be directed at the body in suicide, self-harm or severe perversions, or at the mind through severe drug abuse or deep depressions (Laufer and Laufer 1984; Rosenfeld 1987; Bion 1957, 1962a, 1962b). Some borderline patients move between normal and very severe disturbance at different times. With this most disturbed group of adolescents, there may be different functions of the personality, an 'adolescent function' and a 'borderline function' (cf. Bion 1957, 1963, for his theory of functions; Rosenfeld 1965). Clinically, it is refreshing when a patient who has been quite borderline, or confused and deluded, becomes disturbing in an ordinary adolescent way! There is a return to what Winnicott would term the playfulness of adolescence, driven by strong, even if often highly disruptive and disturbing, life forces.

Britton's views (1989) on the Oedipus complex serve as a link between Freud's view and the later views of Klein and Bion, as applied here to adolescence. Just as in the depressive position some capacity to tolerate and accept loss of immediate satisfaction is necessary, so in Oedipal relationships it becomes necessary to accept exclusion and restriction by not being part of the parental couple and their sexuality, and hence to be able to take up what Britton calls 'the third position'. When internalised, this capacity to accept an actual excluded third position enables the individual to have a concept of the external, the other, in terms of his own experience of being an 'other'. This capacity to accept the other is an essential part of the adolescent's ability to take his/her place in the world outside, the bigger scheme of things away from parents and family. When this does not happen – when there is, in Britton's terms, 'an Oedipal illusion' – the relation to the outside world is disturbed.

Finally, here are two clinical examples of adolescent girls to illustrate the radical shifts in processes of projection and introjection during adolescence.

Case four

Penny, aged 18, continuously showed swings between cooperative and purposeful efforts, and bombastic and destructive behaviour. She has now finished a year's psychoanalytical treatment in an inpatient adolescent unit (a therapeutic community), and is so far managing independently. (For the complexity of the transference in such work, cf. Chapters 4–7; also see Chapters 11 and 12, and Day and Flynn 2003 for further description of the work of the Adolescent Unit.) Penny was loud, aggressive and uncontained. She was thrown out of everywhere, school and home, and she had been through 30 placements over the previous three years. She drank heavily, used drugs, had casual unsafe sex, and had sunk to living rough on the street in gangs, sometimes thieving and mugging. In her favour, she had developed a strong and ongoing relationship with a persistent social worker and psychiatrist, had managed some outpatient psychoanalytic psychotherapy and some family meetings, and wanted to change. Penny had an over-close and over-involved relationship with her father, who, although very fond of her, would also violently hit her, or impulsively throw her out. She openly hated her mother and was derogatory about her. She denied her parents had a real life as a couple. Penny had had a history of bowel problems and sphincter control as a child, requiring years of intrusive anal procedures. In treatment, as before, she enacted all of this, with angry verbal and occasionally physical attacks on any social boundary.

My feeling at assessment, my countertransference, was that 'something was missing', although I could not put my finger on exactly what it was. Through months of struggle with her, dealing with angry projections that dismantled or blew apart achievements in terms of understanding or containment of feelings by other patients, or us ourselves, and distorted introjections of what she perceived the treatment was doing to her ('messing her up'), this question of 'what was missing?' remained with me. I thought she had communicated something to me, which I had to hold and work with. At times I wondered if it was some hidden incestuous sexual abuse, but over time I discounted this idea, although her intense incestuous phantasies about her relationship with her father, and her experiences of degrading and shaming intrusive physical procedures, confused her, with consequent masculine identifications that were linked with power and violence. Yet this could be worked on, as long as we held on to a hope that she could change.

In the end I thought something was being played out in Penny's enactments that had to be felt and experienced by me and others before she could bear to re-experience it herself and begin the task of trying to hold on to and contain it mentally and emotionally herself. At one level what was missing related to her difficulty of taking something in, retaining it and holding on to it. At another level it was simple: what was missing was her mother – shown repeatedly in her mistrust of femininity, of productiveness, and of her growing talents. In treatment her feelings about her femininity were slowly changing, in particular in her psychotherapy with her female psychotherapist working through a transference about a 'useless mother'. But as Penny worked on this she increasingly experienced what lay beneath, her deep despair and shame.

A turning point in getting in touch with this despair and shame was her re-experiencing, and living through quite traumatically, two events she had until now kept secret, from the time when she was at her lowest on the streets: the first was when she beat up another girl, a stranger, for no reason, in the toilet in a night club; the second was when she was gang-raped by a group of boys. Painfully she put together what had happened to her and what she did to others, and herself, in these events and at other times. She needed to be in touch with, and own, her aggression and guilt, and to accept an understanding of how this contributed to her chaotic and destructive behaviour. There ensued a period of intense crisis, in which she thought she might end her life by acting on impulse, but she came through as she faced her despair and the ill effects of her destructiveness. She had now begun to take in a real belief in her own value, and in the future growth of her talents. Her normal adolescent self, her humour and playfulness, were strengthened, and she was now much better able to hold within herself her own anxious expectancy about the future. An engaging, though at times somewhat overbearing, ordinary adolescent side now became more dominant. Penny was for the first time actively and consistently pursuing a course in the performing arts, using her capacity for drama to good effect. With a lessening of her negative projective identification, something less intense and destructive could now come through. Shortly before leaving treatment she boasted half playfully, half anxiously, 'You should get my autograph now, while you can, before I become famous!'

Penny's case illustrates the operation of both negative and positive projective identification during adolescence. Her use of excessive negative projective identification led to serious confusion of internal and external reality, especially when she was highly disturbed and deeply antisocial. The case also highlights the need for those attempting to contain her to be able to receive and deal with negative projective identification, through understanding and by setting adequate boundaries, and to differentiate it from positive projective identification, which although sometimes also disturbing could allow ordinary adolescent development to continue.

Case five

My final case example is Anne, who had a borderline personality disorder (for a detailed account of work with borderline adolescents see Chapters 11 and 12). Anne suffered from self-harming attacks on her body and psychotic distortions in her mental states when her projections could not be adequately received. Anne's treatment showed the importance for her, and others, of an inpatient adolescent setting, which is described in the next chapter, where her projections could be adequately received and contained, so that she could re-establish a safer and more securely based psychic growth.

> Anne, aged 17, had been out of school since the age of 10, with no subsequent outside schooling. She had been unable to maintain any sustained social contact or commitment outside the family; she no longer had any contact with groups of peers, and only seldom met anyone her own age or any adult apart from a teacher for a few hours per week of home tuition. As a consequence she suffered chronic social and personal isolation. She had one daily activity and her lifeline – three times weekly private psychotherapy for two years. She was reportedly rude and contemptuous to her analyst, but nevertheless made some progress.

Anne had been a bright and happy child until her parents' acrimonious divorce when she was 5 years old. She then developed an omnipotent need to take responsibility, and progressively felt her needs neglected. For two years in early adolescence, there were a number of psychotic symptoms, including a psychotic fear of holding a pen, which meant Anne could do no schoolwork for a long period. Also from the age of 14 and puberty she had been partly anorectic and severely self-harming through disfiguring burns on her arms and legs and cuts to her face. Anne attended a younger age adolescent unit for nearly two years. She then returned home with the hope of more progressive social integration but immediately reverted to her patterns of isolation. Although her symptoms had subsided to a degree, she did not change and remained socially isolated. There remained at the beginning of inpatient treatment a very high risk of suicide.

Anne continued periodically and secretly to harm herself. She was prone to idealised love phantasies of older men, and was controlling in a regressed way, typified by her insistence that people including (even especially) professionals use a babyish form of her name. Many complied. The psychotic symptoms were not always or easily apparent, but there appeared a continuing disposition to psychotic beliefs and thinking (Wollheim 1999), and any real underlying change, for her to be able to take on an ordinary life, had also not occurred.

Her first month in the inpatient Adolescent Unit was an ordeal for her, which she made herself get through, sticking it out. Anne slowly began to manage the challenge of social relationships, but only so long as she kept herself emotionally distant. She and staff struggled with this, in work groups, activities and within the twice weekly adolescent therapy group, where her tendency to take on the role of the person responsible for keeping it all going was again particularly noticeable. In her individual psychotherapy what came out was her fear of putting experiences together (literally 'linking' and 'thinking', cf. Bion 1959, 1962a, 1962b), and having her own viewpoint, for fear of going mad. Frequently, after gaining some understanding she would evacuate it again, saying she had forgotten what happened. She could easily be forgotten by staff and some patients, and remain at an emotional distance from others. An exception to this occurred quite atypically with one adolescent, who challenged her social withdrawal as due to her personal but hidden hatred of what she located in other people. This adolescent (Penny above) partly bullied her, but in effect also hounded her in a most useful way into a real relationship with her, and to be more connected with her real needs and angry feelings!

Progressively, with her psychotherapy and her life in the unit, Anne became stronger. With a developing ego-strength, she then became more able to face more disturbing aspects of her symptoms. For several months, she seemed to have remained on the brink of moving forward to something more normal, shown by her weight remaining just below a level where she could have regular periods until nearly the end of treatment. As she progressed, she began to take some GCSE classes, and to take more challenging roles inside and outside the hospital. In several family meetings, separately with both her father and her mother's side of the family, she began to express more about what she felt about what had happened and to understand more about her role within the family. She was temporarily less confused and isolated. Her precocious over-identification with her father, and the sexual fixations on older men, were still however more apparent to us than to her, as was her mother's depression and incapacity to bear feelings. It was now apparent that there had been a chronic pattern of almost complete denial of emotionality within the family at crucial times, particularly after the divorce.

A significant point of progress in her treatment came when Anne allowed herself to re-experience towards the end of treatment a reactivation of her suicide wishes. A particularly stressful and terrifying incident occurred at home on one of the final weekends in the run-up to discharge. Anne tried to jump out of a second floor window, and had to be restrained by her stepfather. What happened could then, after many months of treatment and family work, be recognised by Anne and her parents, and subsequently be thought about and discussed within Anne's treatment. Anne had learnt and now could see that this alarming behaviour could represent something. She now had an increased capacity to allow her real feelings to be expressed, however disturbed. This allowed her to work to differentiate more her powerful but largely hidden emotions, and to use projective identification, less in a negative way, by breaking links of understanding, leading to psychotic manifestations, and acts of self-harm, but as more of a communication (cf. Bion 1962). In this very disturbing incident she had experienced an outburst of pathological jealousy. There had been a trip out with her family to a café that Sunday afternoon, when Anne had felt that those there, particularly her mother, were more interested in another girl they had met than in her. This outburst of intense pathological jealousy could be understood in terms of the persistent jealousy of her younger sister, with whom she unconsciously identified this girl. It could be seen as part of a pattern of her intense emotions, and other conflicts about her mother and father, on an infantile level, and as a child after the divorce – rather than something that was simply mad.

Shortly after this, when Anne had had time in her psychotherapy and with her nurse to process some of what had happened, in a meeting of the adolescents near the end of treatment, she talked with some clarity about her feelings and wishes. Noticeably she seemed to have a 'thicker skin' and withstood some of the conflict and hostility coming at her from other adolescents within the meeting. For a while she was listening and fiddling about continuously with a pen between her fingers. I noticed the pen had her real name on it, 'Anne', which, as mentioned above, she normally would never use or want others to use. She knew I always used the name Anne, much to her annoyance, and never the shortened babyish form of her name she usually insisted on. Something important was symbolised in this small act. With her increased capacity for social relationships, and her increased ego-strength, I thought she was beginning to build a new clearer identity, less regressed and hostile, but with a sense too of where she stood socially. The pen that had once been feared in a psychotic way she now could hold. It was just a pen, and she fiddled about with it nervously, as she struggled within the group meeting. Previously her fear of the pen had created enormous disabilities for her, taking away her education and social life. Now, since she had more capacity to contain her emotions and experiences, the pen was more like, in Winnicott's terms, a transitional object (Winnicott 1971). Anne was learning she could leave behind her some of her infantile identifications and could begin to manage within a group of adolescents and be able to contain herself.

In conclusion I have proposed an outline of a psychoanalytical theory of adolescence that brings together Freud's early emphasis on the body and biological development, with the reworking of infantile sexuality as an approach to maturity and adulthood, and later developments in theory by Anna Freud and Melanie Klein, and also Winnicott and Bion. More recent psychoanalytic work with adolescents has enabled us to develop more coherent accounts of adolescent states of mind and has given us the possibility of differentiating normal adolescent developments from pathological changes. I shall now develop this further in the last two chapters.

Chapter 11

The containment of borderline adolescents

> To that truth which has the look of falsehood
> A man should always close his lips, if he can . . .
> (Dante, *The Divine Comedy; Inferno*, Canto XVI, 124)

Introduction

In this chapter I look at the containment of borderline adolescents, as they begin or undergo treatment in an adolescent unit in a therapeutic community setting at the Cassel Hospital, UK. Comparisons can be made with other psychoanalytically run adolescent units in the USA (Rinsley 1971a, 1971b, 1974; Carter and Rinsley 1977). There are 12 adolescents and young persons on the unit of both sexes and between the ages of 16 and 23. They have had extensive previous use of mental health and social service involvement over a number of years, including periods in other younger age adolescent units or acute settings. They have experienced a breakdown in their social situation, with their families or carers, and their capacity to manage everyday life, especially to stay safe. Most belong to the middle and severe end of the borderline personality spectrum (Herman and van der Kolk 1987; Herman, Perry and van der Kolk 1989; Pynoos 1990; van der Kolk and Fisler 1994; Day and Flynn 2003). Some of these patients have, from time to time or in the past, experienced some psychotic symptoms or episodes, along with major self-harm, severe depression, eating disorders, psychosomatic complaints and suicide attempts, and may, like many disturbed adolescents, fear the occurrence of a major psychotic breakdown. We normally exclude patients with prodromal psychotic conditions and schizophrenia, those with severe and active addiction problems to alcohol or street drugs, and those with a high risk of violence to others. My outline and examples will indicate how closely we test the limits of treatability by psychotherapeutic methods with such groups of patients, as their 'last chance' instead of going to adult psychiatric services.

A number of research studies by Chiesa and Fonagy describe the overall clinical effectiveness of the Cassel Hospital approach to personality disorder and give strong indications that better beneficial outcomes occur when a first phase intensive inpatient psychotherapeutic work is followed by a second phase of outreach work in the young person's locality (Chiesa 1997; Chiesa and Fonagy 2000). We are currently adapting this outcome from adult studies to adolescents in offering now a two-phase programme of treatment – nine months to one year inpatient, followed by one year outreach. Here I shall limit what I say to the first phase of work, to our current experience of the inpatient treatment.

Containment in an inpatient setting includes the complex task of understanding the meaning of the adolescent's symptoms, their mental states and their social behaviour. There are particular problems of containment for borderline adolescents, who may undergo temporary psychotic or delusional states. Some such adolescents can in some circumstances be contained in a therapeutic community setting, but others however cannot be so contained, and need to transfer to an acute unit, at least temporarily, and be treated by medication and continuous observation. First, I describe the context or setting of therapeutic treatment, in particular from a nursing perspective. The focus is on both the minimal and optimal conditions where learning and change can take place. Second, I make use of psychoanalytic ideas about adolescents with borderline psychotic conditions as outlined in the last chapter, and ideas about containment from Chapter 1, in some composite treatment examples of individual adolescents.

When treating the very disturbed adolescent, the diagnosis, our knowledge of the history and aetiology of their problems, and our views and reactions, may change as the adolescent changes. It is important then to have a treatment modality that is sensitive both to the overall general development of adolescents, and to severe forms of adolescent disturbance and behaviour, including possible incipient forms of psychosis. I believe that it is important to hold on to the idea that therapeutic forms of treatment and management for highly disturbed adolescents may offer something useful at different points in their development and at different stages of their disturbance.

The context of therapeutic treatment

As described in Chapters 4 to 7, the whole approach to treatment is underpinned by psychoanalytic understanding of individual and group behaviour. It combines group and individual psychoanalytic psychotherapy and psychosocial nursing within an inpatient therapeutic community structure (Day and Flynn 2003; Kennedy et al. 1987). I describe a continuous movement in the work between an individual and a group perspective. A shift of thinking took place when Bion, Rickman, Tom Main, Maxwell Jones and others developed the idea that neurosis was not simply an individual problem but was a problem of the group: 'Neurosis needs to be displayed as a danger to the group; and its display must somehow be made the common aim of the group' (Bion 1961: 13, 14). Within life in institutions, neurosis becomes manifest and is experienced in the group, as an interference to group functioning, or, in Bion's later terms, to the 'work group'. When this happens individuals can take responsibility as members of the group to become 'self-critical' (p. 18) to change the group functioning. Bion's and Main's further work uncovered the underlying psychotic processes in individual and group behaviour (Bion 1962b; Main 1957/1989). We now understand that particularly with borderline patients severe disturbance becomes manifest not just in individuals but in disturbed group and institutional functioning.

Normally young people come for a year's treatment in the inpatient Adolescent Unit at the Cassel Hospital. The structure of the Adolescent Unit is similar to the other units, and we have described it fully in the above chapters and elsewhere (Flynn and Turner 2003). Both aspects of treatment, psychotherapy and nursing, are seen to be in the psychoanalytic sense 'mutative', i.e. they can lead to lasting psychic change. The complex processes of this treatment, and the stresses on individuals and groups, need to be understood in a series of meetings, which review the progress of patients and which look at the staff countertransference and possible unconscious enactments, individually or collectively.

Patients have an active part in treatment, both in the day and at night. The central message or philosophy is that the patients can contain themselves with help and support from each other and staff. The emphasis is on their functioning and strength rather than their collapse. Issues that arise from crises which patients face at night can be brought back into the day for consideration within nursing structures and in psychotherapy. For those people who have difficult night times, unable to settle from the day, or with nightmares and flashbacks, there is a system of night contacts. Here a patient will ask another patient to be his/her night contact so that they can then call on them during the night for support, if necessary. In an everyday way the patients deal with the impact of disturbance, their own and that of other patients on each other, and share responsibility at looking at it. One of the major factors that determines whether the patient has the capacity and the support to stay in this form of treatment is whether they are forming relationships with other patients, and whether they are accepted by those patients. We assess the impact of the adolescent on the community and, vice versa, the impact of the community on the adolescent. In doing this we assess the culture of the adolescent group within the therapeutic community.

To guide these relationships, there are three clear boundaries for patients about acceptable behaviour within the unit, which we attempt to apply consistently. These are: no alcohol or street drugs, no violence, and no sexual relationships. These are clear, minimal and straightforward. In effect they emphasise the wide areas of choices the adolescents actually do have in treatment. These rules have been the subject of discussion by the community management team (CMT), so this means the community of patients owns the rules and it increases the likelihood that they will be adhered to. Obviously with adolescents the rules get 'tested'. But if all attempts to work with and collaborate with a person have failed, and there is no agreement about being in treatment, ultimately they may be discharged. However, the measure most frequently used is 'short leave'. This is time out for both the individual concerned and the community and the staff, and a time to think about the effect of the behaviour, the reasons for it, and how it can be different, plus how it relates to central reasons for being in treatment. Usually, once a boundary has been re-established by saying no to certain behaviour, patients can resume treatment and can often move on. At the end of short leave there will be a 'management meeting', normally with the senior nurse and consultant to discuss with the patient an understanding of what was happening and how this may make treatment different.

Judy

Judy is an 18-year-old girl with a history of sexual abuse by her stepfather. Following his prosecution and imprisonment for this offence, Judy was totally rejected by her family. On the day of the court verdict she had been given half an hour to grab her belongings and leave the family home. She began to self-harm severely by burning and cutting, eventually needing several skin grafts. She lived in an adolescent unit for two years and had been allowed to stay much longer than anybody before her. She then moved to a social services hostel in preparation for her admission to the Cassel. She had established friendly relationships with professionals that included inappropriately meeting up at weekends or spending holiday time together. In effect these professionals became substitute caring figures and had been pulled out of role. There was a huge effort to understand Judy's self-harm and be sympathetic to its causes. Although she was given a lot of help to stop the self-harm, this did not happen, and the self-harm and negative behaviour got much worse. She was becoming, in Main's sense in 'The Ailment', a 'special patient' (Main 1957).

The senior nurse and consultant met her prior to her admission to the Cassel to start to establish some boundaries, clearest of which was the requirement to curb severe self-harm. Otherwise we would not be able to work with her. She had attended this meeting on crutches after having had a skin graft on her leg, due to another serious episode of self-harm. She was so furious with this meeting, feeling we did not understand her, that she turned down admission. The already lengthy assessment was put on hold. Several months later however, after another admission to hospital for self-harm, she wrote to ask to be reconsidered and was then reassessed and subsequently admitted.

During her six-week assessment she mostly kept herself safe but remote, and there was just one incident of superficial burning during this time. Judy remained obsessed by self-harm and yet always presented herself as struggling with it, so that in fact, it was extremely hard to get to know her. Then her psychotherapist went on holiday leaving her with her male nurse. Judy went on weekend leave early, saying there was nothing at the hospital for her. At the end of the psychotherapist's holiday, when it was becoming clear that Judy felt abandoned and envious of the family she assumed her therapist to have, she lacerated her wrists, needing surgery to repair the damage.

Judy then missed the first session she was to have had on her psychotherapist's return from leave. In the usual morning meeting between nurses and patients Judy claimed there was no connection between her self-harm and her psychotherapist's holiday. She felt that she should be able just to continue as she was at the hospital and gave a bland, perfunctory understanding of why she had done what she had. She was met for a management meeting and sent on short leave. Judy was furious, and only then in her rage did she express her feelings about being disappointed, and how this made her self-harm. Up until then she had not as yet expressed this at all or in any way really attempted to work with what she felt. She just thought we should 'understand' her reasons, without her owning them or struggling with change. There was a ring of falsity about this and an appeal from injured narcissism. (I refer you to the quote from Dante at the beginning of the chapter, and Freud 1914.)

Judy was outraged then that she would be sent away. When she returned after a week, however, she was much more thoughtful, more open about her anger, more willing to express it and more realistic about what she needed to do in treatment. It was the last time she self-harmed in her treatment, and she has since looked upon this management meeting as a turning point in her growth towards health and independence. Our use of the sanction of short leave in this situation underlined our view that her self-harm was perpetuated by her unthinking and others' collusive acceptance of her destructive and narcissistic behaviour, which prevented the development of other more ordinary and sane attachments. We shall return to this theme again below.

Some may be shocked and, like Judy initially, see this type of management as cruel, perpetuating patterns of cruelty a traumatised adolescent has suffered. But I have stressed the need to confront the destructive narcissistic base of the disturbance (Rosenfeld 1971; Steiner 1993), as well as giving space to help the patient recognise and work through repetitious cycles of self-harm. One can also see that over and above Judy's reaction to her psychotherapist's break there was an underlying pattern of transference to me and 'the institution'/'the treatment as whole', which was part of and crucial to her repetitious patterns of abuse on her own body. We were seen as like the parent of whom she is frightened, but involves herself with repeatedly in a negative way. (Refer to my discussion in Chapter 6, especially pages 101–3 and 111–12, which is relevant here.) Understanding these issues as aspects of Judy's transference to treatment was an important part of the work, which was then taken further and deeper in her psychotherapy and nursing work. In managing severe self-harm in an adolescent unit, it is important to recognise that the tyrannical organisation (and 'psychic retreat') is turned to not simply because the child is trapped by fear and dread (which would make it a defensive reaction) (Steiner 1993) but *because* the destructiveness itself is libidinised, becomes exciting and an alternative satisfaction to healthy growth (Rosenfeld 1971).

In crisis situations, patients are expected to help with the management of other patients and have opinions on what may best help. This includes taking on responsibility for supervision of individuals who are especially vulnerable or at risk in planned arrangements with other patients or alongside staff members. Medication is not given as a quick fix. Many adolescent patients dispense with psychotropic medication before or during treatment. We expect patients to ask each other for help, i.e. to spend time with them, talk to them or involve them in activities. An individual patient who is in crisis is expected to make a plan for him/herself with others' help, and to be involved in saying what they need for that particular time. In other words they are expected to be active, not passive, and to take active control in dealing with symptoms, their illness and their progress.

Living in the community is perhaps the aspect of treatment that is hardest. This is because it involves 24-hour living together, a troublesome sense of belonging, and the need to keep the hospital running as an ordinary place to live, with meals being planned and prepared, and activities and therapeutic structures kept going. Often the intimacy of sharing bedrooms and general living space means that the feedback and observation patients can offer each other is crucial. Patients get to know in a very immediate and real way that the behaviour, mental states and actions of others affect them individually and as a group. The community experience can be the first time that people feel they have belonged anywhere and the first time they may realise that their feelings, behaviour and history are not unique. They may find that they are not alone, strange or misfits, and they may discover in interactions with others how their functioning may need to change.

A lot of thought goes into a patient's discharge from the community and a specific date is set at least two months in advance in order to begin the process of leaving the hospital and saying goodbye. We help to prepare young people to leave by always offering a space to talk about it and in practical ways, with adolescents, make links with local education or set up workers' meetings to work out further therapeutic provisions following discharge. We encourage patients to attend college during their treatment and try to arrange psychotherapy times and roles in the community that allow them to do this, provided this is consistent with other aims in treatment.

Change in severely emotionally disturbed adolescents

I have described the context of inpatient treatment, and some detailed psychoanalytic theory about change in adolescence in Chapter 10, which I refer you back to. I would now like to illustrate the work in further detailed case examples. We are used to the idea from psychoanalysis that it is the operation of powerful psychological mechanisms in infancy that shapes the personality, a shape that is modified but essentially the same at later stages of development. Adolescence is a substantially new period of experience, growth and change in the personality. For underlying the changes in adolescence, just as in infancy, there are major shifts in the relation of the super-ego and ego to the increased id drives, and continuous processes of projective identification, splitting and fragmentation of the ego, which alter the boundaries of internal and external reality, and change the shape of the personality in a fundamentally new way (Klein 1932, 1946; Freud 1936). Adolescents with borderline disturbances exemplify these changes in a particularly marked way.

Some borderline patients move between normal and pathological positions at different times, so that with this most disturbed group of adolescents, there may be different functions of the personality, an 'adolescent function' and a 'borderline function'. Bion differentiated movements of the personality between neurotic and psychotic positions, and later the operation of different functions of the personality (Bion 1957, 1965). Each position or function needs to be separately identified and understood, then addressed, as we shall illustrate in the examples below. There may be movement backwards and forwards between different functions, sometimes progressively over long periods of time, sometimes erratically in a see-saw effect. There needs, too, to be a different understanding of transference in respect of each function, of normal or 'neurotic transference' and delusional or 'psychotic transference'.

Much of the therapeutic work in an inpatient unit with borderline adolescents involves bringing individuals out of pathological states of mind and back to more healthy ways of interacting, allowing attachments and relationships to grow. It also involves understanding group processes in which individuals negatively affect the group and the group negatively affects individuals – a kind of contagion effect. Groups of adolescents may be passive, withdrawn and sometimes worryingly compliant. I have also learnt to be anxious when there is a mood of depression, often presaging a spate of acts of self-harm or an individual suicide attempt. Most worryingly, I find, is a manic state often irritable and excitable, with a hidden arrogant devaluation of staff, which can erupt in a supposedly 'harmless incident', followed by blame and despair, and further serious self-harm. Such incidents can cause 'riots' of feeling, what Bion called 'highly organised', 'fight–flight' responses (Bion 1961). Painstaking work over many weeks or months is necessary to bring most of the patients back fully into a treatment alliance. Such work by staff and patients most fully earns the title of 'culture of enquiry', which sometimes otherwise can seem a bit self-congratulatory. Careful management of the whole range of tasks of the unit – the 'primary task' of containment – including the tasks of understanding and supporting staff, especially those under strain or attack, is the most essential aspect of leadership of an adolescent unit (Menzies Lyth 1988).

Clinical examples

I shall now discuss two further clinical examples of borderline adolescents. These two cases, Joan and Maureen, illustrate recovery from psychotic functioning and intra-psychic growth, with concomitant improvement in social relationships and functioning. In my later discussion I shall discuss Joan and Maureen, as well as Judy above, and Anne and Penny whom I discussed in detail in the last chapter.

Joan

Joan, aged 16, used a number of aspects of therapeutic community treatment to overcome a severe depression. In particular I shall illustrate how she experienced in the here and now of the treatment, especially in its later phases, a depth of feelings which enabled her to complete the year-long inpatient experience in an emotionally real way. She had taken six overdoses since the age of 14, the last of which nearly killed her, putting her in a coma for some days. She was on a Section 3 until the week before admission because she had said that after her GCSEs she planned to kill herself. (A Section 3 is a compulsory treatment section, valid for six months, of the Mental Health Act 1987.) It was quite unusual to transfer after just a weekend's break from an acute adolescent unit to the Cassel Hospital. We would normally require a minimum interval of two weeks between transfer at home, or in a non-hospital setting. We did so in this case because of the intense anxiety about her.

Joan's parents had divorced when she was one, and she had lived first with her mother and then her father after an extended and relentless custody battle. Joan's mother suffers from a chronic and severe manic depressive psychosis, with schizophrenic tendencies, and Joan was left with her alone for many of the early months of her life. Her grandmother had actually mothered Joan until she was 6 years old. Then her father remarried and her grandmother went back to Scotland, where she later died without

Joan ever seeing her again. The anger she felt about this was repressed and then displaced onto the stepmother. The situation was exacerbated further when the stepmother 'persuaded' her to ask her mother to stop all contact with her when she was aged 10, because contact had been bizarre and upsetting for Joan. In her upbringing Joan had clearly been disturbed by her mother, and unable to express and work through her sense of responsibility for her mother and her confused and intense sense of guilt. She had attempted to cut off and kill off her unwanted thoughts, which left her feeling more desperate and alone, and then she tried the overdoses, to kill herself off.

This pattern of cutting off from others repeated itself in the early part of treatment. The Cassel Adolescent Unit is more open and free than the heavily structured unit she had been in, where she had 'buried' herself in her GCSE work. Gradually she became more involved. Renewed attachments were formed within her family, with her father and stepmother, especially with the support of family meetings. She made new relationships in the therapeutic community and importantly she worked through broken relationships with changes of first nurses. Joan was amazed that people were genuinely interested in how she was and what she felt, especially in her individual psychotherapy. From these experiences she began to understand more about the central underlying problem of separation, which underlay her suicidality. She experienced separations as that person dying, and due to her complex unconscious guilt that she had killed off the person. She felt this in relation to her mother and her grandmother. She was also frightened of her natural mother pushing things into her. It seemed evident that there had been, at a very early age and continued to be, as a matter of reality, some level of psychotic impingement from the mother. In her transference to her psychotherapist and in her relation to nurses, Joan had to work to discriminate what was 'mad' from what she could accept. This problem of 'taking in' may have been related to the eating problem she had, and to her resistance to hearing what people were saying to her about what she would need. To avoid this painful 'taking in', if she could set aside the loving feelings she had had for her grandmother, she could set aside also the feeling that she had killed her. However, the result of this was that she became even more cut off from her needs.

Despite work on this, Joan still managed to keep a degree of her real affect and some aspects of her whole development out of treatment. A relationship, partly sexual, to another young woman who had left the hospital kept the transference within the hospital a bit diluted, as well as keeping to the side issues of her personal and sexual identity. Joan wanted instead to get back to school to do A levels, and to be coated again with a secure sense of normality. She complained about how 'mad' we all were to expect her to engage any more in treatment. Her dispute with us over her leaving date – she wanted to leave earlier by about a month – brought all this to a head. We challenged her and this brought out an open disagreement on the issue for about two months. Her full anger and fury were now expressed, about endings and the separation from the hospital, in a way that clearly helped her see her real level of feelings in many other areas too.

This intense resurgence of her affect, around the issue of separation from treatment, and its containment, helped in effect to re-engage Joan in treatment in a crucial way and at a crucial time. The immediate problems of her conflict with us in the therapeutic community setting recreated problems from the past and core intra-psychic issues for her. Essentially she experienced the plans and care of the hospital and her workers about the timing of her leaving as a psychotic impingement – we 'were mad' – like a continued impingement of her schizophrenic mother, and the strange unexplained loss, death, of her primary carer during infancy, her grandmother. All of this connected to the fundamental dynamic of her suicidal feelings, and her anger with all her close parental figures. Eventually, as she worked on these issues, a compromise was reached that worked well, whereby Joan started classes outside the hospital but came back for about two further weeks of psychotherapy and her final review. This gave the needed time to think about and work on these issues, and carry it over into her post-discharge work.

Maureen

My final example describes our understanding of delusional symptoms that occurred during inpatient treatment and were part of a pattern of disturbance of an abused young woman, Maureen, who has a severe borderline personality disorder. I aim to show that those who suffer from borderline personality disorders may move between more normal/neurotic positions and more psychotic positions (Bion 1957, 1965; Rosenfeld 1965, 1987). In other words at times of severe disturbance, normal and neurotic levels of functioning break down, and such patients show a psychotic level of disturbance. This needs to be understood, in order to work to re-establish a more normal and neurotic level of functioning.

Maureen is a young woman of 21, who came to the Cassel following a very disturbed upbringing. She was one of two children in a family, where the parents were together but both had had considerable mental health difficulties. The mother made repeated self-harm and suicide attempts, frequently in front of her daughter, who then had to call for help. The father had suffered major depression, and was felt by Maureen to be cruel, undermining and useless, in that 'he did nothing for the family'. Maureen had suffered sexual abuse from a family friend over a prolonged period between the ages of 9 and 13. She was involved between her parents in their recurring violent conflicts, and became incapable of secure long-lasting external attachments outside the family. The severe conflicts were now internalised and repeatedly enacted in her pathology. She had been continuously disturbed making multiple self-harm and suicide attempts since the age of 14. The dependence of her parents on psychiatric services now translated into Maureen's parasitic dependence on psychiatric services, especially recurrent and ineffective inpatient psychiatric admissions. Bion described how such parasitic relationships destroy both sides (Bion 1970: 103).

On admission Maureen complained of not knowing who she was. She had a very confused identity, a pattern of obscure obsessional rituals and extensive concrete thinking. Examples of this come out below. She was very overweight, although she had had a period of being very slim when infatuated with a female teacher. Prior to admission to the Cassel she used alcohol excessively. Two types of self-harm were most prominent. There had been multiple severe depth slashes by a knife or razor on both arms. To someone seeing these first off they have a gruesome effect and could make one feel sick. There was also the ever-looming possibility that a serious attempt would be made on her own life, in a final way that would end everything. Behind this was her recurring fear of going mad.

What also became prominent within the treatment were major worrying incidents where threats were made on the lives of staff working with her. Due to states of confusion her aggression against people outside would often be seen by her to be legitimised. Following a first aggressive incident, Maureen was away from the hospital for three to four weeks, some of the time back in her local psychiatric hospital. Later on, there was another absence from the hospital, when she was on short leave for nearly two weeks. There were then severe anxieties about her capacity to sustain our sort of treatment. I shall return to this period of absence and short leave below to look at the meaning of her self-harm.

Maureen was one of the most worrying adolescents on the unit at that time. Her obsessional rituals manifested themselves across the hospital, particularly in the activities and work groups, preventing her being really involved. It was always difficult to get at what exactly Maureen's emotional state was, as there was extensive splitting of her experience. Simultaneous traits existed, of mocking withdrawal and manic excited exuberance, and she evoked complicity by seduction with some staff, and anger and rejection in other staff. It was difficult to get through to Maureen, and there was a doubt about whether she could take anything in. The significance of this may date from her earliest infantile experience, for we knew that as an infant Maureen suffered from seizures and was also hospitalised because of being unable to digest milk.

Within treatment Maureen had now settled into a pattern in which she used alcohol outside the hospital each weekend, thereby blotting out her capacity to react to and further her involvement, and preventing real advances in treatment. A first serious violent incident occurred when, rejecting the night nurse's involvement with her, she brandished a knife at her, again under the influence of alcohol. We understood the violence to have erupted because she was being challenged. Her obsessional rituals had served to keep out troubling and conflicting emotions, but at a deeper level they served too to keep out a psychotic level of confusion. When her behaviour was challenged she began to act in a bizarre and dangerous way. We decided only to allow her to return to the hospital after she had agreed a contract not to use alcohol within her treatment. This was stricter and less flexible than rules about alcohol with other patients.

However, such stricter boundaries allowed for more productive periods of treatment, when she could listen, and so be less paranoid and less constantly misunderstanding of the motives of others. She could then develop some relationships in the community, where she became in time increasingly well liked, and for some patients almost indispensable for their treatment. This reflected within the therapeutic culture how Maureen could be again, as in her family, the indispensable helper who could set herself apart from personal conflicts. This was a kind of Oedipal illusion, in Britton's sense, where she could be the only helpful one and there was seen to be no helpful parental couple or parental authority (Britton 1989).

I shall describe now the build-up over a two to three week period; setting the scene to the second period away from the hospital, and our understanding then of her behaviour and her disturbance. Maureen had the staff split in her mind. There were just one or two figures that were helpful and most figures were mistrusted. Sometimes now she had an obsessional, paranoid belief that Mr Flynn, the Head of the Adolescent Unit, was out to kill her. There were other disturbing examples of concrete thinking. Helpful and genuine interventions were treated either with disdain or as directly provocative and troubling. Evident in her, at a deeper level, was a destructive envy and a fateful hopelessness.

Maureen kept stressing at this time how crazy her mother was, and how 'her mother kept upsetting her', particularly at weekends. Nevertheless, when in her flat at weekends she had to be in contact with her parents three times a day, otherwise she would not manage. She was upset also about a worker from the voluntary society that had helped her who had recently left. All the signs were there of a recurring pattern for her of an idealised relationship, or infatuation, with some degree of over-involvement by the worker with her. This could be understood as a splitting of the bad intrusive mother (her real mother) and the replacement idealised mother (the worker, and sometimes in treatment, her psychotherapist).

Maureen had always had a pride in her own flat that she kept comfortable and pristine. Every effort and most resources were put into keeping the flat so. By contrast it was very difficult to get her to put the same level of emotional resources into her own treatment. A worrying warning sign occurred one weekend when she smashed a number of treasured ornaments in her flat in a fit of rage.

Also over this time Maureen became increasingly and continuously pre-occupied that something would get into her flat to spoil it and ruin it from the inside. This seemed to fit with a level of paranoid thinking, in every aspect of contact with her, that something evil or bad would destroy her from the inside. Contamination could get into everything and could get anywhere. Suddenly this fear became a reality for her when she discovered some maggots in her flat. Evidently a neighbour who used to go fishing had been breeding maggots in his flat and somehow or other some of these had evidently got into her flat. It was difficult to know how real the problem was. There was something confused and unreal about the whole thing, but whilst she was preoccupied with this there was no way that anything at the Cassel could be real and thought about. All attention had to be paid to the infestation within the flat. Maureen was now becoming more worrying within the hospital. Some of what she said seemed confused and had a psychotic feel about it, although there was no evidence that she was hallucinating in a formally psychotic way.

During this time Maureen had her first family meeting with her mother and father, with her nurse and myself, the head of the unit. To the workers, and indeed the family at the time, there was a sense that some under-standing of various matters had been shared. It was noticeable, however, how Maureen's mother did continuously interrupt or talk over her, indeed invade her, as she remained obliviously and continuously preoccupied about herself. In turn Maureen obliterated anything helpful her father said and he was not capable of pulling anything together. Maureen mentioned, but her parents passed over, the incidents in childhood with the family friend, and it seemed the issue of sexual abuse could not be talked about. Going over such painful personal matters with her family was now as before particularly difficult.

Following the family meeting, nevertheless, Maureen seemed temporarily less disturbed for a day or two. However, her mind was bent on going off for a week on short leave to sort out the issue of maggots in her flat with the environmental health officer, and various other issues about benefits, which did need dealing with. She was prevailed upon to reduce this period to two days and therefore was going to return on the Tuesday night instead of the Sunday night from the weekend at home. There was some break-down in the communication between staff about the arrangements: some thought the short leave of two days had been agreed, others thought it was going to be a week and others thought it had been refused altogether. These disagreements could later be seen as a sign of our confusion about Maureen and as evidence of a splitting process.

On the Monday night, the first day of short leave, a very serious incident occurred when Maureen severely cut herself at her flat, in a similar manner to previous severe acts of self-harm. She had been distressed that she could not convince the environmental officer and other workers outside that her flat was still infested with maggots. She was admitted to her local psychiatric hospital, reportedly with some depersonalisation and a risk of suicide.

However, as had frequently happened before, on the psychiatric ward her behaviour returned to normal within a few days. After some ten days and several meetings with the psychiatrist there and the workers here she returned to the Cassel and settled back into treatment. Similar patterns have occurred since. Maureen's treatment continued and there were periods of progress and periods of acute disturbance, and in an overall sense some improvement.

For my purposes now, I shall attempt to use our understanding of what happened, and what led to this episode of self-harm, to illuminate changes in Maureen's underlying psychic functioning. I shall describe the transition to an increased level of psychotic functioning, followed by more cooperation in treatment and progress, with the re-establishment of a normal or neurotic level of functioning.

The meaning of Maureen's self-harm on this occasion can be understood, but only in a very complex way, and only by putting together many aspects of the treatment. In particular we needed to examine her relation to the tasks and activities in the hospital, her relationships with the nurses, and what she was able to work through in an individual transference within her psychotherapy. It would seem that Maureen had been deeply affected by continuous worrying and meaningless intrusions, particularly from her mother. Her own thinking and mind was continuously invaded. This repeated the effect of her mother's suicidal and self-harming attacks during her childhood, which had also brought with it a real level of emotional deprivation. Maureen then had suffered a further type of intrusion, in terms of the sexual abuse by the family friend. It is unclear whether there was parental complicity in this but it is clear at least that there was some negligence.

Maureen's own mental functioning developed in a way that had made her mistrustful, paranoid, prone to severe splitting, and patterns of destructive fragmentation leading to confusional states. This type of functioning is well described by Herbert Rosenfeld (1965), Wilfred Bion (1957), and Melanie Klein (1946). Central to this is the severe splitting of mind and body. Freud spoke of the ego as 'a bodily ego'. Maureen, with her severe level of splitting, could enact a destructive threat on herself by attacking her body, hence the severe cutting. When this splitting occurred, there were the good and bad workers, there was the good place and the bad place, the good place being the idealised flat, the bad place being the troubling and disquieting Cassel Hospital. Anna Freud (1952a) has described how, at a neurotic level of functioning, severely deprived children often enact a split within themselves in which the body is neglected and mistreated but then needs to be looked after by someone. Effectively then the child internalises a helper and a helped. Maureen's concentration in an obsessional way on cleaning her flat, and indeed her self-appointed role of helper of other patients on the unit, was this helping activity in relation to the damaged part of the self. So long as Maureen could keep up this idealised form of care, at a relatively static level of severe neurotic conflict, regarding herself as able to maintain her flat and her place within the unit, there was less likelihood of a psychotic level of reaction. Below her level of ordinary or neurotic difficulties then, and the obsessional symptoms, was potentially a psychotic level of mental activity and disturbance. It was when her neurotic level of adaptation eventually entirely broke down on the Monday, and her flat went from being very good, or ideal, to very bad and contaminated (as her beliefs about the maggots had transformed into a delusional belief), that Maureen reverted to a psychotic level of functioning, and with renewed severe splitting made the severe attacks on her body. This led in turn to a severe sense of hopelessness and a more worrying danger that a real suicide attempt would be made.

These delusional ideas took over Maureen when she was pushing away and withdrawing from contact and treatment. Her thinking had become more concrete (Segal 1957), she was attacking the unit and its head, but then the projective identification was returned in a concrete form in her paranoid idea that 'he was out to kill her', and she needed to get out of the hospital (Bion 1954, 1956; Freud 1911a: 63). Her ideas became progressively more paranoid and her previous idealisations, about her previous worker and her flat, broke down, leading her to experience fully the terrifying splitting and fragmentation within herself, leading then to attacks on herself, the severe self-harm, and danger of a suicide attempt.

In our work with this patient from this time we tried to incorporate what we had learnt about the build-up to this self-harm, so that as a result the level and type of splitting and destructive fragmentation decreased. We have felt it necessary to work, particularly in the individual psychotherapy, with the way sometimes rather incomplete and indeed thin levels of contact become idealised. Maureen would then become obsessed with the idea that she was going to lose what little she had. All the while, however, contact within the therapeutic community, that was indeed potentially more helpful, richer and could have a more purposeful direction, would get overlooked.

There was a calmer aspect to Maureen as she took on some of this. She now found ways of talking about her disturbance in the hospital, in psychotherapy and particularly in group situations. She then began to use more normal therapeutic community structures as a vehicle for expression of her conflicts, as illustrated in the following example about her use of the work group to express feelings in her relationship with her nurse.

Maureen was habitually meticulously tidy, both at home and in her room in the hospital. She had always taken tasks at the Cassel to do with such cleaning very seriously, even when she had been most uncooperative in other areas. She was in a work group with her nurse, cleaning the common room. Usually her nurse had been able to rely on her attendance. As discharge loomed, Maureen stopped attending and she continually had to be woken in the mornings. Her nurse began to find her behaviour infuriating. As Maureen was now not attending structures or being active in community life, the issue was discussed in a morning meeting. It became clear that Maureen was furious with staff for discharging her and was reacting in a way she knew would be noticed and questioned, but was nevertheless *safe*. As a serious self-harmer, this was very important. She had used the structures, the context of the morning work group, to contain her angry feelings and enactments within treatment, rather than express them in a self-destructive way, attacking the boundaries of treatment itself.

Conclusion

The cases described here, Judy, Joan and Maureen, plus Anne and Penny described previously (Chapter 10) are all adolescents who have been diagnosed with a borderline personality disorder, or 'borderline adolescents'. Using the conceptual distinctions when describing the borderline child (Chapter 3), Joan, Anne and Maureen would fit into cluster A of borderline adolescents, as being more clearly psychotic at times, with a fragile reality sense and thought disorganisation (Bleiberg 2000: 41–4). Judy and Penny would fit into cluster B, who are in the severely neurotic range, have a 'dramatic' personality disorder, including intense dramatic affect and hunger for social response.

Bion's distinction (1957) between psychotic and non-psychotic parts of the personality is crucial in treating these most disturbed adolescents. Unless the psychotic elements are recognised as such, and carefully managed so that the adolescent can recapture their more healthy functions, their disturbance may well be seen as unitary, yet still will be experienced as erratic and incomprehensible, allowing no coherent therapeutic approach. Conversely, if undue emphasis is placed alone on the psychotic elements, then important issues of adolescent development or maturation are missed. Work to identify difficulties in development, which all adolescents experience to some degree, is equally important. These issues include the development of health and personal self-care, a recognition of and a relationship to their more sexual body and greater capacity for aggression, increased mental capacities and capacities for social interaction, stronger peer relationships and new processes of attachment to others, while there is a process of detachment from the parents.

The setting of the Adolescent Unit provides many opportunities both for adolescent development and for the experience and treatment of severe pathology and disturbance. Maureen's use of a therapeutic structure, the morning work group and the following firm meeting, to express her anger, allowed her to work to try to develop more ordinary and reliable adult attachments, integrating intense feelings of disappointment and betrayal if things did not work out. Something was strengthened, reducing the likelihood of a return to the frequent splitting and excessive projective identification I have described above, which would lead to psychotic disturbance and recurrent acute psychiatric admissions. Different features of the inpatient setting are important for different adolescents: for Penny it was to remain caring and firm while responding to frequent outbursts of aggression and antisocial behaviour; for Anne it was to find significance and make sense of frightening personal emotional experiences, which had meant a social isolation; for Joan it was to recognise experiences of loss in relation to the beginning and end of treatment itself; and for Judy it was to recognise painful trauma while not colluding with a narcissistic specialness which tended to justify and augment self-harm of her body and self-destructive strategies in relationships.

In all these case descriptions we can see adolescents who were able to use aspects of the therapeutic community and psychoanalytical psychotherapy. They were able to recover from states of acute disturbance, characterised by delusional states and psychotic symptoms, so creating again a push for ordinary adolescent expression, change and development. Bion (1962b) introduced the concept of 'containment', using the example of the child's earliest object relations in relation to the breast, to describe the modification of infantile fears. The infant projects a part of its psyche, namely its bad feelings, into a good breast: then, in due course, they are removed and re-introjected. During their sojourn in the good breast they are felt to have been modified in such a way that the object that is re-introjected has become tolerable to the infant's psyche. The 'container' is that into which an object is projected, and the 'contained' is that which can be projected into the 'container' (Bion 1962b: 90). Adapting this theory of containment to the study of adolescents, the 'contained' in the Adolescent Unit may at times be certain bizarre and psychotic manifestations from the adolescent, and at other times more lively yet still disturbed expressions of adolescent change and development. The 'container' is both the receptive emotional capacities of the staff, nurses and psychotherapists, and their thoughtful structures for realistic communal living, in the therapeutic culture of the unit and the hospital, as devised through the cooperative capacities of therapeutic community residents. I have described in the examples how in this applied context therapeutic work, derived from psychoanalytic thinking and the patients' engagement in socially productive roles, may help them move away from illness and develop new active ego strengths, to create real internal and external change.

Chapter 12

The eclipse of adolescence

Assessment of normal and pathological aspects

Introduction

I have defined adolescence, understood psychoanalytically, as a developmental process in which the young person acquires new sexual and aggressive powers, including a new powerful and sexual body, as they rework Oedipal relationships in the light of new tasks in life. The young person acquires a new sense of themselves and their physical, mental and emotional capacity, including a sense of their individuality and their personal value (see Chapters 10 and 11). If very severe disturbance takes hold of the adolescent during this developmental process, then the whole process may be halted, or at the least obscured. This is the eclipse of adolescence.

Eclipses occur when one body or object blocks or obscures the light between two other bodies or objects. In solar eclipses, the moon passes between the sun and earth, obscuring the light of the sun on the earth, and in lunar eclipses the earth passes between the sun and moon, obscuring the light of the sun on the moon. For young people, eclipses of adolescence occur when a process of severe disturbance obscures or obliterates the light or the life forces of normal development. The converse can happen too, that the very powerful life forces in the adolescent process obscure darker destructive or death forces that have been evident in childhood and may become evident again in adulthood. I shall not deal with this latter situation so much here. Eclipses that occur are important. The study of solar and lunar eclipses from the time of Galileo and Newton was important for the development of the theory of dynamics (Sharratt 1994). Equally, viewing changes in terms of eclipses of adolescent development can become an opportunity to understand the psychodynamics of adolescence. It gives us a new way to look at adolescent experiences of excitement and disturbance.

Clinical example

Let me give an example of an eclipse of normal developmental processes in adolescence. Lucy, who was nearly 16 when she came into treatment with us in an inpatient adolescent unit, had had intensive treatment as a major suicide risk since her early teens. At 13 she had overdosed with 75 paracetamol: she vomited afterwards but not on purpose and was disappointed she did not die. There had been other serious but unsuccessful overdoses, cutting and self-harm, and an attempt to hang herself. Another time in a previous hospital she had carefully planned a vicious assault on a female member of staff, calling her quietly into a room on her own for a confidential word and then smashing her in the face. At one point she had had a suicide pact with another 13-year-old girl. When Lucy backed out of this she was convinced the girl was out to kill her. Lucy was described as much of the time gentle, friendly and cooperative with an intelligent understanding. Yet she had had acute disturbances since early childhood, especially severe nightmares, and problems of concentration and memory, which, despite the fact she had won a scholarship to a very good school, caused her to drop out of education completely when she was 14 (in year 9). She remained a substantial suicide risk, especially because of secretive planning and her rather uncanny good humour before any serious suicide attempt that could put workers off the scent of danger. There were also a range of other problems, with eating, some use of drugs and so on.

I will not go into the full history here. There were, however, no obvious antecedent events or trauma that could easily explain or sum up such behaviour. Lucy was an only child and she had lived with her mother. Her father was around for just a few months after her birth and there were secrets about him: he may have been a criminal and could not be talked about in the family. Her mother was bright and worked professionally, but at referral she had not yet been identified as having mental health problems, although there was a major history of mental illness on her side of the family. She was a foster parent, with a succession of children coming and going in the family, until Lucy was 12. There was then the appearance of normality in the family. During the years of Lucy's worsening problems there had been some family work, but it had repeatedly reached impasse, because either Lucy or her mother prevented any real moves forward.

At assessment for inpatient treatment Lucy could not sustain any understanding about why she was as she was. She fended off particularly any suggestion that there was anything amiss between her and her mother. She was also angry that every psychiatric assessment seemed to make something of the absence of her father. She stressed she had got used to this and it was not a problem for her. However, she made a curious distinction that I felt was genuine and would open the way to understanding the complex types of thought confusion she suffered from. She said it was not *what* had happened to her, or the events, but her *perceptions* about what happened to her that were the problem. She seemed to imply in this the possibility that her view of the external and the real may result from her distortions of thinking and feeling. There was also some measure of engagement with the therapeutic process and me. She felt I had been very direct with her about key issues (i.e. her destructiveness), and she had felt very down between the two assessment meetings, so she knew that she had been deeply affected, but she was pleased she had come up again. She mentioned she had previously not been able to do this. This indication of a capacity to get in touch with her underlying depression, rather than enact it in murderous phantasies and actions, was a key prognostic indicator for change.

During the course of treatment with us, one could see there were two sides of this girl, an adolescent side and a very disturbed, borderline or pathological side, so that progress could only occur by working with both sides. As treatment proceeded she was not so caught up with thoughts of death, and she struggled to develop what she now recognised was her rather empty life. Her adolescent side could be more apparent in ordinary ways, her mixing with peers, her chattiness, her sense of fun, her dress, her slim figure, her interest in rock music and pop festivals, even to a degree her exploratory use of street drugs, which, as she has got a bit better, she had laid off, recognising it made her so much worse in her bad periods.

One time I had to meet her for a management meeting to assess her acute suicidal state and she was wearing a tee-shirt with 'Rage against the Machine' on the front. She had been experiencing treatment in a paranoid way as a method of killing her off, crushing the life out of her, and we were seen I thought to be like a huge industrial psychiatric/psychotherapy machine working her over, so she needed to fight us off, rage against us and prevent us getting to her. This she duly did, by not attending the thera- peutic structures she was required to and being determinately negative about treatment. While thinking with her about her feelings, as she struggled to recognise and alter her wish to self-harm and for suicide, and she thought about her acute state of confusion and unhappiness, I did also acknowledge her tee-shirt. She beamed with pleasure and told me of the forthcoming rock concert at Wembley that she was planning to go to, to see the rock group 'Rage against the Machine'.

There were many facets to such management meetings that provided her with a degree of containment. Lucy could be difficult with many male staff, especially the senior nurse, a black man, who got the brunt of her negative paternal transference. But with me, perhaps partly because of my role as a substitute father figure (who accepted her for treatment and chaired her reviews and was in her family meetings) in a positive paternal transference, she seemed to be able to be more responsive, which could help her strengthen a life-directed side.

Family meetings had exposed many elements of a mutually destructive relationship between Lucy and her mother, which each worked to alter, eventually making many weekends much better and more contained for Lucy. Positive and destructive elements from both mother and adolescent were identified, so that for a time a third position of understanding and holding on to the life side of Lucy became possible. Later on however this progress was again affected when Lucy's mother becoming seriously disturbed and ill with a manic depressive illness, so she was unable to continue the family meetings.

Nevertheless the adolescent side of Lucy was strengthened, with her increased recognition of real difficulties, with her doing some school exams, and planning her weekends and her future. All this was an integral part of strengthening a life-directed side of her, which very easily could be overcome and squeezed out by something very negative. Such attempts to differentiate and strengthen these adolescent aspects were likely to disturb the death-orientated equilibrium previously held (a rather fixed partial eclipse of life forces), which had continuously brought her back to more depression and disturbance.

Lucy now candidly expressed an awareness of how she was just hanging on in treatment, she knew her relationship with her mother was fraught and destructive for each of them. More positively she began saying how depressed and fragile she felt and expressing her inner states. As she did, other adolescents responded more to her so that she was in fact less isolated. She did not then have to bear the empty days and the frightening nights on her own.

The type of splitting that then occurred in the treatment process seemed less a chaotic fragmentation than part of an attempt to differentiate good and bad, which viewed in an overall way could be seen as part of a normal developmental process. Let me illustrate this with regard to the two main relationships she had in treatment, with her psychotherapist and her nurse. *Her psychotherapy* had been putting her in touch with violent feelings of hatred and rage that she found very distressing. In the transference to her female psychotherapist, she was seeing herself as confused and mixed up with a mother figure whom she hated so much she wished to destroy her. For this reason she felt she had to miss her sessions or leave early, to prevent her acting out her wish to destroy her psychotherapist. She then sometimes felt regret, but as the pattern repeated itself continuously she became more aware how she experienced her psychotherapist as untrustworthy, and at such times could not experience her as a container of more disturbed feelings. This increasingly brought inner conflict and the emergence of a wish to overcome something she increasingly felt was negative. There was the theme of fusion, as well as confusion, in the psychotherapy. When she was very depressed she felt it was her psychotherapist who was depressed. What is more, she did a lot to induce chaotic, depressed and desperate feelings in her psychotherapist (Joseph 1989; Sandler 1976, 1988), to make it a reality. The relationship was becoming a mirror image of that with her mother, or more strictly her internal mother. Although she was not yet able to see this, the seeds were there for her to work through important aspects of her relationship with her mother in her transference to her psychotherapist. There were dangers in this development, particularly as instead of having plans for death, Lucy now, as she had more fluid and ready access to her feelings, was more immediately in touch with impulses, and could suddenly act on them, and on a recent occasion had indeed cut herself (but not severely) in an impulsive way.

Lucy's relationship to her nurse was different entirely and reflected the splitting processes I referred to above. She attempted only to engage her nurse about practical issues or physical issues to do with her health and kept away from her feelings and emotions, being vague and evasive when these were touched on. She only let her nurse in when she was on the point of a crisis. Attention was usually only given to the exciting things outside, the disco or the pop concert. There were two levels of engagement, one of excitement in these outside things, and the other of depression and withdrawal, not turning up to activities and therapeutic structures, and going back to bed. What was different however about the relationship to the nurse was that there was *not* a confused involvement between them, nor any enmeshment. Lucy showed more clearly with her how she defended herself against disturbance, either by taking flight in an excited way or by withdrawal. The earlier death pact, suicidal planning and behaviour, had had this highly excited side, which with her increased capacity for depression was now to a degree transformed into depression about her destructive capacities. This withdrawal allowed her to give in and be overwhelmed by her depression (Steiner 1993). Both these reactions to her nurse could then be taken up with her as ways of relating, connected to complex internal phantasies or perceptions that acted as defences. They could be addressed as ordinary psychological work to do to help her to cope better.

As I have illustrated here and above (see Chapter 11 on Maureen and Chapter 7 on Susan and Ann), if splitting processes can be understood, even in such severe and complex cases, then the containment within the inpatient process and coordinated collaborative work between nurse and psychotherapist can facilitate progress. This coming together of important elements (by 'reversing' the splits) happened with Lucy in the later phases of treatment, as it can in successful treatments of other borderline adolescents, so she could work towards a less destructive adolescent life style after treatment.

Central issues in assessment

The assessment of severely disturbed adolescents involves differentiating elements that are normal from those that are pathological, that is elements that go far beyond what is seen in the more 'healthy disturbance' of ordinary adolescents. In assessing any adolescent, the most crucial and difficult question is: 'Is this adolescent's behaviour or anxiety normal, or are there signs of present or future pathology?' (Kernberg 1984; Laufer and

Laufer 1984: 178; Laufer 1995; Anderson 1998; Bleiberg 2000; Waddell 2002). Above, and in Chapter 11, I have described changes, indeed sometimes frequent oscillations, between normal and more pathological sides in the adolescent. Here I would like to look at how in assessing the adolescent for treatment one needs to relate to and engage with both these sides.

Facing the 'full stream of adolescent turmoil', the adolescent's disturbing and uncomfortable projections, their 'agitation of inexperience' (Copley 1993: 57), or coming in contact again not just with one's own adolescent feelings and memories but with 'the adolescent habitat, with its groupishness, its predilection for mindlessness and sensuality, its self absorption and aversion to external world demands' (Waddell 2002: 368), poses challenges to all those in contact with adolescents, professionals and not least parents. However it is only with relatively few adolescents that it is clear that tendencies towards destructiveness outweigh more positive aspects and innate capacities for sexual and psychological growth, which then turn into a total hatred of his/her own development (Anderson 1998: 71). In some such adolescents the process of attacks on the self can form a closed system inside the self so that communication of deep anxiety and all other real communication is stymied and effective relational contact even to do an assessment is very difficult (Anderson 1998: 75). Great persistence will be required to get the adolescent to open up and discover the seriousness of their disturbance. Once however an adolescent becomes engaged in the therapeutic process, time is on his/her side – the therapeutic process itself can temporarily enable the conflicts of adolescence to remain fluid (Laufer and Laufer 1984: 178). This opening is vital, especially with suicidal adolescents, because after a suicide attempt there may be in phantasy a part of themselves that is dead to which they continue to maintain a relationship. Time is of the essence then to intervene before an adolescent's enactment of this phantasy brings a successful suicide (Laufer and Laufer 1984: 189, 204; cf. too Winnicott 1963a on 'Fear of Breakdown').

Kernberg (1984) identifies seven areas where the normal may be confused or mixed up with the pathological, and each needs to be separately identified and differentiated in assessment of severely disturbed adolescents. The seven areas of differentiation are as follows:

1   *Severe anxiety and depression* of a normal adolescent's overall functioning at home, in school and with peers, may resemble the severer social breakdown typical of borderline conditions.
2   *Rapidly shifting identifications* with this or that social ideology or group, as part of the adolescent tendency to identity crises, may look over a few months like a radical pathological change in the personality.
3   *Conflicts with parents, siblings, school authorities* and so on may reflect neurotic dependent and rebellious needs, or they may reflect severe pathology.

4   *Antisocial behaviour* in adolescence may be 'normal' or reflect severe character pathology and borderline personality organisation.

5   *Infantile narcissistic reactions* so frequent in adolescence may be more normal or mask a severe narcissistic personality structure.

6   *Perverse or promiscuous sexual trends* that may be a normal or transient part of adolescence or mask the predominance of aggressive conflicts that are typical in borderline personality organisation.

7   *Borderline conditions* may mask slowly developing psychotic conditions such as schizophrenic illness or severe depression (the other type of eclipse).

Kernberg raises an intriguing question: 'Do all adolescents present some degree of identity diffusion and hence are their symptoms and behaviour indistinguishable from later borderline personality organisation?' This is a question I have attempted to address in these chapters. Such features are distinguishable, but only if the assessment brings out and tests what is normal and what pathological, and treatment has strategies to contain both aspects.

In practice in the diagnostic assessment interview of the adolescent I would be looking (see Kernberg 1984) at three crucial elements:

1   *A capacity for reality testing*: in both normal and pathological adolescent functioning primitive defensive operations such as splitting, denial and projective tendencies come into use, and there can be the lack of an integrated sense of self and a differentiated concept of others. It is the presence or absence of reality testing in a strict sense that permits diagnostic differentiation, especially with the severer types of narcissistic personality who may come for assessment.

2   *A capacity for recognition of 'the other'*: this is a central capacity that can help to differentiate normal adolescent turmoil when coming up against a combination of omnipotent control, grandiosity, and devaluation with violent rebelliousness against the parents in the adolescent. This underlies any more normal Oedipal functioning (see Chapter 10 and Britton 1989).

3   *A capacity for experiencing guilt and concern*: this is important in working in particular with adolescents who are suicidal or engage in severely destructive self-harming behaviour.

While it is true that it is only after intensive psychotherapeutic treatment and substantial change that the borderline adolescent will develop these capacities, there will need to be at least some element of each of these three capacities present in order to start psychotherapeutic treatment. This is essential for a treatment alliance and the basis for the 'adolescent function' to establish more 'territory' in the internal and external life of the adolescent in relation to the 'borderline function'.

It is important for the adolescent to take a full part in deciding about the treatment he/she receives, what the arrangements are and what their commitments are. The adolescent needs to acknowledge his/her need for treatment and be able to accept that the assessor's arrangements for treatment are part of their recognition that the adolescent is at risk or ill. A back-up acute psychiatric bed may be needed, and arrangements need to be agreed and in place for readmission to an inpatient acute psychiatric bed if this is required during the treatment period. I believe that knowledge of this by the adolescent allows them a freedom to express themselves within the inpatient psychotherapeutic context of the unit, and indeed offers a further degree of containment, knowing there is a safety valve (Winnicott 1963b). Importantly, it also allows for the possibility of acting out within treatment, and hence testing the reality of the phantasies and types of relationship underlying their disturbance. It therefore contributes importantly to working with more normal developmental aspects of the adolescent and differentiating these from other aspects that involve a hatred of growth and reality. This is in line with Rosenfeld's important argument allowing for the possibility of acting out in analysis (Rosenfeld 1965), and Betty Joseph's emphasis on the inevitability and importance for learning and self-growth of 'acting in' the transference, or enactments, during psychoanalytic treatments (Joseph 1989).

Anderson notes particularly vis-à-vis the suicidal adolescent that 'a primary problem faced in development is how to manage our hatred and that of others in order to protect ourselves and others whom we love and need' (Anderson 1999: 71). Awareness of the limits of treatability implies a curb on therapeutic omnipotence (Winnicott 1949; MacCarthy 1987; Abram 1996: 172–82). The situation with very disturbed adolescents is complex and fluid and one that needs to be faced with uncertainty and with limited preconceptions in order to understand the adolescent (Waddell 2002). Workable and comprehensible boundaries of the setting of work are also essential if the psychoanalyst or psychotherapist is to be able to deal with his/her own countertransference: 'We are frightened, provoked, filled with anger and sometimes even hatred. We are made to feel responsible and guilty . . . and there is no way round this often bewildering and upsetting situation' (Anderson 1999: 77).

Assessment of adolescents involves giving adequate weight to the history of the patient, their symptoms and diagnosis, and to the impression they give in the here and now of the assessment interview, especially about their capacity to respond to therapeutic intervention and to change (Limentani 1972; Baker 1980). But predicting treatability on the basis of diagnostic classification and history alone is not a clear guide of what will be effective treatment. In voluntary treatments, where the capacity to take responsibility for treatment and the capacity for gaining insight is being assessed, it is important if possible to identify the developmental stage in early life where the problems originated, and for the adolescent to be able to make links between these problems, his/her symptoms and history (Glover 1954). Other important elements to assess are the need to identify the types of underlying anxieties and the resulting defences (Freud 1936; Baker 1980; Garelick 1994) and the relationship between the patient and the assessor, so that factors internal to the patient can be scrutinised, such as motivation and the capacity for constructive synthesis of the psychotherapeutic experience (Limentani 1972).

A key issue is the degree of the assessor's activity. Too much attention to history and symptoms can clutter the assessor's mind and keep out the freshness of their own feelings and perceptions, including their deeper countertransference, and their 'total affective response' (King 1978). This can obscure not just the psychotherapist's own personal responses but the all-important issue of the patient's presentation in the assessment and their emerging transference and attitude towards treatment. Elucidation of the unconscious transaction between the patient and the assessor gives us the key aspects of the transference and the psychodynamic formulation upon which treatment is based (Steiner 1976). Coming to a psychodynamic formulation, however tentative and tenuous, is an important function of assessment and is based on three levels of object relationship:

• the current life situation
• the infantile object relationships as described in the patient's history
• the relationship with the assessor which to all intents and purposes is the beginning of the transference (Hinshelwood 1991; Sandler 1988).

For successful assessment of adolescents, the assessor's capacity to form a treatment alliance with the adolescent is vital, to help the adolescent to be psychologically minded, to help the adolescent feel listened to (Appelbaum 1972), and to link relief of psychic pain with self-knowledge (Coltart 1988). The assessor should have developed their own position regarding recommendations for treatment, have an internal model of psychic change that they use, know where they stand on the continuum between insight and corrective emotional experience, and then be prepared to say what is the most appropriate treatment (Coltart 1988; Limentani 1972).

Others (Laufer and Laufer 1984) play down the importance of the assessor's own personal skills in the interaction with the adolescent, in favour of devoting very close energy to understanding the nature of the problem and the deep unconscious levels of the disturbance, importantly recognising a breakdown that has occurred. They describe a group of adolescents whose depression make it very difficult to get in touch with the urgency of the problem. They are anxious and perhaps terrified but do not know why: 'when seen for assessment they can describe themselves as dead, not caring, feeling hopeless, hating themselves and not knowing what to do with themselves, but without the awareness they have given up already.' An important function of the analytic assessment is to make conscious the extent of their desperation and the risk to their lives from suicide if they feel that all else has failed (Laufer and Laufer 1984: 201–2).

The first assessment session then is vital in bringing together a view of the adolescent, what has happened to them, how they relate and reveal aspects of their inner world and functioning and how they relate to the possibility of treatment. Important aspects of the unconscious transaction between the adolescent and assessor can be looked at, perhaps providing a tentative early psychodynamic formulation, which will no doubt change as assessment and treatment progresses. I invite the adolescent to bring whatever they wish to bring, facilitating the possibility of free association. This permits a rigorous scrutiny in the here and now of the interaction between the patient and the psychotherapist, particularly the nature of the contact at the affective level and the degree of access to the patient's inner world (Garelick 1994). The presence and quality of emotional contact in the session is important, as well as the patient's capacity to think and understand. It is also an opportunity for the assessor to point things out in the here and now and to monitor the reaction of the patient. I would also ask and try to gauge from the adolescent what they think treatment is and what they want out of it. Having two assessment interviews gives the opportunity of seeing what happens both within and between sessions, and is particularly valuable for seeing changes and responses in the adolescent's expectations of treatment.

Remembering Bion's injunction to eschew memory and desire (Bion 1970), I prefer to have read and then partially put to one side in my mind the major known facts about the adolescent, and the treatment expectations and desires of the adolescent and others, and hear directly afresh. Some opportunity to say what their problems are can facilitate contact with the adolescent, and give them the opportunity to tell their version of events and of themselves. It is rare when this approach does not bring out something new. This establishes something about their ownership of themselves and their treatment. It accords too with one of Freud's earliest papers on psychotherapy, where he states that 'one should look beyond the patient's illness and form an estimate of his whole personality'; those who are clearly unsuitable for psychotherapy are 'those who are not driven to seek treatment by their own suffering' (Freud 1905a).

We can try to assess ego strength – the tolerance of anxiety, adaptability, reality testing, object relationships and motivation – but there are doubts and difficulties in ascertaining the 'elusive quality' of ego strength (Limentani 1972). What perhaps we are looking for more than ego strength per se is a capacity in the ego to utilise its own regression and then learn from it during treatment (Namnum 1968). Again, as Freud mentioned (1905a), what is more important than ego strength is an awareness of some deficiency of ego strength, and a wish to change.

For those patients who as yet are totally unaware of their impulses, there can be no accurate predictor of treatability. Such patients may for a time be unsuitable for psychotherapeutic treatment and need a period of supportive containment. As Kernberg puts it succinctly:

> There is a type of denial that is a very deep-seated defence, linked with primitive splitting and projective mechanisms, that perpetuates and reinforces such mechanisms and which is alien to the development of insight. The patient is aware of the fact that at this time his perceptions, thoughts and feelings about himself or other people are completely opposite to those he has had at other times; but this memory has no emotional relevance, it cannot influence the way he feels now.
>
> (Kernberg 1975: 31)

For treatment to be possible then one needs to find a non-conflictual sphere of the ego and be able to develop a treatment alliance that includes an agreement about the limitation of impulses. Problems occur in treatment when a patient shows some degree of ego strength, insight, cooperation and keenness during the preliminary stages, but at some later point when there is some psychological movement he/she begins to reveal a hard core of basic mistrust that is a serious stumbling block in the treatment.

Patients who present their neurotic difficulties, but who split off, disown and project the psychotic part of the self, may seek treatment to maintain their own psychotic defences and be difficult to assess, particularly if one has no prior knowledge of their psychiatric history. A clue to such a problem could be the feeling in the assessor of something missing, or of a discrepancy between the patient's presentations and their difficulties in the external world. To elucidate such a dynamic requires an active attempt on the part of the assessor to locate the split off aspects of the person (Rosenfeld 1978, 1987).

Clinical examples

I shall now look at two examples of initial assessments of severely emotionally disturbed adolescents to illustrate some of these issues. In particular I hope to bring out what was necessary in a minimal way for these young people to be able to engage in psychotherapeutic treatment within the applied setting of the young persons inpatient unit at the Cassel Hospital.

Roland

Roland, aged 19, was referred by a community consultant psychiatrist for inpatient treatment after a long history of emotional problems and depression, deliberate self-harm and suicide attempts, including hanging attempts on at least three occasions. Roland was severely suicidal, very emotionally volatile and he had considerable identity problems. His parents were from widely different ethnic groups and their violent marriage had broken up when he was 10, leading to prolonged conflict and acrimony. When originally seen at that point in a child guidance clinic, Roland was in a very upset state, feeling dejected, depressed and 'possibly suicidal'. After further years of conflict when his depressed mother was still caught up emotionally with her ex-husband, Roland's problems seemed worse than ever. He was very unstable and deteriorated after each inpatient psychiatric admission. He had no friends or structure to his day, his sleep was poor and broken and he did not eat properly. He was clearly more suicidal and following a short spell at his father's house was developing homicidal ideas against his father.

In the *outpatient consultation* Roland presented as a strong young man of mixed-race appearance who seemed gentle yet forceful and visibly anxious. He was open and candid, particularly about his failings including his significant repeated lack of impulse control. He was not particularly depressed but felt he was not currently functioning, said he was suicidal and afraid of his violence and felt he needed to do something about it. He expressed anger and hatred against both his parents indiscriminately – even his mother who had looked after him and stood by him – because he felt his mother had allowed his father to abuse him emotionally. He could remember the time when the family were together and his father repeatedly beat up and mistreated his mother. He had felt terrorised in the middle of it. I thought he repeatedly relived and was traumatised by these experiences, but also there was a quality of obsessive return to the themes of hatred and anger, after which he tipped back into depression.

Throughout the interview Roland seemed to hold back tears and an upset that was almost bursting through the surface. He spoke of the effect of the emotional abuse – being shouted at continuously by his father and fearing his continuous violence against his mother – as there being 'nothing alive in him'. He said he wanted to kill his father, and he had nightmares from which he awoke punching the walls and finding his knuckles red with blood. As he said this he went through a long display of cracking his knuckles in front of me. I said to him that I thought he might use the hatred to keep himself alive. My impression was that his hatred could be very directed at the father and then the mother, and then come out in other situations, and potentially with me, the man who controlled access to treatment. I thought that Roland would need to make a particular effort to avoid angry and violent outbursts in the therapeutic setting. I put this to him and told him that violence would not be tolerated against staff or other patients. In his reply I felt Roland seemed unsure about whether he would manage this but he would try. I thought this was a crucial issue of the assessment.

Roland then told me something about his upbringing and development. Between the ages of 10 and 15 was a very bad period. He underperformed at school and in exams, then started a performing arts course at college but said he did not fit in 'with the thespians' and dropped out. Later, after I had got more of a whole impression of him, I said that I thought there was 'something of the performer about him' too, thinking that he could work himself up into an angry and hateful state out of a sense of hurt and injustice. He again acknowledged this, although somewhat painfully.

Roland described the best period as being when he worked for some jewellers for 16 months, like his father did – a job he enjoyed, when he had a girlfriend and friends. He told me in nonchalant but still fascinated tones that he thought his father might have been involved in some violent activities. He said he had wanted to get on with his father but after getting into yet another violent confrontation with him his mental state rapidly deteriorated and he ended up again in psychiatric hospital. I thought that there was some not so hidden idealisation of violence and identification with a hateful aggressor that ran deep in Roland's personality. I thought his depression may relate to these violent phantasies, which were rooted in abuse and the disturbance of primary relationships he had suffered.

I explained something of the nature of treatment to him, stressing how we try to understand the meaning of behaviour and difficulties about taking responsibility and moving on. Roland responded by saying that he knew he had difficulties with his impulses and control of violence. He said he was 'like a glass, which is always three-quarters full, which only takes a small amount to overflow'. Roland talked about his use of self-harm as a getting by mechanism, to bring pain and then let it go away again. He then showed me various cuts on his arm. What made a lasting impression on me after we met was that there was something intensely direct and involving about his contact with me.

When I saw him *with his mother* after a short break I saw more directly his lack of self-control. Roland very suddenly became angry with her as he recalled what had gone wrong in the past and he then spoke angrily about how unprotected he felt when as a child his mother had returned him to his father for access visits. He suddenly lost control, began exclaiming loudly and angrily and gesticulating in an agitated way, how he could not now travel back 'with her' on the bus. His mother seemed passive and immobilised. When I intervened and put it to him that I thought there was something very domineering in the way he talked about his mother, he partially recovered and later settled down before they left. On reflection afterwards I realised that despite all his noise and bluster I felt that momentarily he was easy to forget or wipe out of my mind. I wondered if this was an aspect of countertransference, conveyed unconsciously by him to me about his experience of being forgettable and overlooked by parents caught up in a chronic sadomasochistic relationship.

Overall I found Roland likeable but very confused and very distressed. I thought that without containment he was at a significant risk of another serious suicide attempt or a dangerous attack upon someone else. I thought his level of insight into his own behaviour was minimal, in particular into his own investment in hateful fantasies and violent acting out.

Roland subsequently on another day made a three-hour journey to be at the *nursing assessment* for 9.30 am. During a four-hour visit he met other adolescents, had a detailed interview with the senior nurse, and experienced at first hand some of the structures of the inpatient setting, including some therapeutic meetings. He seemed unusually calm in the first morning meeting with the adolescents, but when he met the senior nurse he spoke at length in a rambling way, hardly making any eye contact. His train of thought seemed very disconnected, leaving the nurse feeling confused. He seemed full of self-hatred for 'messing things up', and felt this was one of the triggers for his breakdown. He talked of a previous suicide plan when he was going to jump in front of a moving train but his mobile phone rang when he was about to jump. He thought someone he could not identify talked him out of it. The senior nurse remembered from the notes that it was his mother who had made this vital telephone call, but Roland denied this. He was unable to give his mother any credit for this intervention.

Roland had read up about the unit and said he knew why he needed a therapeutic community – to help him with the structure of the day and his relationships. The nurse asked him to try to contain some of his rage against his parents in the run-up to admission two weeks later. Roland stayed in treatment several months, but then left prematurely after an increase of aggressive behaviour and a wish by him to resume his full social life and college outside. I shall discuss the assessment in the light of his treatment below and now proceed with discussion of the second assessment case.

Erna

Erna, aged nearly 16, had had emotional problems since puberty resulting in self-harm and severe suicide attempts. There had been dramatic fluctuations in her mental state from her being relatively stable to her becoming extremely depressed and suicidal. She had had chronic urinary tract infections as a child between the ages of 2 and 10 requiring repeated investigations. In contrast to her brothers, during her childhood she was seen as a bright, feminine and capable child for whom her parents had high expectations. Then at the age of 12 her mother blurted out in a row that her father had another family. She then learnt for the first time that her father was not married to her mother but married with another family and had a separate household.

In a *telephone conversation with the referring consultant*, prior to my seeing Erna, I learnt that she had nearly killed herself three months before, having snatched a bottle from a medication trolley and overdosed on the contents, and for a while she had been on a Section 3. He thought she was depressed and was developing a narcissistic personality disorder. Erna had begun psychotherapy and made use of it, and could see her difficulties may relate to a deprivation of emotional attention throughout her childhood, and her fascination with satanism may relate to how her value system was turned upside down by the revelations about her father's second life. The consultant thought that, despite some useful work with the parents, in the long term Erna's relationship with them was not going to work and he mentioned significant personality difficulties in Erna's mother.

Erna completed our *detailed questionnaire* well, writing candidly about her problems, which she described as depression, anger and emotional pain. She wrote of feeling 'plastic', thinking 'death is a good option'. She repeatedly self-harmed, had difficulties with eating and suffered massive mood swings. She described her most important problem as 'feeling that she does not belong anywhere'. She had not spoken to her father for three years between the age of 12 and 15, and said how there was still anger and strain in their current relationship.

I met Erna on her own for an hour in the *first outpatient consultation*. She was of medium height, slim, with an open smiling face, relaxed and composed. She wore a casual black top and largish jeans. I was struck by how black and dyed her hair was – unremittingly 'Gothic'. In response to my suggestion that she tell me about her difficulties and how our unit might help, Erna talked of her swings of mood and her continuing self-harm, then described herself as 'floating at the moment', not knowing what was going to happen. I then found the interview divided between the two sides that the referrers had described well. The earlier part was about her self-harm and had a heavy purposeless feel, while in the second half I found Erna much lighter, more talkative and more hopeful. In the earlier part she talked in a somewhat nonchalant way about having taken ten overdoses and having 'knocked her liver to bits' with paracetamol. She described taking tablets, going on a bus, not knowing or caring where she was going or what would happen. She spoke of finding London and its atmosphere 'awful' but travelled through it aimlessly in a semi-comatose state.

The sense Erna gave of her experience of mental distress and self-destructive behaviour was that there was a part of her that was inaccessible to thinking or indeed to a more reasonable part of her that could be more connected and could relate. I was struck by a comparison between her experience of her mental state and her experience of her family: in other words that there was a part, an area that was inaccessible to her that could not be processed or thought about.

As she talked I thought that Erna experienced a palpable hurt about the disturbances within her family and about her father's secretive other life, and there was a connection between all this and Erna seeing something deeply wrong with herself. I found myself feeling worried and uncertain. Erna clearly had a low sense of self-esteem. She was hurt and angry with her father and could easily flare up with him, but strangely there was something more direct with her father. She described her mother as 'helpful and approachable', but even early on I sensed that there was a strong sense of protection of her, and really there were more difficulties there between them. She described herself as having an idyllic childhood up to the point of the revelations about her father: she was the one child in the family who was seen to be normal and she was dressed up in girly dresses. But Erna left out any mention about her recurrent childhood hospitalisations. I was left asking myself questions about the possible impact on Erna, from an early age, of disturbed family relationships, and their effect on her mind and body. At one point I suggested to Erna that some of her self-destructive behaviour might be part of an angry attack upon her father and what he had done. Erna was thoughtful and said she had not thought about that before. She was then able to tell me a certain amount more about herself and her experience at her current unit.

After a short break I met *Erna with her parents* for a further half an hour. The level of their denial was high without a crack and Erna's mother described her problems as being 'hormonal'. There seemed little recognition of the destructive effect of cancelling out Erna's own emotionality. She also seemed actively angry and somewhat domineering. Her manner perhaps hid her own very collapsed side. She did not want foster parents involved, as her family 'did not believe in them' since 'they would not be as good as her family'. Erna's father sat quietly with a show of open (false) confidence, but could not acknowledge any difficulties to which he may have contributed. At one point he shed some tears about how difficult it was *for him* with Erna having the difficulties she had. He spoke somewhat sentimentally of her as his 'princess' for whom he 'would do anything'. I found myself with very little room for thinking in this part of the assessment, and Erna largely clammed up as she had said beforehand that she would. There had clearly been a shift in feeling towards Erna, from her being a very special child who did not have the same difficulties as their other children, to someone from 12 onwards who was a problem, was not allowed to complain, and instead herself blamed. This seemed to have something to do with the severely destructive behaviour Erna then got into.

My conclusion, following the first interview, was that there were some very complex and disturbing family dynamics that continued to affect

Erna's mental state in an ongoing way. Her severe blaming of herself, which may perhaps have underlain her bodily symptoms as a child, had developed into a severely dangerous form in early adolescence, as her internal despair matched the chronic stuckness of her external family circumstances. In the assessment process Erna was keen to continue therapeutic work and I thought may become more contained and less dangerous if she could commit herself to ongoing work in a realistic way. Erna was seen again for a *second outpatient consultation* and a *nursing assessment* before admission. She was in inpatient treatment for a full year and made considerable improvements, especially after the halfway mark. She is now discharged, managing in the outside community, living separately from her family, pursuing her education, and undergoing ongoing psychotherapy.

Discussion

Both these adolescents had been through extensive periods of treatment so far but the patterns of acting out in self-harming, dangerous and suicidal ways persisted and each was being referred for further intensive psycho-therapeutic treatment in an inpatient setting. A key issue was whether each was motivated for and could sustain a commitment to such treatment. More negative and more positive sides were in evidence in both. With Roland there was some splitting of his presentation at different times with different assessors, with me in the outpatient consultation and with the senior nurse in the nursing assessment. In the outpatient consultation I could see patterns of enactment of excited and angry hatred, but he responded to interpretation of this, and some degree of paternal contain-ment. With the senior nurse Roland's thought seemed disconnected and deeply confusing, and yet he moved out of this or sidestepped it by assum-ing a nonchalant calmness and aloofness at times with other adolescents. With Erna there was more continuity, but there was still a split presentation *within* the interviews, a heavy purposeless feel as she was preoccupied in an uncaring and anarchic way about self-harm and self-destructive thoughts, but as the interview progressed she was able to think more, make pur-poseful links, and be more talkative and hopeful. This change from negative to positive types of communication, and shifts in the type of projective identification, from a dumping of negative and harmful thoughts and actions to a more vulnerable opening up, was most important.

Roland, despite evidence of a quality of splitting at the start that in part indicated that he was not wholly accepting of his own need for help and need to change, was intensely motivated to make an impact – hence my countertransference feeling of this. There was however another side of my countertransference – how easy he was to forget or wipe out. Essentially he recognised his own vulnerability to suicide and his need to work to understand this and get over his frequent acute psychiatric crises. When he eventually left treatment, albeit prematurely, he did say he was no longer acutely suicidal and was shocked to remember how unstably suicidal he had been at referral. He clearly had now made significant use of the treatment setting to understand more about himself and to begin to change in a consistent way, rather than lurch from crisis to crisis. Through family meetings alongside his individual psychotherapy Roland had also managed to develop a better relationship with his mother more based on respect. On the unit a lot of work was done about his position of scapegoat in the family and at times his tendency to bully and scapegoat others (Waddell 1999).

What was crucial at the outset for Roland, before treatment was possible, and what was important for my assessment, was some recognition by him of his volatility and potential for violence, and some level of commitment to control this and understand it. For this he needed to show some sense of his need for a containing object, to find ways to deal with disturbing thoughts and unthinking actions other than in violent enactments or in relieving but directionless self-harm, such as cutting, or ultimately suicide.

With Erna what was most worrying prior to assessment was her inaccessibility and the severity and unpredictability of her self-harming and suicidal behaviour. It was essential for her to recognise that her own mental states could be inaccessible to her. When I monitored my countertransference, my being 'worried and uncertain', I thought she could and would communicate about herself and her own more split off and disowned parts, as she had unconsciously to me. She was indeed highly worrying because of the risk of suicide and we felt this, but we needed to know she may also come to feel this and recognise it during treatment. In the assessment I had a sense that she could get over the complex situation of her parents' relationship, could adjust to working with the immense relationship difficulties of this situation and could bring together in her mind separate deep-rooted senseless areas.

In conclusion then, as I hope I have illustrated in these two examples of severely disturbed adolescents, the task in assessment of adolescents is to try to contain and understand the adolescent's different types of communication, including distinguishing different types of projective identification, and to try to foster a capacity for a life-directed transference relationship. Some initial capacity for reality testing, some recognition of 'the other' and acceptance of the minimum conditions of treatment, in particular agreement about the safety of oneself and others, and some capacity for experiencing guilt and concern, are essential prerequisites for beginning psychotherapeutic treatments. Such indicators in assessment can show how possible or successful it may be to undertake psychoanalytical psychotherapeutic treatment in applied settings even for very severely emotionally disturbed adolescents.

Bibliography

Association of British Adopting and Fostering Agencies (ABAFA) Research Series (1989) *Access to Birth Records.*

Abel-Hirsch, N. (2003) 'On Bion's concept of suffering pain and pleasure', unpublished paper read at conference on philosophy and psychoanalysis at the British Psychoanalytical Society, 8 March.

Abram, J. (1996) *The Language of Winnicott*, London: Karnac.

Aichhorn, A. (1931) *Wayward Youth*, trans. A. Bloggs, New York and London: Viking and Putnam.

Ainsworth, M., Blehar, M. C., Waters, E. and Wall, S. (1978) *Patterns of Attachment: A Psychological Study of a Strange Situation*, Hillsdale, NJ: Erlbaum.

Alvarez, A. (1992) *Live Company: Psychoanalytic Psychotherapy with Autistic, Borderline, Deprived and Abused Children*, London: Routledge.

—— (2000) 'A developmental view of "defence": the borderline psychotic child', in T. Lubbe (ed.) *The Borderline Psychotic Child: A Selective Integration*, London and Philadelphia: Routledge.

Anastasopoulos, D., Laylou-Lignos, E. and Waddell, M. (eds) *Psychoanalytic Psychotherapy of the Severely Disturbed Adolescent*, London: Karnac.

Anderson, R. (1998) 'Suicidal behaviour and its meaning in adolescence', in R. Anderson and A. Dartington (eds) *Facing It Out: Clinical Perspectives on Adolescent Disturbance*, London: Duckworth.

Appelbaum, A. (1972) 'A critical re-examination of the concept "motivation for change" in psychoanalytic treatment', *International Journal of Psychoanalysis* 53: 51.

Auestad, A.-M. (1992) 'I am father's baby – you can have the turtle: psychotherapy in a family context', *Journal of Child Psychotherapy* 18(1): 57–74.

Baker, R. (1980) 'The finding "not suitable" in the selection of supervised cases', *International Review of Psychoanalysis* 7: 353.

—— (1993) 'The patient's discovery of the psychoanalyst as a new object', *International Journal of Psychoanalysis* 74: 1223–34.

Balint, M. (1933) 'On transference of emotions', in M. Balint *Primary Love and Psycho-Analytic Technique*, London: Karnac.

—— (1937) 'Ego developmental states of the ego. Primary object-love', in M. Balint *Primary Love and Psycho-Analytic Technique*, London: Karnac.

Balint, M. (1950) 'Changing therapeutic aims and techniques in psycho-analysis', *International Journal of Psychoanalysis* 31: 117–24.
—— (1959) *Thrills and Regressions*, London: Hogarth.
—— (1968) *The Basic Fault: Therapeutic Aspects of Regression*, London: Routledge.
Bandler (Bellman), D. (1987) 'Working with other professionals in an inpatient setting', *Journal of Child Psychotherapy* 13(2): 81–9.
Barnes, E. (ed.) (1967) *Psychosocial Nursing*, London: Tavistock.
Barnes, E., Griffiths, P., Ord, J. and Wells, D. (eds) (1997) *Face to Face with Distress: The Professional Use of Self in Psychosocial Care*, London: Butterworth Heinemann.
Baumann, C. (1999) 'Adoptive fathers and birth fathers: a study of attitudes', *Child and Adolescent Social Work Journal* 16(5): 373–91.
Bentovim, A. (1986) 'Bereaved children', *British Medical Journal* 292(6534): 14–82 (June 7).
Bentovim, A., Elton, A., Hildebrand, J., Tranter, M. and Vizard, E. (eds) (1988) *Child Sexual Abuse within the Family: Assessment and Treatment*, London: Butterworth.
Bertram, P. (2003) 'Some Oedipal problems with adopted children and their parents', *Journal of Child Psychotherapy* 29(1): 21–36.
Bion, W. (1954) 'Notes on the theory of schizophrenia', *International Journal of Psychoanalysis* 35, reprinted in W. Bion *Second Thoughts* (1967) London: Karnac.
—— (1956) 'Development of schizophrenic thought', *International Journal of Psychoanalysis*, reprinted in W. Bion *Second Thoughts* (1967) London: Karnac.
—— (1957) 'Differentiation of the psychotic from the non-psychotic personalities', *International Journal of Psychoanalysis* 38, reprinted in W. Bion *Second Thoughts* (1967) London: Karnac.
—— (1958) 'On hallucination', *International Journal of Psychoanalysis*, reprinted in W. Bion *Second Thoughts* (1967) London: Karnac.
—— (1959) 'Attacks on linking', *International Journal of Psychoanalysis* 40: 5–6, reprinted in W. Bion *Second Thoughts* (1967) London: Karnac.
—— (1961) *Experiences in Groups*, London: Tavistock.
—— (1962a) 'A theory of thinking', *International Journal of Psychoanalysis* 42: 4–5, reprinted in W. Bion *Second Thoughts* (1967) London: Karnac.
—— (1962b) 'Learning from experience', in W. Bion *Seven Servants* (1977) New York: Jason Aronson.
—— (1963) 'Elements of psychoanalysis', in W. Bion *Seven Servants* (1977) New York: Jason Aronson.
—— (1965) 'Transformations', in W. Bion *Seven Servants* (1977) New York: Jason Aronson.
—— (1967) *Second Thoughts*, London: Karnac.
—— (1970) 'Attention and interpretation', in W. Bion *Seven Servants* (1977) New York: Jason Aronson.
Black, D. (ed.) (1993) *When Father Kills Mother: Guiding Children through Trauma and Grief*, London: Routledge.
Bleiberg, E. (2000) 'Borderline personality disorder in children and adolescents', in T. Lubbe (ed.) *The Borderline Psychotic Child: A Selective Integration*, London and Philadelphia: Routledge.

Blos, P. (1962) *On Adolescence*, New York: Free Press.
—— (1972) *The Young Adolescent*, New York: Free Press.
Blum, H. P. (1983) 'Adoptive parents: generative conflict and generational continuity', *Psychoanalytic Study of the Child* 38: 141–63.
Boardman, J., Griffin, J. and Murray, O. (eds) (1986) *The Oxford History of the Classical World*, Oxford: Oxford University Press.
Bollas, C. (1989) *Forces of Destiny: Psychoanalysis and Human Idiom*, London: Free Association Books.
Bott-Spillius, E. (1990) 'Asylum and society', in E. Trist and H. Murray (eds) *The Social Engagement of Social Science*, vol. 1, London: Free Association Books.
Bowlby, J. (1971) *Attachment*, London: Penguin.
—— (1973) *Separation*, London: Penguin.
—— (1998) *A Secure Base: Clinical Applications of Attachment Theory*, London: Routledge.
Brenman-Pick, E. (1985) 'Working through in the counter-transference', *International Journal of Psychoanalysis*, 66: 157–66.
Brinich, P. M. (1980) 'Some potential effects of adoption on self and object representations', *Psychoanalytic Study of the Child* 35: 107–33.
Brinich, P. M. (1995) 'Psychoanalytic perspectives on adoption and ambivalence', *Psychoanalytic Psychology* 12(2): 181–99.
Britton, R. (1989) 'The missing link: parental sexuality in the Oedipus complex', in R. Britton, M. Feldman and E. O'Shaugnessy (eds) *The Oedipus Complex Today*, London: Karnac, pp. 83–102.
—— (1998) *Belief and Imagination: Explorations in Psychoanalysis*, London: Routledge.
—— (2002) 'Forever father's daughter: the Athene–Antigone complex', in J. Trowell and A. Etchagoyen (2002) *The Importance of Fathers: A Psychoanalytic Re-evaluation*, London: Routledge.
Brody, H. (2001) *The Other Side of Eden*, London: Faber and Faber.
Brodzinsky, D. M. *et al.* (1990) *Open Adoption*, New York: Oxford University Press.
Burlingham, D. (1952) *Twins: A Study of Three Pairs of Identical Twins*, New York: International Universities Press.
Burman, R. (1987) 'Regressive distortions in a therapeutic community', in A. Heymans, R. Kennedy and L. Tischler (eds) *The Family as In-patient*, London: Free Association Books.
Byng-Hall, J. (1979) 'Re-editing family mythology during family therapy', *Journal of Family Therapy* 1: 103–16.
—— (1985) 'The family script: a useful bridge between theory and practice', *Journal of Family Therapy* 7: 301–5.
Canham, H. (2003) 'The relevance of the Oedipus myth to fostered and adoptive children', *Journal of Child Psychotherapy* 29(1): 5–20.
Carpy, D. (1989) 'Tolerating the counter-transference; a mutative process', *International Journal of Psychoanalysis* 70: 287–94.
Carter, L. and Rinsley, D. B. (1977) 'Vicissitudes of "empathy" in a borderline adolescent', *International Review of Psychoanalysis* 4: 317–26.
Casement, P. (1985) *Learning from the Patient*, London: Tavistock.
Cath, S. and Shopper, M. (eds) (2002) 'Step parenting: creating and recreating families in America today', Hillsdale, NJ: Analytic Press.

Chiesa, M. (1997) 'A combined inpatient/outpatient programme for severe personality disorders', *Therapeutic Communities* 18: 297–309.

Chiesa, M. and Fonagy, P. (2000) 'Cassel Hospital personality disorder study: methodology and treatment effects', *British Journal of Psychiatry* 176: 485–91.

Cicchetti, D. and Barnett, D. (1991) 'Attachment organisation in preschool aged maltreated children', *Development and Psychopathology* 3: 397–411.

Coltart, N. (1988) 'Diagnosis and assessment for suitability for psychoanalytic psychotherapy', *British Journal of Psychotherapy* 4: 127–34.

Coombe, P. (1995) 'The inpatient treatment of mother and child at the Cassel Hospital; a case of Munchausen syndrome by proxy', *British Journal of Psychotherapy* 12: 195–207.

Copley, B. (1993) *The World of Adolescence*, London: Free Association Books.

Dante, A. (1321/1993) *The Divine Comedy*, trans. Sisson, London: World Classics.

Dartington, A. (1994) 'Where angels fear to tread: idealism, despondency and inhibition of thought in hospital nursing', in A. Obholtzer and V. Z. Roberts (eds) *The Unconscious at Work*, London: Routledge, pp. 101–9.

Day, L. and Flynn, D. (eds) (2003) *The Internal and External Worlds of Children and Adolescents: Collaborative Therapeutic Care*, London: Karnac.

Derdeyn, A. P. and Graves, C. L. (1998) 'Clinical vicissitudes of adoption', *Child and Adolescent Psychiatric Clinics of North America*, 7(2): 373–88.

Dorner, S. and Atwell, J. D. (1985) 'Family adjustment to the early loss of a baby born with spina bifida', *Developmental Medicine and Child Neurology*, 27(4): 461–6 (Aug).

Ekstein, R. and Wallerstein, J. (1954) 'Observations on the psychology of borderline and psychotic children', *Psychoanalytic Study of the Child* 9: 344–69.

Enke, H. (1965) 'Bipolare Gruppenpsychotherapie als Moglichkeit Pscyhoanalytischer Arbeit in der stationaren Psychotherapie', *Zeitschrift fur Psychotherapie und Medizinishe Psychologie* 15: 116–24.

Erikson, E. H. (1968) *Identity, Youth and Crisis*, London: Faber.

—— (1977) *Childhood and Society*, London: Paladin.

Evans, J. (1998) *Active Analytic Group Therapy for Adolescents*, London and Philadelpia: Jessica Kingsley.

Ezriel, H. (1950) 'A psychoanalytic approach to group treatment', *British Journal of Medical Psychology* 23: 59–74.

—— (1952) 'Notes on psychoanalytic therapy II: Interpretation and research', *Psychiatry* 15: 119–26.

Flynn, C. (1993) 'The patient's pantry: the nature of the nursing task', *Therapeutic Communities* 14(4): 227–36.

Flynn, D. (1987a) 'The child's view of the hospital: an examination of the child's experience of an in-patient setting', in A. Heymans, R. Kernberg and L. Tischler (eds) *The Family as In-Patient*, London: Free Association Books.

—— (1987b) 'Internal conflict and growth in a child preparing to start school', *Journal of Child Psychotherapy* 13(2): 77–90.

—— (1988) 'The assessment and psychotherapy of a physically abused girl during in-patient family treatment', *Journal of Child Psychotherapy* 13(2): 77–91.

—— (1992) 'Adolescent group work in a hospital in-patient setting with spina bifida patients and others', *Journal of Child Psychotherapy* 18(2): 87–108.

Flynn, D. (1998) 'Psychoanalytic aspects of inpatient treatment', *Journal of Child Psychotherapy* 24(2): 283–306.

—— (1999) 'The challenges of in-patient work in a therapeutic community', in M. Lanyado and A. Horne (eds) *The Handbook of Child and Adolescent Psychotherapy*, London: Routledge.

—— (2000) 'Adolescence', in *Adolescence*, London: Institute of Psychoanalysis.

—— (2002) 'The adoptive father', in A. Etchagoyen and J. Trowell (eds) *The Importance of Fathers*, London: Routledge.

Flynn, D. and Turner, J. (2003) 'Containment of borderline adolescents', in L. Day and D. Flynn (eds) *The Internal and External Worlds of Children and Adolescents: Collaborative Therapeutic Care*, London: Karnac.

Folkart, L. (1964) 'The role of a child psychotherapist in an inpatient setting', *Journal of Child Psychotherapy* 1(2): 44–5.

—— (1967) 'Some problems of treating children in an inpatient setting', *Journal of Child Psychotherapy* 2(1): 46–55.

Fonagy, P. (1991) 'Thinking about thinking: some clinical and theoretical considerations in the treatment of a borderline patient', *International Journal of Psychoanalysis* 72: 639–56.

Fonagy, P. and Target, M. (1996a) 'A contemporary psychoanalytic perspective: psychodynamic development therapy', in E. Hibbs and P. Jensen (eds) *Psychosocial Treatments for Child and Adolescent Disorders: Empirically Based Approaches*, Washington, DC: APA and NIH.

—— (1996b) 'Predictors of outcome in child psychoanalysis: a retrospective study of 763 cases at the Anna Freud Centre', *Journal of the American Psychoanalytical Association* 44: 27–77.

Fonagy, P. and Target, M. (2000) 'Mentalisation and personality disorder in children: a current perspective from the Anna Freud Centre' in T. Lubbe (ed.) *The Borderline Psychotic Child: A Selective Integration*, London and Philadelphia: Routledge.

—— (2003) *Psychoanalytic Theories: Perspectives from Developmental Psychopathology*, London and Philadelphia: Whurr.

Fonagy, P., Leigh, T., Steele, M., Steele, H., Kennedy, R., Mattoon, G., Target, M. and Gerber, A. (1996c) 'The relation of attachment status, psychiatric classification, and response to psychotherapy', *Journal of Consultation in Clinical Psychology* 64(1): 22–31.

Foulkes, S. H. (1948) *Introduction to Group-Analytic Psychotherapy*, London: Heinemann.

—— (1986) *Group Analytic Psychotherapy: Method and Principles*, London: Maresfield.

Frankel, S. A. (1991) 'Pathogenic factors in the experience of early and late adopted children', *Psychoanalytic Study of the Child* 46: 91–108.

Freud, A. (1936) *The Ego and Mechanisms of Defence*, London: Hogarth.

—— (1952a) 'The role of bodily illness in the mental life of children', in *The Psychoanalytic Study of the Child*, vol. 7, New York: International Universities Press.

—— (1952b) '"Yale Law School lecture", quoted in Schecter, 1967; "Psychoanalytic theory as it relates to Adoption"', *Journal of the American Psycho-Analytical Association* 15: 695–708.

Freud, A. (1965) *Normality and Pathology in Childhood, Writings* 6, New York: International Universities Press.

Freud, S. (1893) *Studies in Hysteria*, S.E. 2, 125–34, London: Hogarth and The Institute of Psycho-Analysis.

—— (1900) *The Interpretation of Dreams*, S.E. 4 and 5, ibid.

—— (1905a) 'On psychotherapy', S.E.7, ibid.

—— (1905b) *Three Essays on the Theory of Sexuality*, S.E. 7, 125–243, ibid.

—— (1905c) 'Fragment of an analysis of a case of hysteria', S.E. 7, 7–124, ibid.

—— (1906) 'Psycho-analysis and the establishment of facts in legal proceedings', S.E. 9, 103–13, ibid.

—— (1909a) *Analysis of Phobia in a Five year old Boy (Little Hans)*, S.E. 10, 5–152.

—— (1909b) 'Family romance phantasies'. S.E. 9, 236–41, ibid.

—— (1911a) *Psycho-analytical Notes on an Autobiographical case of Paranoia (Schreber)*, S.E. 12, 3–82.

—— (1911b) 'Formulations on the two principles of mental functioning', S.E. 12, 218–26, ibid.

—— (1912) 'The dynamics of transference', S.E. 12, 97–108, ibid.

—— (1913) *Totem and Taboo*, S.E. 13, ibid.

—— (1914) 'On narcissism', S.E. 14, 73–102, ibid.

—— (1916) *Introductory Lectures on Psychoanalysis*, S.E. 15, 16, 13–477.

—— (1917) 'Mourning and melancholia', S.E. 14, 243–58, ibid.

—— (1918a) *From the History of an Infantile Neurosis*, S.E. 17, 3–122, ibid.

—— (1918) *Inhibitions, Symptoms and Anxiety*, S.E. 20, 77–175, ibid.

—— (1919) 'A child is being beaten', S.E. 17, ibid.

—— (1920) 'Beyond the pleasure principle', S.E. 18, 3–66, ibid.

—— (1923) *The Ego and the Id*, S.E. 19, 3–66, ibid.

—— (1924) 'The economic problem of masochism', S.E. 19, 157–72, ibid.

—— (1925) 'Book review of *Wayward Youth*' by Aichhorn (German edn), S.E. 19, 272–5.

—— (1931) 'On female sexuality', S.E. 21, 221–46, ibid.

—— (1939) *Moses and Monotheism*, S.E. 23, 2–140, ibid.

Garelick, A. (1994) 'Psychotherapy assessment: theory and practice', *Psychoanalytic Psychotherapy* 8(2): 101–16.

Gay, P. (1988) *Freud, A Life for Our Time*, London: Macmillan.

Geleerd, E. R. (1946) 'A contribution to the problem of psychosis in childhood', *The Psychoanalytical Study of the Child* 2: 271–93.

—— (1958) 'Borderline states in children and adolescents', *Psychoanalytic Study of the Child* 13: 279–95.

Glasser, M. (1998) 'On violence: a preliminary communication', *International Journal of Psychoanalysis* 79: 887–902.

Glover, E. (1954) *The Technique of Psychoanalysis*, London: Baillière.

Goldstein, J. and Goldstein, S. (1998) '"Put yourself in the skin of the child", she said', *Psychoanalytic Study of the Child* 51: 46–55.

Green, André (1979) *The Tragic Effect: The Oedipus Complex in Tragedy*, trans. Alan Sheridan, Cambridge: Cambridge University Press.

Green, A. H. (1981) 'Developmental and psychodynamic factors in child abuse', *International Journal of Family Psychiatry* 2: 3–4.

Green, A. H., Gaines, R. W. and Sandgrund, A. (1974) 'Child abuse: pathological syndrome of family interaction', *American Journal of Psychiatry* 131: 8.

Griffiths, P. and Pringle, P. (eds) (1997) *Psychosocial Practice in a Residential Setting*, London: Karnac.

Grinberg, L. (1962) 'On a specific aspect of countertransference due to the patient's projective identification', *International Journal of Psychoanalysis* 43: 436–40.

Hanley, C. (1987) 'The assault on truth: Freud's suppression of the seduction theory', *International Journal of Psychoanalysis* 67: 517–21.

Harvey, P. (1937) *The Oxford Companion to Classical Literature*, Oxford: Clarendon Press.

Healy, K. (2003) 'Adolescence: a transitory world', in L. Day and D. Flynn (eds) *The Internal and External World of Children and Adolescents: Collaborative Therapeutic Care*, London: Karnac.

Healy, K. and Kennedy, R. (1993) 'Which families benefit from in-patient psychotherapeutic work at the Cassel Hospital', *British Journal of Psychotherapy* 9(4): 394–404.

Healy, K., Kennedy, R. and Sinclair, J. (1991) 'Child psychical abuse observed: comparison of child-abusing and non child-abusing families in an in-patient psychotherapy setting', *British Journal of Psychiatry* 158: 234–7.

Heimann, P. (1950) 'On counter-transference', *International Journal of Psychoanalysis* 31: 1–2 and in M. Tonnesmann (ed.) *About Children and Children-No-Longer*, London: Routledge.

—— (1960) 'Counter-transference', *British Journal of Medical Psychology* 33: 9.

Herman, J. and van der Kolk, B. (1987) 'Traumatic antecedents of borderline personality disorders', in B. van der Kolk (ed.) *Psychological Trauma*, Washington, DC: American Psychiatric Press.

Herman, J., Perry, C. and van der Kolk, B. (1989) 'Childhood trauma in borderline personality disorder', *American Journal of Psychiatry* 146: 490–5.

Hinshelwood, R. D. (1987) 'The psychotherapists role in a large psychiatric institution', *Psychoanalytic Psychotherapy* 2(3): 207–15.

—— (1991) *A Dictionary of Kleinian Thought*, 2nd edn, London: Free Association Books.

—— (1991) 'Psychodynamic formulation in assessment for psychotherapy', *British Journal of Psychotherapy* 8: 166–74.

—— (1994) *Clinical Klein*, London: Free Association Books.

—— (1999) 'Countertransference', *International Journal of Psychoanalysis* 80: 797–818.

Hinshelwood, R. D. and Skogstad, W. (2000) *Observing Organisations*, London: Routledge.

Hinton, P. (1980) 'How a ten-year-old girl faced her death', *Journal of Child Psychotherapy* 6: 107–16.

Hinton, J. (1967) *Dying*, London: Penguin.

Hobbes, T. (1651/1962) *Leviathan*, London: Fontana.

Hodges, J. (1990) 'The relationship to self and objects in early maternal deprivation and adoption', *Journal of Child Psychotherapy* 16(1): 53–74.

Hodges, J., Berger, M., Melzak, S., Oldeshulte, R., Rabb, S. and Salo, F. (1984) 'Two crucial questions: adopted children in psychoanalytic treatment', *Journal of Child Psychotherapy* 10: 47–56.

Holmes, J. (2000) 'Attachment theory and abuse: a developmental perspective', in U. McCluskey and C.-A. Hooper (eds) *Psychodynamic Perspectives on Abuse: The Cost of Feer*, London and Philadelphia: Jessica Kingsley.

Hopkins, J. (2000a) 'A case of shoe and foot fetishism in a 6-year-old girl', in T. Lubbe (ed.) *The Borderline Psychotic Child: A Selective Integration*, London and Philadelphia: Routledge.

—— (2000b) 'Overcoming a child's resistance to late adoption: how one new attachment can facilitate another', *Journal of Child Psychotherapy* 26(3): 335–47.

Ibsen, A. (1968) *Little Eyolf*, trans. Michael Meyer, London: Methuen.

Isaacs, S. (1952) 'The nature and function of phantasy', in J. Riviere (ed.) *Developments in Psycho-Analysis*, London: Hogarth and Institute of Psychoanalysis, pp. 67–121.

Jacobs, T. J. (1988) 'On having an adopted sibling', *International Journal of Psychoanalysis* 15(1): 25–35.

Jaffe, B. and Fanshel, D. (1970) *How They Fared in Adoption: A Follow-up Study*, New York: Columbia University Press.

Janssen, P. (1987) *Psychoanalytic Therapy in the Hospital Setting*, London: Routledge.

James, O. (1984) 'The role of the nurse/therapist relationship in the therapeutic community', *International Review of Psychoanalysis* 11: 151–62, reprinted in A. Heymans, R. Kennedy and L. Tischler (eds) *The Family as In-Patient* (1987), London: Free Association Books.

Jaques, E. (1953) 'On the dynamics of social structure', *Human Relations* 6: 10–23.

Jaques, E. (1955) 'Social systems as a defence against persecutory anxiety', in M. Klein, P. Heimann and R. Money-Kyrle (eds) *New Directions in Psychoanalysis*, London: Tavistock.

Jones, E. (1922/1948) 'Some problems of adolescence', in E. Jones *Collected Papers*, London: Maresfield.

—— (1962) *The Life and Work of Sigmund Freud*, London: Hogarth.

Jordan, P. (1995) 'The mother's role in promoting fathering behaviour', in J. Shapiro, M. Diamond *et al. Contemporary Social, Developmental and Clinical Perspectives*, Springer series on men, 8, 69–71.

Joseph, B. (1978) 'Different types of anxiety and their handling in the analytic situation', *International Journal of Psychoanalysis*, reprinted in E. Bott Spillius and M. Feldman (eds) *Psychic Equilibrium and Psychic Change*, London: Routledge.

—— (1985) 'Transference; the total situation', *International Journal of Psychoanalysis*, reprinted in E. Bott Spillius and M. Feldman (eds) *Psychic Equilibrium and Psychic Change* (1989), London: Routledge.

—— (1989) E. Bott Spillius and M. Feldman (eds) *Psychic Equilibrium and Psychic Change*, London: Routledge.

Judd, D. (1989) *Give Sorrow Words*, London: Free Association Books.

—— (1990) 'Psyche/soma issues for an adolescent with spina bifida and mental handicap', *Journal of Child Psychotherapy* 16: 83–97.

Kazak, A. E. and Clark, M. W. (1986) 'Stress in families of children with Myelomeningocele', *Developmental Medicine and Child Neurology* 28(2): 220–28 (April).

Kennedy, R. (1987) 'The work of the day: aspects of work with families at the

Cassel Hospital', in A. Heymans, R. Kennedy and L. Tischler (eds) *The Family as In-Patient*, London: Free Association Books.

Kennedy, R. (1989) 'Psychotherapy, child abuse and the law', *Bulletin Royal College of Psychiatrists* 13: 471–6.

—— (1997) *Child Abuse, Psychotherapy and the Law*, London: Free Association Books.

Kennedy, R., Heymans, A. and Tischler, L. (eds) (1987) *The Family as In-patient*, London: Free Association Books.

Kennedy, R. and Coombe, P. (1995) 'Family treatment of Munchausen syndrome by proxy', *Bulletin of the Australian Association of Group Psychotherapists* 15: 1–8.

Kernberg, O. (1972) 'Menninger Foundation psychotherapy research project', *Bulletin of the Menninger Clinic* 36: 179–276.

—— (1975) *Borderline Conditions and Pathological Narcissism*, New York: Jason Aronson.

—— (1984) *Severe Personality Disorders: Psychotherapeutic Strategies*, New York: Yale University Press.

Kernberg, P. (1983a) 'Borderline conditions: childhood and adolescent aspects', in K. Robson (ed.) *The Borderline Child*, New York: McGraw-Hill.

—— (1983b) 'Issues in the psychotherapy of borderline conditions in children', in K. Robson (ed.) *The Borderline Child*, New York: McGraw-Hill.

King, P. (1978) 'Affective responses of the analyst to the patient's communications', *International Journal of Psychoanalysis* 59: 329–34.

Klein, M. (1925) 'A contribution to the psychogenesis of tics', in *Collected Writings*, vol. 1, London: Hogarth.

—— (1928) 'Earlier stages of the Oedipal conflict', in *Collected Writings*, vol. 1, London: Hogarth.

—— (1929) 'Personification in the play of children', in *Collected Writings*, vol. 1, London: Hogarth.

—— (1930) 'The importance of symbol formation in the development of the ego', in *Collected Writings*, vol. 1, London: Hogarth.

—— (1932) 'The psycho-analysis of children', *Collected Writings*, vol. 2, London: Hogarth.

—— (1933) 'The early development of conscience in children', in *Collected Writings*, vol. 1, London: Hogarth.

—— (1935) 'A contribution to the development of manic depressive states', in *Collected Writings*, vol. 1, London: Hogarth.

—— (1936) 'Weaning', in *Collected Writings*, vol. 1, London: Hogarth.

—— (1937) 'Love, guilt and reparation', in *Collected Writings*, vol. 1, London: Hogarth.

—— (1940) 'Mourning and its relation to manic-depressive states', in *Collected Writings*, vol. 1, London: Hogarth.

—— (1945) 'The Oedipus complex in the light of early anxieties', in *Collected Writings*, vol. 1, London: Hogarth.

—— (1946) 'Notes on some schizoid mechanisms', *International Journal of Psychoanalysis*, 27, reprinted in *Collected Writings*, vol. 3, London: Hogarth.

Klein, M. (1952) 'The origins of transference', in *Collected Writings*, vol. 3, London: Hogarth.

—— (1955) 'On identification', in *Collected Writings*, vol. 3, London: Hogarth.

—— (1957) 'Envy and gratitude', in *Collected Writings*, vol. 3, London: Hogarth.

—— (1961) *Narrative of a Child Analysis*, in *Collected Works*, vol. 4, London: Hogarth Press.

Kraemer, S. (1991) 'The origins of fatherhood: an ancient family process', *Family Process* 30(4): 377–92.

Landerholm, L. (2001) 'The experience of abandonment and adoption, as a child and as a parent, in the psychological motivational perspective', *International Forum of Psychoanalysis* 10(1): 12–25.

Lanyado, M. and Horne, A. (eds) (1999) *The Handbook of Child and Adolescent Psychotherapy: Psychoanalytic Approaches*, London: Routledge.

Laplanche, J. (1987) *New Foundations for Psychoanalysis*, trans. D. Macey, Oxford: Blackwell.

Laplanche, J. and Pontalis J.-B. (1973) *The Language of Psychoanalysis*, London: Hogarth.

Laufer, M. (ed.) (1995) *The Suicidal Adolescent*, London: Karnac.

Laufer, M. and Laufer, M. E. (1984) *Adolescence and Developmental Breakdown: A Psychoanalytic View*, New Haven and London: Yale University Press.

Likierman, M. (2001) *Melanie Klein: Her Work in Context*, London and New York: Continuum.

Limentani, A. (1972) 'The assessment of analysability: a major hazard in selection for psychoanalysis', *International Journal of Psychoanalysis* 53: 351.

Linton, R. (1936) *The Study of Man*, New York: Appleton-Century.

Locke, J. (1690/1924) *Two Treatises on Civil Government*, London: Dent.

Lubbe, T. (ed.) (2000a) *The Borderline Psychotic Child: A Selective Integration*, London and Philadelphia: Routledge.

—— (2000b) 'Two forms of mindlessness in the borderline psychotic child', in T. Lubbe (ed.) *The Borderline Psychotic Child: A Selective Integration*, London and Philadelphia: Routledge.

Lui, J. (1997) 'An intergenerational comparison of child-rearing attitudes and ideas in Shanghai', *Psychological Science, China* 18(4): 211–15.

MacCarthy, B. (1987) 'Incest victims', *Psychoanalytical Psychotherapy* 2: 157–68.

McWhinnie, A. M. (1976) *Adopted Children: How They Grow Up*, London: Routledge and Kegan Paul.

Mahler, M. (1952) 'On child psychosis and schizophrenia: autistic and symbiotic infantile psychosis', *Psychoanalytic Study of the Child* 7: 286–305.

Main, M. and Hesse, E. (1990b) 'Parents' unresolved traumatic experiences are related to infant disorganised attachment status: is frightened and/or frightening parental behaviour the linking mechanism?', in M. Greenberg, D. Cicchetti and E. M. Cummings (eds) *Attachment in the Preschool Years: Theory, Research and Intervention*, Chicago, Illinois: University of Chicago Press, pp. 161–82.

Main, M. and Solomon, J. (1986) 'Discovery of an insecure-disorganised/disoriented attachment pattern', in T. B. Brazelton and M. W. Yogman (eds) *Affective Development in Infancy*, Norwood, NJ: Ablex, pp. 94–124.

Main, T. (1989) 'The hospital as a therapeutic institution', in T. Main *The Ailment and Other Psychoanalytic Essays* (1989), London: Free Association Books.

Main, T. (1957/1989) 'The ailment', *British Journal of Medical Psychology* 30: 129–

45, reprinted in T. Main *The Ailment and Other Psychoanalytic Essays* (1989), London: Free Association Books.

—— (1975/1989) 'Some psychodynamics of large groups', in Kreeger (ed.) *The Large Group*, London: Constable, reprinted in T. Main *The Ailment and Other Psychoanalytic Essays*, London: Free Association Books.

—— (1989) *The Ailment and Other Psychoanalytic Essays*, London: Free Association Books.

Marsden, L. (2003) 'School children in the Cassel community', in L. Day and D. Flynn (eds) *The Internal and External Worlds of Children and Adolescents: Collaborative Therapeutic Care*, London: Karnac.

Masson, J. (1984) *The Assault on Truth: Freud's Suppression of the Seduction Theory*, New York: Farrar, Straus and Giroux.

Masterson, J. and Rinsley, D. (1975) 'The borderline syndrome: the role of the mother in the genesis and psychic structure of the borderline personality', *International Journal of Psychoanalysis* 56: 163–77.

Matthews, E. (2002) *The Philosophy of Merleau-Ponty*, Chesham: Acumen.

Mead, M. (1956) *New Lives for Old*, New York: William Harrow.

Meadow, R. (1977) 'Munchausen syndrome by proxy: the hinterland of child abuse', *The Lancet* 2: 343–5.

Meltzer, D. (1967) *The Psychoanalytic Process*, London: Heinemann.

—— (1973) *Sexual States of Mind*, Strath Tay: Clunie Press.

—— Bremner, J., Hoxter, S., Weddell, D. and Wittenberg, I. (1975) *Explorations in Autism*, Strath Tay: Clunie Press.

—— (1994) *Sincerity and Other Works*, London: Karnac.

Menninger, W. C. (1936) 'Psychoanalytic principles applied to the treatment of hospitalised patients', *Bulletin of the Menninger Clinic* 1: 35–43.

—— (1981) 'Bion's contribution to thinking about groups', in J. S. Grotstein (ed.) *Do I Dare Disturb the Universe?*, London: Maresfield.

Menzies Lyth, I. (1988) 'The functioning of social systems as a defence against anxiety', in I. Menzies Lyth *Containing Anxiety in Institutions*, London: Free Association Books.

—— (1975) 'Thoughts on the maternal role in contemporary society', *Journal of Child Psychotherapy* 4: 5–14.

—— (1988) 'Staff support systems: task and anti-task in adolescent institutions', in L. Menzies Lyth *Containing Anxiety in Institutions*, London: Free Association Books.

Merleau-Ponty, M. (1945/2002) *Phenomenology of Perception*, London: Routledge.

Mill, J. S. (1863/1910) *Utilitarianism*, London: Dent.

Miller, E. (1993) *From Dependency to Autonomy: Studies in Organisation and Change*, London: Free Association Books.

Milner, M. (1955) 'The role of illusion in symbol formation', in M. Klein, P. Hermann and R. E. Money-Kyrle (eds) *New Directions in Psychoanalysis*, London: Tavistock.

Milton, J. (1994) 'Abuser and abused: perverse solutions following childhood abuse', *Psychoanalytic Psychotherapy* 8(3): 243–55.

Money-Kyrle, R. (1978) 'Normal countertransference and some of its deviations', in R. Money-Kyrle *Collected Papers*, ed. D. Meltzer, Strath Tay: Clunie Press.

Money-Kyrle, R. (1978) *Collected Papers*, ed. D. Meltzer, Strath Tay: Clunie Press.

Montaigne, Michel de (1958) *Essays*, trans. J. M. Cohen, London: Penguin.

Morice, L. and McCluskey, S. (2003) 'The darkling plain: the inpatient treatment of a severely disturbed borderline adolescent', in L. Day and D. Flynn (eds) *The Internal and External Worlds of Children and Adolescents: Collaborative Therapeutic Care*, London: Karnac.

Muir, B. (1987) 'Is in-patient psychotherapy a valid concept?', in A. Heymans, R. Kennedy and L. Tischler (eds) *The Family as In-patient*, London: Free Association Books.

Namnum, N. (1968) 'The problem of analysability and the autonomous ego', *International Journal of Psychoanalysis* 49: 271–5.

Nickman, S. L. (1985) 'Losses in adoption: the need for dialogue, *Psychoanalytic Study of the Child* 40: 365–98.

Nickman, S. L. and Lewis, R. G. (1995) 'Adoptive families and professionals: when the experts make things worse', *Journal of the American Academy of Child and Adolescent Psychiatry* 34(1): 122.

Noy-Sharav, D. (2002) 'Good enough adoptive parenting – the adopted child and selfobject relations', *Clinical Social Work Journal* 30(1): 57–76.

Obholtzer, A. (2002) 'Some thoughts on managing and consulting to organisational dynamics', paper read at Opus conference, London, 22 November.

Obholtzer, A. and Roberts, V. Z. (eds) (1994) *The Unconscious at Work*, London: Routledge.

Ogden, T. (1989) *The Primitive Edge of Experience*, New Jersey and London: Jason Aronson.

—— (1992) *Projective Identification and Psychotherapeutic Technique*, London: Karnac.

O'Shaughnessy, E. (1992a) 'Enclaves and excursions', *International Journal of Psychoanalysis* 73: 603–11.

—— (1992b) 'Psychosis: not thinking in a bizarre world', in R. Anderson (ed.) *Clinical Lectures on Klein and Bion*, London and New York: Routledge.

Parkes, C. M. (1972) *Bereavement*, London: Penguin.

Petot, J.-M. (1990) *Melanie Klein: Volume 1: First Discoveries and First System, 1919–1932*, Connecticut: International Universities Press.

—— (1991) *Melanie Klein: Volume 2: The Ego and the Good Object, 1932–1960*, Connecticut: International Universities Press.

Pincus, L. and Dare, C. (1978) *Secrets in the Family*, New York: Pantheon Books.

Pynoos, R. S. (1990) 'Posttraumatic stress disorder in children and adolescents', in D. Garfinkel, G. A. Carlson and E. B. Weller (eds) *Psychiatric Disorders in Children and Adolescents*, Philadelphia: W. B. Saunders.

Quinodoz, D. (1996) 'An adopted analysand's transference of a "hole-object"', *International Journal of Psycho-Analysis* 77(2): 323–36.

—— (1999a) 'The Oedipus complex revisited: Oedipus abandoned, Oedipus adopted', *International Journal of Psycho-Analysis* 80(1): 15–30.

—— (1999b) 'Deux grands méconnus: Les Parents adoptifs d'Oedipe. Du dedouble-ment des imagos parentales au dedoublement des affects', *Revue Française de Psychanalyse* 63(1): 103–22.

Quinton, A. (1973) *Utilitarian Ethics*, London: Macmillan.

Racine, J. (1963) *Iphigenia*, trans. John Cairncross, London: Penguin.

Racker, H. (1957) 'The meanings and uses of countertransference', *Psychoanalytic*

Quarterly, 26, and reprinted in H. Racker *Transference and Countertransference* (1968), London: Maresfield.

—— (1968) *Transference and Countertransference*, London: Maresfield.

Rayner, E. (1991) *The Independent Mind in British Psychoanalysis*, London, Free Association Books.

Raynor, L. (1980) *The Adopted Child Comes of Age*, London: George Allen and Unwin.

Reder, P. and Lucey, C. (1995) *Assessment of Parenting: Psychiatric and Psychological Contributions*, London: Routledge.

Reder, P., Duncan, S. and Gray, M. (1993) *Beyond Blame: Child Abuse Tragedies Revisited*, London: Routledge.

Revans, R. W. (1959) 'The hospital as an organism: a study in communications and morale', in *Preprint No. 7, Sixth International Meeting at the Institute of Management Sciences, September 1959*, Paris: Pergamon.

Rice, A. K. (1963) *The Enterprise and the Environment*, London: Tavistock.

—— (1965) *Learning for Leadership*, London: Tavistock.

Riesenberg-Malcolm, R. (1999) *On Bearing Unbearable States of Mind*, London: Routledge.

Rinsley, D. B. (1961) 'Psychiatric hospital treatment of adolescents: verbal and nonverbal resistance to treatment', *Bulletin of the Menninger Clinic* 25: 249–63.

—— (1971a) 'The adolescent inpatient: patterns of depersonification', *Psychiatric Quarterly* 45: 3–22.

—— (1971b) 'Theory and practice of intensive residential treatment of adolescents', in S. C Feinstein, P. L Giovacchini and A. A. Miller (eds) *Adolescent Psychiatry*, vol. 1, New York: Basic Books.

—— (1974) 'Residential treatment of adolescents', in G. Caplan (ed.) *American Handbook of Psychiatry*, vol. 2, New York: Basic Books.

Roberts, V. Z. (1994) 'The self-assigned impossible task', in A. Obholtzer and V. Z. Roberts (eds) *The Unconscious at Work*, London: Routledge, pp. 110–20.

Robinson, R. O., Lippold, T. and Land, R. (1986) 'Body schema: does it depend on bodily-derived sensations?', *Developmental Medicine and Child Neurology* 28(1): 49–52 (Feb).

Rosenfeld, H. A., (1965) 'The psychopathology of hypochondriasis', in H. A. Rosenfeld *Psychotic States*, London: Hogarth.

—— (1965) *Psychotic States*, London: Hogarth.

—— (1971) 'A clinical approach to the psychoanalytic theory of the life and death instincts: an investigation into the aggressive aspects of narcissism', *International Journal of Psychoanalysis* 52: 169–78.

—— (1978) 'Notes on the pathology and psychoanalytic treatment of some borderline patients', *International Journal of Psychoanalysis* 59: 215–21.

—— (1987) *Impasse and Interpretation*, London: Tavistock.

Rosenfeld, S. and Sprince, M. (1963) 'An attempt to formulate the meaning of the concept "borderline"', *Psychoanalytic Study of the Child* 18: 603–35.

—— (1965) 'Some thoughts on the technical handling of borderline children', *Psychoanalytic Study of the Child* 20: 495–517.

Rousseau, J.-J. (1762/1913) *The Social Contract* London: Dent.

Rutter, M. (1972) *Maternal Deprivation Reassessed*, London: Penguin.

Rutter, M., Birch, H. G., Thomas, A. and Chen, S. (1964) 'Temperamental characteristics in infancy and later development of behavioural disorders', *British Journal of Psychiatry*, 110: 651–61.

Salinger, J. D. (1945/6) *The Catcher in the Rye*, London: Penguin.

Salo, F. (1990) '"Well, I couldn't say no, could I?": Difficulties in the path of late adoption', *Journal of Child Psychotherapy* 16(1): 75–92.

Sandler, J. (1976) 'Countertransference and role-responsiveness', *International Review of Psychoanalysis* 3: 42–7.

Sandler, J. with Freud, A. (1985) *The Analysis of Defence*, New York: International Universities Press.

—— (ed.) (1988) *Projection, Identification and Projective Identification*, London: Karnac.

Scharff, J. S. and Scharff, D. E. (1998) *Object Relations Individual Therapy*, London: Karnac.

Schechter, M. D. (1967) 'Psychoanalytic theory as it relates to adoption', *Journal of the American Psychoanalytical Association* 15: 695–708.

Segal, H. (1957) 'Notes on symbol formation', *International Journal of Psychoanalysis* 38: 391–97.

—— (1964) 'Phantasy and other mental processes', *International Journal of Psychoanalysis*, reprinted in H. Segal *Delusion and Artistic Creativity and Other Psychoanalytic Essays* (1986), London: Free Association Books.

—— (1973) *Introduction to the Work of Melanie Klein*, London: Hogarth.

—— (1977) 'Countertransference', *International Journal of Psychoanalytical Psychotherapy*, reprinted in H. Segal *Delusion and Artistic Creativity and Other Psychoanalytic Essays* (1986), London: Free Association Books.

—— (1979) *Klein*, London: Fontana/Collins.

Shakespeare, W. (1964) *King Lear*, London: Methuen.

Sharma, A., McGue, M. and Benson, P. (1998) 'The psychological adjustment of United States adopted adolescents and their non-adopted siblings', *Child Development* 69(3): 791–802.

Sharratt, M. (1994) *Galileo: Decisive Innovator*, Cambridge: Cambridge University Press.

Shengold, L. (1979) 'Child abuse and deprivation: soul murder', *Journal of the American Psychoanalytical Association* 27(3): 533–59.

Sherick, I. (1983) 'Adoption and disturbed narcissism: a case illustration of a latency boy', *Journal of the American Psychoanalytical Association* 31(2): 487–513.

Simmel, E. (1929) 'Psychoanalytic treatment in a sanatorium', *International Journal of Psychoanalysis*, 10: 70–84.

Sinason, V. (1988) 'Richard III, Hephaestus and Echo: sexuality and mental/ multiple handicap', *Journal of Child Psychotherapy* 14(2): 93–105.

Skogstad, W. (2003) 'Internal and external reality in in-patient psychotherapy: working with severely disturbed patients at the Cassel Hospital', *Psychoanalytic Psychotherapy* 17(2): 97–118.

Smart, J. J. C. and Williams, B. (1973) *Utilitarianism: For and Against*, Cambridge: Cambridge University Press.

Smith, S. L. and Howard, J. A. (1999) 'Promoting successful adoptions: practice with trouble families', *Saga Sourcebooks for the Human Services Series* 40.

Spillius, E. (1988) *Melanie Klein Today, Volume 1: Mainly Theory*, London and New York: Routledge.

—— (1988) *Melanie Klein Today, Volume 2: Mainly Practice*, London and New York: Routledge.

Stark, G. D. (1977) *Spina Bifida: Problems and Management*, Oxford: Blackwell.

Steele, B. (1976) 'Psychodynamic factors in child abuse', in C. H. Kempe and R. E. Heifer (eds) *The Battered Child*, Cambridge: Ballinger.

Steinbeck, J. (1952) *East of Eden*, London: Heinemann.

Steiner, J. (1976) 'Some aspects of interviewing technique and their relationship to the transference', *British Journal of Medical Psychology* 49: 65–72.

—— (1982) 'Perverse relationships between parts of the self: a clinical illustration', *International Journal of Psychoanalysis* 63: 241–51.

—— (1993) *Psychic Retreats*, London: Routledge.

—— (1994) 'Patient-centred and analyst centred interpretations: some implications of containment and countertransference', *Psychoanalytic Inquiry* 14: 406–22.

Stern, D. (1985) *The Interpersonal World of the Infant*, New York: Basic Books.

Stewart, H. (1996) *Michael Balint, Object Relations Pure and Applied*, London: Routledge.

Strachey, J. (1957) 'Editor's note to *Instincts and their Vicissitudes*', S.E. 14: 111–16.

Sutherland, J. D. (1952) 'Notes on psychoanalytic group therapy: therapy and training', *Psychiatry* 15: 111–17.

—— (1965) 'Recent advances in the understanding of small groups; their disorders and treatment', *Proceedings of the Sixth International Congress of Psychotherapy*, Basle: Karger.

Szur, R. (1983) 'Sexuality and aggression as related themes', in M. Boston and R. Szur (eds) *Psychotherapy with Severely Deprived Children*, London: Routledge.

Target, M. (1998) 'The recovered memories debate', *International Journal of Psychoanalysis* 79: 1015–28.

Tausk, V. (1933) 'On the origin of the "influencing machine" in schizophrenia', *Psychoanalytic Quarterly* 2: 519.

Tew, B. *et al.* (1985) 'The results of a selective surgical policy on the cognitive abilities of children with spina bifida', *Developmental Medicine and Child Neurology* 27: 606–14.

Thomas, A., Bax, M. and Smyth, D. (1987) 'The provision of support services for the handicapped young adult', research document, Dept. of Child Health, Charing Cross and Westminster Medical School.

Thompson, L. and Joseph, A. (1944) *The Hopi Way*, Chicago: University of Chicago Press.

Tischler, L. (1987) 'Nurse–therapist supervision', in R. Kennedy, A. Heymans and L. Tischler (eds) *The Family as In-Patient*, London: Free Association Books.

Tizard, B. (1977) *Adoption – A Second Chance*, London: Open Books.

Triseliotis, J. (1973) *In Search of Origins – The Experiences of Adopted People*, London: Routledge and Kegan Paul.

Trist, E., Higgin, G., Murray, H. and Pollock, A. (1963) *Organisational Choice: Capabilities of Groups at the Coal Face Under Changing Technologies*, London: Tavistock.

Trowell, J. (1982) 'Possible effects of emergency caesarian section on the mother/child relationship', *Early Human Development* 7: 41–51.

Trowell, J. and Etchagoyen, A. (2002) *The Importance of Fathers: A Psychoanalytic Re-evaluation*, London: Routledge.

Van der Kolk, B. and Fisler, R. (1994) 'Childhood abuse and neglect and loss of self-regulation', *Bulletin Menninger Clinic* 58: 145–68.

Vas Dias, S. (2002) 'Inner silence: one of the impacts of emotional abuse upon the developing self', in U. McCluskey and C. A. Hooper (eds) *Psychodynamic Perspectives on Abuse*, London and Philadelphia: Jessica Kingsley.

Voltaire (1759/1972) *Candide*, Paris: Editions Gallimard.

Waddell, M. (1988) *Inside Lives: Psychoanalysis and the Growth of the Personality*, London: Duckworth.

—— (1999) 'The scapegoat', in R. Anderson and A. Dartington (eds) *Facing It Out, Clinical Perspectives on Adolescent Disturbance*, London: Duckworth.

—— (2002) 'The assessment of adolescents', *Journal of Child Psychotherapy* 28: 3.

Weil, A. P. (1953a) 'Certain severe disturbances of ego development in childhood', *Psychoanalytic Study of the Child* 8: 271–87.

—— (1953b) 'Clinical data and dynamic considerations in certain cases of childhood schizophrenia', *American Journal of Orthopsychiatry* 23.

—— (1970) 'The basic core', *Psychoanalytic Study of the Child* 25: 442–60.

Welldon, E. (1992) *Mother, Madonna, Whore*, London: Guilford.

Wilson, S. (1986) 'Reflections on violence and the perversion of meaning', *British Journal of Psychotherapy* 3(2).

Winnicott, D. W. (1945) 'Primitive emotional development', in D. W. Winnicott *Through Paediatrics to Psychoanalysis* (1982), London: Hogarth.

—— (1949) 'Hate in the countertransference', in D. W. Winnicott *Through Paediatrics to Psychoanalysis* (1982), London: Hogarth.

—— (1956) 'Primary maternal preoccupation', in D. Winnicott *Through Paediatrics to Psychoanalysis* (1982), London: Hogarth, pp. 300–5.

—— (1960) 'The theory of the parent–infant relationship', in D. W. Winnicott *Through Paediatrics to Psychoanalysis* (1982), London: Hogarth.

—— (1963a) 'Fear of breakdown', in D. W. Winnicott *Through Paediatrics to Psychoanalysis* (1982), London: Hogarth.

—— (1963b) 'Hospital care supplementing psychotherapy in adolescence', reprinted in D. W. Winnicott *The Maturational Process and the Facilitating Environment* (1965), London: Hogarth.

—— (1963c) 'Communicating and not communicating leading to a study of certain opposites', in D. W. Winnicott *The Maturational Process and the Facilitating Environment* (1965), London: Hogarth.

—— (1965) *The Maturational Process and the Facilitating Environment*, London: Hogarth.

—— (1969a) 'The use of an object and relating through identifications' in *International Journal of Psychoanalysis* 50: 711–16, reprinted in D. W. Winnicott *Playing and Reality* (1971), London: Penguin.

—— (1969b) 'The use of an object in the context of Moses and Monotheism', in D. W. Winnicott *Psycho-Analytic Explorations* (1989), London: Karnac.

—— (1971) *Playing and Reality*, London: Penguin.

Wittenberg, I., Henry, G. and Osbourne, E. (1983) *The Emotional Experience of Teaching and Learning*, London: Routledge and Kegan Paul.

Wollheim, R. (1999) 'Emotion and the malformation of emotion', in D. Bell (ed.) *Psychoanalysis and Culture, A Kleinian Perspective*, London: Duckworth.

Wordsworth, W. (1995) *The Prelude, The Four Texts (1798, 1799, 1805, 1850)*, London: Penguin.

Zelkowitz, P. and Milet, T. (1997) 'Stress and support as related to postpartum paternal mental health and perceptions of the infant', *Infant Mental Health Journal* 18(4): 424–35.

Zetzel, E. (1968) 'The so-called good hysteric', *International Journal of Psycho-Analysis* 49: 256.

—— (1970) *The Capacity For Emotional Growth*, London: Hogarth.

Zola, E. (1972) *Nana*, trans. D. Holden, London: Penguin.

Index

Index compiled by Frank Pert